Praise for _Seasons_

"Danielle Dulsky is the poet of th   g the
magical art of storytelling and ritual into our lives with _Seasons of Moon
and Flame_. If we listen closely, we find that her voice is running through
our very blood and bones and holds the keys to our ancestral wildness."

— **Ora North,** author of _I Don't Want to Be an Empath Anymore_

"Bold, exquisite, empowering, and healing in its concoction and execution, _Seasons of Moon and Flame_ is an exceptional achievement and an
essential read."

— **Mat Auryn,** author of _Psychic Witch:
A Metaphysical Guide to Meditation, Magick & Manifestation_

"There's a stern spirituality about this book, the whiff of a potent po-
tion and strong medicine cooking by the fireside. A hint of surprise. To
wander through the textual landscapes conjured once again by the mag-
isterial stroke of Danielle Dulsky's pen is to recognize that the world,
like the home of the crone at the edge of the forest, is brimming with
magic. Good, healing, relational, intimate, emergent magic. And we do
need magic today! We need a way of knowing that enchantment has
never been in short supply, even here in the seemingly dour space of the
modern. We need to feel this in our bones, and be touched in a touchless
world. This book is a map that leads not to the exotic faraway, but to the
shocking and orgasmic nearby. Travel at your own risk."

— **Bayo Akomolafe,** author of _These Wilds Beyond Our Fences_
and founding curator of the Emergence Network

"My community and followers know that I would never steer them wrong
when it comes to content that can shift and inspire their lives. Danielle
Dulsky continually creates works of the soul through her writing. The
yearning to come back home, back to the roots of who you are, will en-
velop your bones in this book. A calling not only to remember who you
are but to remember the simplicity of it all in the unraveling of the spirit,
land, and flesh."

— **Juliet Diaz,** author of _Witchery: Embrace the Witch Within_

"As punk icon Henry Rollins once said, 'Knowledge without mileage is bullshit.' Danielle Dulsky is the living embodiment of this truth. *Seasons of Moon and Flame* connects readers to a more intimate relationship with themselves, while also illuminating their uniquely important role in the dance of life. As Danielle explores throughout her book, there's such beauty in the haunting and intoxicating experience of life's seasons. That said, perhaps it's apropos that I write these words at 3:13 AM accompanied by a beautifully deafening silence — embracing my own current season of late-night creative expression. Danielle's guidance, experience, practices, and teachings will spark the revolutionary heart of anyone ready to live their 'year(s) of wild' to the fullest. It certainly did mine."

— **Chris Grosso,** author of *Indie Spiritualist, Everything Mind,* and *Dead Set on Living*

"Danielle Dulsky has given us a rhapsody in celebration of the Holy Wild within and around every awakened woman (and hopefully some men). Come ready to listen to treespeak and crow poetry and encounter lusty egg-bearing grandmothers who can fill an egg-shaped hole in the heart. You'll be invited to step out of linear time into moon cycles and what Australia's First People call the All-at-Once. You'll breathe the medicine smoke of sacred stories and be aroused to step outside the tame land and embody the secret wishes of your soul."

— **Robert Moss,** bestselling author of *The Secret History of Dreaming* and *Dreaming the Soul Back Home*

Seasons of
MOON and
FLAME

Also by Danielle Dulsky

Woman Most Wild: Three Keys for Liberating the Witch Within

The Holy Wild: A Heathen Bible for the Untamed Woman

Seasons of
MOON and
FLAME

the WILD DREAMER'S EPIC
JOURNEY of BECOMING

DANIELLE DULSKY

Foreword by Mat Auryn

New World Library
Novato, California

New World Library
14 Pamaron Way
Novato, California 94949

An early version of the text found on pages 158–59 has appeared on the website *The House of Twigs.*

Text design by Tona Pearce Myers

Library of Congress Cataloging-in-Publication data is available.

First printing, March 2020
ISBN 978-1-60868-642-1
Ebook ISBN 978-1-60868-643-8
Printed in Canada on 100% postconsumer-waste recycled paper

New World Library is proud to be a Gold Certified Environmentally Responsible Publisher. Publisher certification awarded by Green Press Initiative.

10   9   8   7   6   5   4   3   2   1

To the elders I have known

Contents

———◆———

Foreword

—◆—

Throughout recorded history, no portrayal of a woman has been demonized more than that of the hag or crone. She is the projected embodiment of everything patriarchal society resists and condemns. As a result, she is one manifestation of the collective Jungian shadow of our society, in which the things we are taught to fear and avoid take form. Just like the Jungian shadow self, the hag needs to be confronted, embraced, and integrated within ourselves and our society, as she holds the crucial medicine that will heal our global soul-sickness as a species. This mission is more important now than ever before.

The condemnation of the hag surpasses that of the "sinful" yet youthful sexual temptress, sorceress, and nymph archetypes. This is because, as an elderly woman without any children and living alone without a husband, she has seemingly failed to fulfill the patriarchal demand that a woman's role in life is to bear and raise children. She has failed to fulfill the demands to be subservient to others around her, to not want for herself, to be silent, to have her life's worth measured by a man she is bound to, to be uneducated, to be less than. She is sometimes vilified as monstress, demoness, and sinner; at other times as child devourer, soul stealer, murderess, madwoman. But always she is called wicked. The hag's priorities are not those of society around her nor of the roles they dictate for her. She flies via broom, distaff, cauldron, or sometimes a goat through the night sky against a full moon, not giving a flying fuck whether her life, appearance, or desirability is palatable to male appetites.

Sometimes her face is shockingly green like the wisdom of the plant realm and like the color of prosperity — such prosperity that endangered the lives of women, as they were historically killed and tried as Witches for owning land and wealth without a husband. Sometimes her face is frighteningly blue, like the expanse of the midnight sky without limitations or constraints, like the psychic and astral depths of the oceans, or like the immense power of speech. She not only has a voice but uses it as she damn well pleases, a cardinal sin in a society influenced by religious texts demanding that a woman be silent — to be seen and not heard. In fact, she doesn't just use her booming and shrill voice, she cackles, reveling in her own "wickedness" and taking pure delight in it.

The hag lives life on her own terms and plays by her own rules, preferring the companionship of familiars and plants over that of those with weak minds and wills. Relegated to a powerless position in life, the hag doesn't live idly until her time is over — she demands the power that was denied to her and is willing to take it back. She is an educated woman in both traditional and esoteric knowledge. She studies the stars in the sky, communes with the spirits, and learns the forbidden arts of magick to heal and curse, to destroy and transform. No one decides what her truth is; she is in charge of that. Not only has she taken a bite from the fruit of the knowledge of good and evil, it is the main ingredient in her recipe for apple pie.

The hag dwells in our bloodstream as the ancestral memories of our own elders who have come before us. She lives in our souls as memories of when we were once elders ourselves. She lives in our collective consciousness as myths, folklore, fairy tales, and even modern media. She demands attention and will use cunning and trickery or any means necessary to assist her in her goals. She holds stories that need to be heard, truths that need to be understood, and lessons that need to be learned. Unlike that of her male counterpart, the archetype of the old sage and wizened man, her knowledge is seen as dangerous, wild, heretical.

Her mere existence is a harsh reminder that death comes for us all, that beauty fades and our bodies break down — an idea that we as a society are programmed to ignore and try to prevent as long as we possibly can. We are detached from the death process, the destruction of the Earth, how we treat animals, our elders, and ourselves — and will do almost anything to avoid these realities. The hag stands in stark contrast to this willful ignorance, being a mirror of these things about ourselves, our world, and fatality that we don't want to look at but need to.

Yet if you learn to confront and befriend the hag, you will find that she is also the wise crone, the adoptive grandmother, the caretaker of the misfits and the lost, the protectress of the woods and even of nature herself. The hag is the goddess herself. She understands what truly matters in life and that sometimes we need to break arbitrary societal rules to live within our own sovereignty and protect what really matters. She holds a memory of times past, times we have forgotten — a memory of who we once were, how the Earth once was — and thereby holds the keys to paradise lost, and sometimes contempt for how far we have strayed.

In this book, Danielle Dulsky challenges us to confront and befriend the hag, urging us to find that crone within ourselves regardless of our gender, to honor her as a goddess, to unlock the mystery of her cackling and revelry, her severity and mercy, her poison and her healing salve. Thus, Danielle serves as bardess, storyteller, and guide through the forbidden forests of our own psyches and souls. She does it in a fashion that only she herself could do, in an immensely beautiful poetic language that creates a landscape in which the hag not only is able to exist but can gladly thrive without being watered down and without diminishing the nature of who she is and what she stands for. This is seasoned with practical and insightful guidance, rituals, and meditations that enable us to ground and empower the wisdom we glean in these pages.

I invite you to savor this enchanting brew of stories and spells; Danielle's work is a rare and potent balm for the modern soul: bold, exquisite, empowering, and healing in its concoction and execution. *Seasons of Moon and Flame* is an exceptional achievement and an essential read for anyone seeking to honor the mysteries of one of the most powerful archetypes in both modern Witchcraft and folkloric Witchcraft — that of the wild crone. It is a key addition to the libraries of all Witches and the Witch-curious alike.

— Mat Auryn,
author of *Psychic Witch: A Metaphysical Guide to Meditation,
Magick & Manifestation*

Prologue

We — the stubborn dreamers, the raging Witches, and the seer-poets — live in a world where our prophets are few and our fears are many. We seek to remedy our brokenness, repair our severed lineages, and heal over our long-bleeding wounds with return-to-the-earth ceremonies, the medicinal smoke of old stories, and the thick salve of unbridled, collective songs born of old ways and even older lands. We dig for deeper meaning. We re-wild what has been tamed. With great urgency we struggle to grasp what it means to live with care, to belong to a place and a people. In our hungry moments, we aim to master slow living by taking a weekend course; pursuing certification; passing some seemingly great test written by someone we never met in a language we never learned; or finding an authority figure apparently more experienced and educated to grant us permission to reclaim what is already ours, to tell us we are being good, and even to share with us precisely what being *good* means on this ailing planet.

While this thirst for external validation is upheld and reinforced by a hard-hearted culture that depends on hierarchy and speed in order to survive, I have come to believe that maybe, just maybe, this ache for approval emerges from something else: from a painfully persistent understanding of our particular tenderness — from our simultaneously knowing that we need communities where elders are valued and knowing that we are so profoundly divorced from such social contexts where aged wisdom is alchemized in the minds of younger generations and used to shape a new world, a world that not only sees the bleeding wounds of individualism, colonization, and capitalism but can make extraordinary art out of the scars. In what we might still call "the West," there is an in-the-joints longing for that unique sort of relationship between elder and seeker, grandparent and babe, hag and maiden, hunter and youth, but there is also an embodied resistance to such an unfamiliar relationship. What if what we long for is a true teacher who can show us what it means to belong to an ever-widening, ever-healing collective, who can temper our zeal and our certainty just a bit, who can remind us that the dark moon of death awaits us all and that somewhere on the great fabric of space and time are those who are already grieving our absence, already sharing the small and glorious stories of our lives around kitchen tables and campfires?

Stories are the medicine, and time poverty is the enemy of story. In our world, we need our lessons delivered quickly and through few words. We need to be spoon-fed our knowledge in easily swallowed bites and eye-catching captions, and stories leave too much up for interpretation and require too much of our precious time to be told true and well. Like our most potent dreams, stories provide a rich and fertile ground on which to sit and consider, never to solve, the great dilemmas of relationship and mystery, love and the sacred, magick and the emerging brilliance of this wild world. It is the tales that leave us with more questions than we had before we heard them that are the world shapers — and, yes, that is the power of story. Visionary stories can shift perspectives; evoke a discomfort necessary in order to encourage changes being made; and reforge a vital connection to land, creatures, and people. In my life, I feel the imperative of story as primary, as integral to my Witchcraft, my art, my ancestral healing, and my way of being in the world.

The art of living slowly, of taking time to listen to the earth speak and breathe in a rhythm that allows for an appreciation of place, is not taught but rather shared. We long not for those spiritual teachers who will offer us an escape from the real work of transforming this slow-to-heal world or, worse, numb us to the realities that surround us; what we yearn for, what we are willing to wander for, what we wake at midnight having dreamed of, are the elders who will bring us home to ourselves, who will inspire us into collective movements, who will share with us what they know and, in so doing, help us remember what we have never truly forgotten.

Our bones want belonging.

My personal journey of becoming reached a pivotal apex of sorts when I realized that — for all my certificates and feverish pursuits; for all my faraway searching for belonging and esoteric knowledge that might, if I only worked hard enough, grant me some missing piece of the puzzle that was my precious life, the life of a white woman raised in a beautiful boneyard land — I had learned my most nourishing, useful lessons from my grandmother. Grace Dulsky was a woman of strong roots, beloved by many in life and still missed sorely years after her death. Like me, she walked close to the earth, stout and sturdy crone that she was, and her demeanor would waver between a practical, no-nonsense busybodiedness and a softer, stiller, contemplative silence; it was in these moments that her forename made sense, when she was staring long from the window of her mountain cabin at the wind-rocked lake or when she spent the day from dawn to dusk baking with a patience I have never known.

This book is partly structured in accordance with the unintentional and yet somehow quite predictable pattern of visits to her home during what was a volatile, hormonal, and rebellious time in my life, as it is for many young ones, of course. Greeting me in her house slippers, she would first feed me like only a grandmother can feed her granddaughter, with that deeper understanding of exactly what tastes I needed on my tongue to heal whatever wounds were aching that day. My teenage anorexia had no home in Grace's kitchen, and her otherworldly black cat would nose itself against my jutting ribs and wait for crumbs.

In time would come that conversational bite. Never would I see it coming, though it happened so regularly, that small and sharp-edged question that would make me rethink all my plans, prompt me to question my relationships, and stun me into silence. This was the challenge, the piercing sting. This was the precise upset I needed, as if that old woman had flipped over my psychic table and sent all my carefully prepared notes spilling onto the ground. Sometimes, it would be as simple as a raised brow that showed the very skepticism I needed, or sometimes it would be a few poignant words spit out of nowhere, as if all 4'10" of Grace Elizabeth was channeling some dark-winged and long-tongued old Germanic

Goddess of destruction. Whatever its form, it was never long-winded or enduring, never a tirade or a scolding — just a bite.

The wisdom would inevitably follow then. After she'd bitten me, after she'd made me wonder what I was doing with that small life of mine, she'd somehow always seal up our visit in a neater package, offering warm-armed support and the softest, most maternal love I had — and indeed have — ever known. At the end of our visits, she would speak like spirit speaks, with a mysterious, innocent, so-subtle tone that, regardless of the precise shape her words were taking, always said *Yes, dear child. These small moments are what life is made of.*

And right you still are, Grace.

My visits to Grace's house were my Crone School, and her curriculum was not easily learned, nor was it, I am sure, easily shared. If there was a single vision statement for her elder academy, it was this: A more holy gift than the regular enjoyment of — than the daily and embodied kinship *with* — those fleeting moments of contentment and peace does not exist. Living slowly is activism, too. Taking time to listen to the stories of our elder-teachers is the stuff of rebellion, but it is not the stories alone that will shape the emerging future. Find that hallowed meeting place where your life — where your lived experience, passions, wounds, and in-finite hope — encounters the story; this is the edge of wildness, the fringe on which the greatest transformation can occur.

Here, we are beyond language. Here, we are living shrines to who we used to be and who we will become. Here, we are both hopeful prayer and mournful keening.

May we walk the way we hope our ghosts will walk. May we conceive of time as friend and the seasons as elder-teachers; they have been spiral-dancing since long before we were born, after all. May we learn to find sovereignty in our humility, and may we remember the magick of our long-gone ancestors. The hag has much healing wisdom to share with us, if we only listen, so let us build twig-and-stone shrines in the woods to those gray-haired ones who taught us well.

All blessings be.

The Hag's Song

I fell into sleep and dreamt of a hag
She leapt like a youth and crouched on a crag
I know you, I said. Her face was my own
I'll show you, I said, and ran for the crone
Just look! I am you, you wild-boned thing!
She shook and turned blue, then started to sing
Her prayer was so old, bewailing the trees
A keening so bold, for rough times like these
I licked a tear from her eye, the salt from her hair
Then she was I, her hymn mine to share
My bones — how they ached! But my songs were so rich
My voice, how it quaked with the howl of that Witch
I sang for the elders, the dead, and the snow
I moaned for the yew trees, the wolf, and the crow
In time, I grew soft, a soul sopped in song
A Cailleach lost in a rhyme gone too long
I woke in the dark, nudged up by a ghost
The song left its mark, but the hag I loved most.

INTRODUCTION

Our Year of the Wild

Nestled somewhere within the untamed psyche of every wild soul is a wise elder with a salty sense of humor. If we listen, we can hear that cunning hag share her potent medicine with us, singing us songs of haunted autumns, deep winters, and lush-blooming springs. That old one has a long memory, and she speaks the lost rebel language of the wilds with a primal intonation. She helps us make sense of these ever-unraveling and eternally restitched stories of ours, continually offering us an invitation back to those hallowed, heathen lands our deepest selves have never forgotten.

Without the voice of our inner crone, without our well-aged wilderness guide, these flourishing and fertile lands, these ancestral dreamscapes that bud and bloom in our hearts and beyond our walls, rarely offer us definitive answers to our many questions about love, loss, or the sacred. Even gifted with her elusive guidance, we still inevitably struggle to discern what messages the natural world holds for us. Our minds howl for certainty. We want concrete answers. We resist the discomfort of a mystery-riddled life, but the wilds whisper only the softest songs, speaking in a slower and less predictable rhythm than our many screaming, fast-talking screens. The hag tells us of our inextricable belonging to the world, to the wild unseen. In *The Spell of the Sensuous*, David Abram writes: "This breathing landscape is no longer just a passive backdrop against which human history unfolds, but a potentized field of intelligence in which our actions participate." We are creaturely. We are cocreated and dismembered by these wilds over and over again. What persistent unknowns our modern, overbright technologies struggle to illuminate, those holy wilds embrace in moon and flame.

To remember how to hear that inner hag's voice often seems a near-impossible task, an arduous journey home after being away too long, when the comforts of certainty are begging us to rest and stay with all things known. The old ones are whispering, but the devices are shrieking. The haunting lure of the forest beckons, but so does the softness of our beds. We long to remember to listen, but our lives are full of contradictions. Remembering how to hear the hag's voice means making peace with, though rarely resolving, these many beautiful and bizarre conflicts that show us our chaotic complexity, our magickal and messy humanness.

For some, the remembering happens only in dreams, in those subconscious spaces where that primal tongue is spoken through monstrous imagery, overgrown landscapes, or otherworldly spirits. For others, the remembering occurs by light of day, as they take notice of synchronicities, nods from nature, and suddenly realized patterns within their personal myths of wounding and healing. For all, the task is to fall in love with the liminal: the place between the illusion of our separateness and the unnamed sparking and numinous spirit evident in all — the cosmic dance between our feeling flesh, the beloved dead, and the yet-to-be-born; between the human and the beast; and between the stories we live and the stories we share.

Hag Lesson #1

The best stories are not heard but met.

Sovereign within the Collective

To walk with our inner hag requires such remembering, and this remembering is hardly a finite goal to be attained or permanent plateau to be reached; it is a journey of eternal becoming, of a constant and everweaving dance between our singular sovereignty and our intimacy with the collective. Regardless of context, the remembering sparks a subtle stirring in the blood — an ignition, of sorts — that can turn an everyday person first into a mystic and then later, perhaps, into a Witch. To be a mystic is to come home to that fog-filled space of not knowing, time and time again, and to be a Witch is to not only regularly return to liminal space but continually open to those many seasons of confusion and certainty, of shadow and fire, of chaos and order. To be a Witch is not only to acknowledge these many seasons but to humbly and humorously live *of* them, to cocreate a life worth living with time as partner-lover and transformation as teacher-friend. To be a Witch is to have begun learning the greatest lesson the wilds have to teach their human children: Time is a spiral dance of eternal becoming, and to move in that age-old rhythm is to remember the wisdom of not only those crones who have come before us but those yet-to-be-born babes who will be inherited by the new world we leave behind.

To me, the wilds speak in the ancient tongue of the elder-storyteller, and that primal terrain is a burly and resilient beast. In this language of treespeak and crow poetry, there are few words denoting the definite and many words for mystery. Ours is a lexicon of feeling, of beauty, and of the space between. This language includes no concrete truths but favors that pivotal and sacred encounter between the inquiry and the answer. Within these hallowed lands blessed by mist and lit by moon, the Witch finds themselves on an epic journey that is always beginning and always ending. Every year is their wildest year yet. Day by day, they dream their worlds into being. Night by moonlit night, they learn all they can from the fertile dark.

Hag Lesson #2

The revolution will be wildcrafted.

Their annual adventure around the sun is a thirteen-season living-and-breathing ceremony of honoring the wilds as they converge and dance within them. When their memory of magick falls short, they slow their pace. They pay a visit to their inner wise one, and they revisit the stories of their ancestral lines. They feel into the *shaping* more than the shaper or the shape. Their springs are garden altars to healing the human ache, built with much love by the hands of the forebears, an annual mission to uncover the deep medicine of their lines that was carved out, hidden, burned, and demonized. A Witch's summer is an intense and moving spell of gratitude and grace, activism and joy. Their autumn is a sacred séance and beauteous grief ritual spent communing with those knowing ancestors who still walk with them, year by year, moon by moon, and their winters are cocreated rituals of rest and reflection, divination and embodied nourishment, guided by intuition sourced straight from their inner snow-haired elder.

Way of the Witch-Fractal

To live as the Witch lives is to allow your world to be shaped and reshaped by those swelling, cresting, and ebbing wilds to which you already belong. To live as the Witch lives is to continually *remember*, as the magick maker's journey is not solely one of knowledge acquisition but so often one of simple recollection. Whatever particular ancestral medicine runs in your blood, whatever hallowed recipe of many lands, songs, and ceremonies has brewed you, you are a wisdom keeper with much to gift this wounded world. You are a holy confluence of many fertile and fast-running rivers of lineage and land knowledge. What I offer here in these pages is an invitation to awaken that wisdom, that wild and soulful meaning you already embody, to find sanctuary in time's cyclical movements as you would in the warm, firelit home of an elder healer.

I invite you to use your magick to silver-thread not only your own story but also the collective love story we are all living right here, right now, at this pivotal moment when the human community must, simply must, fall in love with this planet. The story has for too long been one of unrequited longing, dragging on and on like a many-millennia-long play ordered in act after act of horror and greed against indigenous people, against the sacred elements — with the wild earth, all the while, waiting for us with an aching patience we do not deserve. Perhaps the play's plot will shift like this: The human animal, faced with the prospect of living in a world of rising seas, will open its ears to the subtle whispers of the beauty beneath its feet; will fall to the ground weeping and begging for forgiveness; and will resolve to do all it can to repair, restore, and rejuvenate what will otherwise be irrevocably lost.

A problem of such magnitude cannot possibly be solved using the same strategies that created it, but what if the way we define these wounds is also part of the injury. Scholar and educator Bayo Akomolafe says, "The times are urgent; let us slow down." No more can we rush away so quickly from the ache, for our shared scars are sacred portals where we just might meet the medicine we need, where we can again know what it means to belong not to a collective trauma but to the whole of our co-created story. We can look one another in the eye here on this hallowed ground, Witch to scientist and believer to skeptic, and say, "I see you. You are hurting, and I am hurting, too."

We are witch-fractals casting our spells and speaking our truths in the name of not only our own liberation but that of all people. We must embrace the knowing that we can be fully empowered, fully and wholly sovereign creatures, but still acknowledge whatever privileges we may have and how racialized trauma and cultural context affect our lives. We can act in ways that are just, center voices that are not our own, and use whatever powers we have been graced with in this life to heal our Earth, the mother that bore us. We can dig out the deep, buried medicine that runs in our blood. We can mend, and we can find the immense pleasures and bountiful treasures that are ours to claim. There is not only discomfort to be found in the unknown but a necessary and humbling delight.

Hag Lesson #3

Joy lives in mystery.

We rush so quickly to solve the unsolvable, to run toward the familiar, but our elders teach us to slow our pulses just a bit, to hear what stories we can, and to listen to those whose input was not valued when this world of ours was built. The poison lies in the absolutes; in the immutable decisions; and in the stubborn refusal to admit that we do not know what *good* means, that maybe, just maybe, there is no solution that does not begin with the strange sanctuary of slowness, and that, importantly, slow living does not mean apathy. May we cease to equate our I-don't-knows with our I-don't-cares, and may we reframe what it means to be wild, empowered, and free.

Wander 'Round the Path

Linear time is the enemy of magick, at best, and the catalyst for hard-edged individualism and colonization, at worst. Perceiving time as only linear encourages fierce movement toward a given goal and the concurrent ignorance of our creaturely cycles. Such rigid thought patterns take us away from the past, from innocence, from memory. The vilest philosophies were used to validate colonial conquests, bound by common and insidious threads of rot called distance, speed, and dominance. We have heralded the stories of ambitious heroes who begin with nothing and end with everything, all the while reinforcing the circle as servant and the line forward as king.

Witches tell the small stories, though, and Witches live on the fringes of society for a reason. If they are too far removed from the wilds, their souls starve and they lose their sense of belonging. If they are too isolated from the human collective, they are unable to effect change, to weave the world they hope will come to fruition. They dance in the great between. They live on the edge, you see. They live on the edge, though not often by choice, to witch their worlds from the inside out. And, to my mind, the greatest lesson the elders, Witches, mystics, and healers can share at this pivotal moment is that of long vision and spiraling time. In *Grandmothers Counsel the World*, Carol Schaefer writes, "The Grandmothers teach us that time is not linear in the Spirit World. All time exists at once, enabling the seeing of events far into the future." This does not mean aggressively and adamantly choosing spiral time over linear time but rather choosing to see the world cyclically when possible — knowing that all birth is also a death, every beginning is an end, and there is a holiness to the dark, to the shadow, which is only wicked when it is shunned and shamed.

What if we loved to live this way? What if we befriended the circle-round again? This is the spiraling path of the embodied Witch, where linear time is often an illusion and each morning's dawn is akin to the new moon, to spring, to youthful joy and conscious innocence. We are sacred workers and magick makers at noonday, feeling the pulse of the full moon and the high fire of summer burn bright on our inner altars, before dusk calls us toward the holy, autumnal energies of the waning moon. We rest, at long last, in the blessed lightlessness of night, our daily dose of winter-tide, held in the arms of the dark moon. This is our dawn-to-dark dance, our opportunity to be dreamed alive not once but over and over again.

You may be thinking that the proverbial real world does not permit such slow movements; how our schedules, calendars, and deadlines rule over us without ever getting our vote; and how helpless we all are to live the way we like. But here is precisely where those on the fringes come into play, entering into our collective story of becoming not with penetrative ambitions of victory but in deep song, sharing their rebels-in-time ways with those who care to listen. We become outlaws by letting our lives breathe as much as possible, by feeling into the emptiness as much as the full, by pushing against and tenderizing the hard edges until they begin to give way. Reflection and rest are radical, and the very systems we wild hearts wish to counter rely entirely on our lack of both.

Given the weight of what is at stake, cultivating a more nourishing relationship with time may seem like a small task, but what if those brief moments of pause are where incremental revolutions begin? What would become of our exhausting quests for perfection if we fell in love with imprecision? This is a lunar journey of becoming, a journey with no destination.

This book is a story of your eternal transmutation, and I invite you to both dream awake and be dreamed alive. Let the place to begin find you, then scry your own way forward. Just like the practice of Witchcraft, this book asks you to begin whenever and wherever you are called, regardless of geography, past study, or access to material resources. You do not need to live in a place where all four solar seasons are neatly defined and easily predicted, for all thirteen moons live within us, just as all the elements, directions, and deep archetypes of light and shadow run in our very blood. Do not look to nature to show you how to feel; rather, look to where nature meets you — look to that space of coming-togetherness, and tend to the spirit of the moment.

You may find yourself in the dead of winter but feel strongly pulled toward the rituals of the summer moons; begin there. You may be raising your hood against the first autumn wind but feel called to read the invocation for the spring season; begin there. You may live in a

Hag Lesson #4
Nonlinear movement is rebellion.

brilliantly sunlit place never visited by ice or snow, or in a seemingly uni-seasonal land of eternal mist and rain. Even so, begin wherever you feel called. This is not a story with a clear beginning and definitive ending but an ongoing, ever-unraveling, and perennial fairy tale of spellcraft, dream visions, small stories, and moon medicine.

Meet the Four Sacred Hags

The archetype of the wild and fearsome hag is found in innumerable tales across countless cultures. She comes as the Cailleach and the Baba Yaga. She comes as the sharp-tongued medicine woman. These wise crones reside in the collective unconscious, tending their cook fires and stirring their cauldrons from their huts, tents, and cottages well hidden within the unmapped terrain of our psychic lands. Dr. Clarissa Pinkola Estés writes in her classic *Women Who Run with the Wolves* that "this old woman stands between the worlds of rationality and mythos. She is the knucklebone on which these two worlds turn." She is not to be overromanticized or made palatable in order to better serve our needs, just as nature does not exist for our consumption. For many, she is the very shadow from which we recoil, the part of our own psyches we have named vile; this is how we know she is our greatest teacher. We are closest to uncovering the hag's bewitching haunts when we find ourselves tender and immersed in nature, brokenhearted but somehow aligned with those deeper rhythms that no linear calendar could ever adequately predict.

In this book, you shall meet four hags who are seasonal gatekeepers, elder-teachers of nature's mysteries, who offer nourishment, challenge, and wisdom to those who dare visit them. There are three lunar seasons for every sun-based season, and it is within these shorter cycles that we truly evolve into more soulful — that is, both uniquely sovereign as well as intimately connected to the collective nature — versions of ourselves. Just as a wise grandmother, just as my own grandmother, might invite you into her home, serve you comfort food by her hearth; confront you with some piece of previously unrealized and hard-to-swallow knowledge; then, finally, provide some invaluably sage advice for moving forward, the three moons of every solar season similarly offer us such cronely education. The first moon of any season provides the sustenance we need, the necessary tastes and psychic nutrition, in order to move on to the challenge offered up by the second moon of the solar season. The last moon is inevitably an initiation to a new level of knowing, where the seeker becomes Priestess and death becomes birth.

In this book, our year is a slow-paced working retreat to the four houses of the hags, an epic apprenticeship of soul that we undergo again and again, each winter finding ourselves once more standing on the bones of who we used to be, reflecting our memories by the soft glow of a dripping candle. Each spring we seek to heal some still-ailing part of ourselves connected to our inherited aches, somehow discovering the precise medicine we need in the depths of our own psyches. Summer finds us at fruition, a swollen version of ourselves, where our magick is sourced straight from our heart-wells of gratitude and compassion, before shape-shifting our particular griefs into banishing magick during the most haunted season of autumn.

This journey is not an unending merry-go-round ride but rather a wondrous and ever-widening spiral. Each season holds for you new gifts, new lessons, newly unlocked opportunities to deepen your mastery, to restore and rebirth your way of being in the world. Your inner wise one does not give you anything you do not already have but only shows you where to look.

Grow the Circle Wider

For me, these pivotal times often spark childhood memories of watching apocalyptic Hollywood films, of aliens and asteroids come to end the human experiment once and for all. My young and recklessly curious mind, shaped considerably by a good deal of born-again Christian indoctrination and the constant threat of many-headed beasts and four horsemen, would wonder if the impending doom of the world was what was required for human beings to come together, forgive one another, rally, and finally save themselves like they always seemed to do in the movies. Did we need to be in the end-times in order to find a collective compassion?

As I grew older, as I traveled, as I began to consider a bigger world than the one in which I was raised, I had to unlearn so much about equality and justice, magick and manifestation — words that meant something very different to me, a white woman, than they did to others with less privilege than I had. Now, in my own few slow and quiet moments when I wonder if an Armageddon is, indeed, upon us, I am aware that the love and unity from the Hollywood movies is not possible without the active dismantling of deeply seated and systemic racism, ableism, sexism, heterosexism, transphobia, and classism, as well as a general fear of otherness.

My hope is that a commitment to your own healing, to your own story of becoming, coexists with a profound conviction, be it a newfound resolution or a long-standing knowing, that we are part of a collective. Our magick is stronger together. The Witch has been harmed by many of the same systems that continue to harm disproportionately people of color, the LGBTQIA+ community, and the beloved planet, and we can, and indeed must, work to grow the circle. It is time to examine the many ways we may be benefiting from and unintentionally doing harm to those people, to those cultures, we claim to love without relinquishing our own wholeness. On the contrary, we are made more whole when we grow our circles wider, when the fringes swallow the center, when we question our beliefs and deconstruct the very systems that privilege us at the expense of others.

To that point, I use the word *grandmother* and the pronouns *she* and *her* in this book when referring to one of the "four sacred hags." This is primarily because, in my mind, all four of these beloved elders are, in part, shades of my own grandmother, and also because our language has not evolved to accurately reflect the complexities of nature. This is not to exclude nonbinary, trans, or other gender-nonconforming individuals from eldership or to herald the gender binary; quite the reverse, I hope this book speaks well and true to anyone with a heathen heart. When I say "woman," I mean anyone who identifies as a woman; this absolutely includes trans women. Our circles can hold it all, and living slowly does not mean living unchallenged. Witches work with nature. Nature is change, and we were not born to be static in our beliefs, judgments, and ways of expressing our beingness in the world.

Hag Lesson #5

Our circles can grow wider and wider still.

Whisper Words of Lineage

I am on an unending journey of restitching my ancestral lineage, as many of us are. The whole of my mother line is of Irish descent, and I have understood this for as long as I can remember. At age eighteen, I impatiently waited until I graduated high school, then immediately boarded a plane for Ireland with neither money nor a plan, committed to a stubborn teenage quest to belong, to feel whole. I lived there for a time, spending the potent summer and autumn seasons encountering much mischief in Dublin and escaping into the mists of the west when I could. Something held me there that did not — that in some ways still does not — hold me here, where I was born and raised, on the land of the Lenni-Lenape, the "true people," outside of Philadelphia, Pennsylvania. Much of the lens — a lens I continually break, mend, then break again — through which I look has been shaped by the Celtic Wheel of the Year, by my brief and brutal stint immersed in traditional Wicca during my twenties, by my many elders and loving and not-so-loving teachers I have known since then, and by my sheer devotion to the wild nature that lives beneath my ribs, that pulses in thick rivers through my veins.

The seasons, the stories, the verses, the spells contained in this book are not intended to speak to any particular lineage, and my sincere hope is that they are accessible to anyone, anywhere. They have a Celtic flavor because I have a Celtic flavor, but I believe this cyclical witchery to be universal. We all live in an ever-changing world, after all. We Witches are animists graced by constant rising and setting suns, waxing and waning moons, ebbing and flowing tides. I claim no mastery, and I am personally suspicious of the motives of modern teachers who teach the old ways as if they own them, as if anyone could ever own them, or as if we are living in the same world as the one within which the human-to-nature kinship was born. We are immersed in a constant flow, and we are all being cocreated by innumerable liquid currents, our old rough parts eroded away and new patterns marked by unforeseen surges. We are all in conversation with one another, with the world, and we must constantly consider and reconsider what we would like to be saying.

Hag Lesson #6

Everything is participation.

Return to Embodiment

The most powerful and harmful systems have benefited considerably from the human animal's detachment from its feeling flesh. We have been taught to frame the intellect as king and reason as god, leaving our holy bodies to be servants, at best, to mind and thought. We have been indoctrinated toward transcendence of the earth, the elements, and our creaturely selves, housing long-standing traumas within our bodies, much to our detriment and that of others and the wounded planet, as these traumas unconsciously play out in our lives. Our bodies are where we meet the world, dissolving the false boundary between our individuality and the infinite, and conscious embodiment is how we integrate that meeting place into our lived-out-loud stories.

As Witches, healers, and wildlings, we intuitively know that our magick is channeled through the body, through our very roots then out, in, up, and down again. Our magick is a dance with the wilds; thus, our breath, our movement, and the sounds we make matter. Our own healing, our own wholeness, matters. Magick is sensual, and there can be no separation between the malleable beauty of our own soft skin and the writhing collective of nature, both seen and unseen, grotesque and lovely. The imperative is to get low to the ground; feel the hum and the pulse not just in our hearts but in our bones; get under our thinking minds; get dirty; and reforge a felt intimacy with the spirits of land, sea, and sky.

Live Cyclically

To live cyclically is to welcome the transitions, to resist tallying the wins and losses that deny this hard Witch's truth: All ends only to begin again. I invite you to reframe time as a living, breathing force that is always swelling and thinning, ebbing and flowing. I invite you to cultivate a renewed sense of in-the-skin nature intimacy by feeling into the words I offer here, and I invite you to come home to the hallowed lands where those wild hags are waiting for you.

Ours is a journey of eternal becoming, an ever-expansive experience of being breathed in and out by nature itself, incarnation after blessed incarnation. To live cyclically is to be more forgiving of the self and, sometimes, of others; to acknowledge that we are all living altars; and to embrace those cocooned seasons of rest, self-care, and rejuvenation as often as those blooming, generative phases of creation, activism, and ferocity.

How do we know when it is time to rest and when it is time to rage? When is it time to reflect on our most pivotal experiences in solitude, and when is it time to use those lessons to make beautiful art, to march to government buildings, or to dismantle broken systems? Listen to the hags; they will tell you. How can we know when we must spend an afternoon engaged in frenzied art making or radical spellcraft? When is it time to wander in mourning or dance in ecstasy? The hags have seen it all, the many heartening joys and well-shed tears, but their wealth of experience has hardly made them apathetic. Let them teach you their cyclical ways, and let them teach you through your own feeling body. These ancient elders, like you, are clever travelers on the path of eternal becoming. Let us listen to them, and this is sure to be our wildest year yet.

House of
INITIATION
The Beginning and the End

Your journey begins here, in the House of Initiation. Take a breath, hum so loudly your teeth rattle, then whisper: "It begins." Imagine this house at the center point of a simple map. To the east lies an ivy-walled cottage surrounded by lush blooms and kept well by the wise Garden Hag. To the south stretches sandy and hallowed grounds ruled by the loving Desert Hag, with the spectral Sea Hag enchanting the gray and salty waters to the west. Finally, in the north looms a haunting snowcapped peak where the Mountain Hag awaits you. Here, you are at the epicenter of your spiral journey. Here, you are the wild and sovereign hag who has learned a softer witchery, remembered how to dance with time, and made peace with her position in this wicked and wondrous world.

The Spiral Journey

Where you go when you leave your House of Initiation is entirely your choice. You might begin by asking yourself to what season you feel most akin. Which of the thirteen moons lives in your soul all year-round? Perhaps begin there. If you are only in need of some story medicine, a quick hag lesson, or a timely ritual, look to the appendices at the end of this book for summarized descriptions and see where the specific themes carry you. Of course, should you be feeling practically minded and find yourself on the cusp of a new moon, look for the chapter that is beginning for you in this moment, according to the season you are in. When all else fails, book divination always serves well. Leave it to the Mystery, flip to a page, and see what word-witchery awaits you. Permit your Craft to breathe. Grant yourself space. Leave out what is not for you, and let these words be invitations to remember, more than instructions to follow.

Hag Lesson #7

What is wild must always change.

Each chapter is a single moon cycle, a single lunar "season," with three chapters dedicated to spring, summer, and winter, respectively. There are four chapters dedicated to the autumn season, accounting for the enigmatic "thirteenth moon." Included in applicable chapters are descriptions of rituals and ceremonies for the celebration of the equinoxes; solstices; and the cross-quarter days, called Beltane, Lughnasadh, Samhain, and Imbolc in the Celtic tradition. Each chapter is organized as if you are a guest, a visiting apprentice, in a magick-rich hag's home. The "Grandmother Speaks" sections describe your mystical encounters with the elder; here, the hag shares her lessons, stories, and words of wisdom for each phase of the moon cycle. The spellwork, ceremonies, and opportunities for reflection are all deeply rooted in the hag's words to you. While the work is sometimes cumulative from moon to moon, know that you are fiercely encouraged to become the outlaw and stray from course from time to time.

Surely, This Babe Wakes Wild

An Ode to Time's Outlaws

She is a keeper of secrets, that old Witch, and she just remembered how to slow-dance with time in those forbidden dips and forgotten lifts that defy all our modern schedules and queer our many labels. She has begun a new naming, an initiation of the Holy Wild fool. Surely, this babe wakes wild on this seemingly mundane morning, for her breath comes easier and she's moving with a certainty only gifted to time's outlaws, only to those who hold hands with the dark and sacred cosmos, touching solid skin to stardust and whispering aloud to all things alien and infinite. Yes, surely this babe wakes wild; you can see it all in her moments of pause, in that stillness and silence that responds to loudmouthed demands for answers. This year will most certainly be her wildest one yet, truth be told, for she's come home to the Mystery and rejected those tired rules and outplayed maneuvers meant to birth the best life.

Surely, this babe wakes wild even now, even as the moon sets

demurely and the sun rises in its daily ceremony of jewel-bright be-
coming. They are time's outlaws, too, you know. The sun and moon
have a good laugh together just now, when they pass one another in
the sky, at the human creatures' bustling and going about their busi-
ness, snickering with an ease that eludes the frantic hearts — but,
surely, this babe wakes wild, for she's taking her lessons from those
crawling celestial orbs now. This is her initiation, and she's set her
tamer ways to burn.

A Softer Witchery

There is much to be said for self-discipline, for keeping our promises to ourselves, for harboring a deep knowing that any new way of being in the world is going to come with moments of intermittent discomfort that must be welcomed as small rituals of growth and learning. No long-held pattern is broken without effort, and to forge a more meaningful relationship with time means not only disrupting our own understanding of aging, of success, and of ambition but doing so within a societal context that heralds speed and pins bright medals to the puffiest and proudest chests. To have a gentler partnership with time is to embrace the paradox, to rebel against the systems that rely on a range of ill-isms in order to maintain their power, including but not limited to capitalism, colonialism, racism, sexism, ageism, heterosexism, ableism, and classism. It is to reject a central tenet of many world religions: that we live, be it once or through multiple incarnations, in order to reach some great goal, receive some immense pardon or reward from a deity far superior to ourselves, and relieve our tired souls from the earthly grind.

In *Weaving the Visions*, Judith Plaskow and Carol Christ write: "God's transcendence is frequently understood to mean that God is different from humanity and nature because God is pure spirit uncorrupted by a physical body. The human body with its connections to nature then is said to keep us from God." The spiritual practices of those who choose to live — physically, psychically, or otherwise — on the fringes of a society undergoing a large-scale and necessary transformation are inevitably ones that resist unquestioned conformity to linear time and embrace the body's sanctity.

Witches live on the fringes of what is socially permissible, and — though they acknowledge the merit of certain structures and systems — they are centrally concerned with nourishing a kinship with what is fundamentally wild and of the earth. There is a humility to their Craft, you see, an acknowledgment that many parts of the human experiment have failed, and a thorough and constant admission that they may not know anything for sure in a world that has evolved to not only support and sustain blatant and egregious economic, political, and societal inequities but embed these ills within our very flesh; this is particularly true if they have benefited from these imbalances, as have the white, cisgender, and able-bodied. Witches are constantly unlearning even the self-taught lessons, all while holding themselves in the fiercest compassion and warmest grace, without running from discomfort.

Here, in this House of Initiation, you are invited toward a softer witchery. Here, magick is more of a wave, a pulsing heart, and a slow dance than a penetrative blade. This is an approach to the Craft at once gently structured and entirely malleable according to where you find yourself now in that epic story you are living. Be wild, trusting that wildness is a never-ending process of reclaiming what belongs to you, of owning your ancestral inheritance and, importantly, acknowledging that you belong to this complex and beauteous web we might only call nature.

Hag Lesson #8

We must be gentle with ourselves.

A key lesson learned in the House of Initiation is that no one can impose any rules or restrictions on a Craft that is fundamentally our own. We Witches must constantly be questioning the extent to which, by denigrating the spiritual practices of others, we sustain or even strengthen the very social norms we are attempting to reject. For some, Witchcraft is a religion. For others, Witchcraft is art; neither approach is superior or more authentic, and to assume so is to reinforce spiritual hierarchies similar to those that brought us to the stakes.

This is your house, Witch. This is a place of beauty and joy, of practice and poetry. Many of those who seek out the Craft do so not because they feel they have been chosen by a deity or born a natural Witch but because they crave slow living — because they sense the majesty in nature, a sense that is now unique and something to be remembered but was once not only a given but the very container for our

Hag Lesson #9

This Craft is yours and ours.

ancestors' bodies, psyches, and spirits. In this house, may you live slowly. May you take time for both somber stillness and frenzied dance, and may you reflect on how the elements have always held you — swaddled you, in fact, like an infant hungry for nothing more than a felt-on-the-skin belonging.

Our Wilder Circles

When you leave this house, when you venture out in whatever direction you feel called, you will be offered occasional opportunities to cast a circle. Consider the circle like you would any other container; it holds what you brew, gives you a psychic and physical place to work, and initiates the sanctity of whatever ceremonial act you are about to begin. The circle, if nothing else, frames that particular moment in time when you were at one with your magick.

As with any other aspect of our Craft that we might hold as holy, we must seek to inspire our circle-casting, to carve away the places where calling the directions becomes rote, when we are reciting words written by someone we have never met or from a tradition that was never ours. Approach the circle from your own experience and write your own incantations. Fall in love with the round. It may serve you to conceive of circle-casting as simply a way of creating sacred space, integral to many animistic traditions; it is a means of both empowering and humbling yourself, of declaring to the elements surrounding you that you are both the maker and what is made, the dreamer and the dream.

The Circle as Story Ritual: Invoking the Witch's Place

Permit the circle to be a story. This is a foundational ritual, a way of connecting to ground and embodying place.

1. Beginning with north, ask: *What does the north mean to me?* Is it the holy direction of craggy rocks, winter, and the earth element, or do you have different associations entirely? Recall a memory that you can fully embody and feel quite viscerally. Do you have a memory of feeling completely whole within the essence of the north? It need not be an objectively epic and

momentous event. Perhaps you were a child watching snow fall outside your window and knowing you would be granted a blissful and blessed reprieve from academia if only for one day. Perhaps you were standing firm on the ground for the first time since you left a constraining relationship, or perhaps you once looked a mother wolf dead in her eyes and became her kin. Ask yourself what north means to you in this moment, and call up a memory you can see, smell, hear, taste, and feel.

2. Do the same with east, that innocent direction of new beginnings, the air element, spring, garden blooms, and possibility; south, that hot and lustful direction of fruition and high fire; and, last, west, the direction of death, mystery, autumn, gray waters, and muse.

3. Gather all four of your seed memories now, one for each direction, then move to stand here in your House of Initiation facing north. Call to mind your memory for this potent direction; speak whatever words you like that honor what lies before you, perhaps starting with "Beloved and ancient elders of the north, those who are my most whole and compassionate kin, I call to you and invite you into this circle." Feel the memory with your entire body, perhaps permitting yourself to move in a spontaneous body prayer. Breathe deep. Soften your knees and feel your foot bones connect to ground.

4. Face east and do the same, allowing your seed memory for this direction to arise in your consciousness, stepping into the memory with your whole being, and inviting the blessed and loving ancestors to join you. Do the same for the bright and wild south and the dark and mysterious west. Feel held from below and blessed from above, perfectly positioned in your own story of becoming, fully nested within your body and warmed by your blood.

Alternative to Circle-Casting: The Pentagram of Being

As an alternative to calling the energies of the directions, the "pentagram of being" is a simple way of grounding, acknowledging sacred space, settling into your skin, rooting into a deep knowing that we are cocreated by many forces, and forging a connection between multiple participants in a circle setting, be it intentionally magickal or any other collective that requires an embodied sense of coming together, of joining one another on common ground.

1. Begin by taking a breath low in the belly, feeling whatever bony parts of the body are connecting to ground. On the exhale, settle into the experience of gratitude, humming softly and calling to mind for what or whom you are grateful in this moment.

2. Inhale again, and on the exhale, call to mind your unique ancestry; this can mean envisioning the lands from which your forebears hail, the names of your beloved dead if you know them, or a more general and unnamed sense of the deeper medicine that runs in your blood.

3. For the third point on the pentagram, feel into the land you are on and acknowledge the indigenous people, the tribes by name if possible, that belong to this ground.

4. The fourth point on the pentagram is your own body; take a breath and on the exhale, without judgment, notice the multitude of sensations present in your creaturely body now, at this moment.

5. Last, inhale deeply, and feel into the current season or moon cycle on your fifth and final exhale.

Moving through the entire pentagram of being takes less than one minute, and it is a simple practice that can be done at the inception and ending of gatherings, solitary ceremonies, and any event that deserves a certain level of dedication and reverence.

To My Pagan Foremothers, I Am Still Here
Word-Witching the Circle-Round

I know not whether I dream of you, you circle of hooded heathens with drums 'tween your legs and smoking pipes dangling from your lips, or if I am, in fact, a living dream of yours. Did you conjure me on some dark-cloaked evening when the thunder rolled and the oldest gods walked heavy on the earth? If I be your vision only, even so, I am still here.

Grandmothers of the North, come to me. Bear witness to this initiation of mine while I face the snowcapped mountains and bid my bones become stone. Grandmothers of the East, come to me. Whisper hushed hymns in an alien tongue while I welcome the warmer winds to bless this naked and aging skin of mine. Grandmothers of the South, come to me. Tend this altar fire while that primal dance takes hold of my flesh and animates these overstiff joints dried out from joylessness. Grandmothers of the West, come to me. Drench me in seawater and weave kelp into my locks so I might remember the old salty mother who bore me.

To my Pagan foremothers, I am still here, held by the loamy ground below and blessed by the vast indigo night above. And so it is.

❖

To Tend a Better Altar, to Write a Better Book of Moon and Flame

The time is nearing now, the time when you will leave this House of Initiation and begin to seek out the hags, as you have many times before within this lifetime and countless incarnations. Before you enter each hag's house, you will be asked to take to your altar, to create a tangible space that will honor the essence, the potency, and the medicine of those particular lunar seasons you find yourself in. Your altar might be simple, a portable tray that can be moved from room to room or a hidden shelf in a cabinet that can be tucked away in the dark. So, too, can your altar be grand and stationary, your holiest of holies in your wild home.

Witchcraft always meets you where you are, and you need not exhaust your precious resources to prepare for this journey. Your altar is a place to work, to make magick, to honor deity if you feel called, to remind you that your witchery is the stuff of beauty, and to serve as hallowed ground, a place to return when life is tugging at your skin. Before you leave this House of Initiation, define an altar space that will support your work, and name it as your own.

Find for yourself, also, a large blank book that will become your Book of Shadows or, if you like, your Book of Moon and Flame, a place to record dream visions, sacred symbols, bizarre images, spellworkings,

word-witchery, and all the secrets learned from those
cunning hags. This is a living text, a book penned by
your hand. You are both author and reader, thus you
cannot misstep in writing upon these pages. Clear your
altar when ready, place your blank book alone on that
surface that will see you through many, many initiations as you journey,
take a breath, feel the tingle of intense potential and vast possibility, and
begin.

Hag Lesson #10

The altar is a touchstone.

An Initiation of Blood and Bone

*This is my initiation of blood and bone. I am naming myself Witch,
and I am seeking out those hidden treasures in my psyche left there
by my heathen grandmothers so long ago. I am taking back what is
mine, and the wildest gods with the greatest stories are dreaming me
into being and naming me their Priestess. Awakened I am on these
precious days, and my most beloved dead are walking with me as
I undertake this great journey and live the wildest year I have ever
known.*

House of the
GARDEN HAG

Opening Spring's Portal

Invocation to the

Crone of the East

❦

Welcome, Witch of Blooming Bud

Paint my face with loam and mud

The scent of birth, this cleansing storm

And you, the hag, in softer form.

The language of spring leaves out the witty banter and proper rhetoric, forsaking the serious grumbles and pensive frowns of winter for those joyous belly-wobbling laughs that can erupt only from their low places on warmer days. Spring is the annual sunrise, the season of possibility dawning and hope subtly realized, if only in those fleeting glimpses of an innocence we once knew when our skin was tighter and our worlds were smaller. We look to the east now, searching for the perpetual dawn in the eyes of newborns and in the tender roots of a garden well nursed through those harsher moons. We find her right there, that Garden Hag who rules this fertile season of hard-blowing storms and resilient hearts, and she tells us tales of ancestral healing and the silver-threaded web of generations. She tells us to check in with our beloveds, to ask for what we need, and to allow ourselves to feel tender. Her stories are those of lightning women; warm, wounded grannies; and wild children, and her wisdom is born of an undying faith in renewal and rebirth.

Overview of the Spring Journey

Season of Tender Roots

Nourishment: Belonging
Story Medicine: The Chicken-Witch of the Grove

Season of the Elders' Altar

Challenge: Heart Healing
Story Medicine: Temple of the Flame Tender

Season of Mud-Caked Hands

Wisdom: Gathering
Story Medicine: Bawdy Betty and the Lady in Beige

The Spring Altar, Handmade with a Wild Innocence

Lay to rest the bones and pine of winter. Now come the moons of erotic innocence and nature lust. Build your spring altar to reflect new beginnings, sensuality, and righteous rejuvenation. Gather things that grow, and tend them well. Honor the air element with sustainably harvested feathers, eggshells, and wildflowers. At altar center place a candle colored or carved in such a way that you might name it "Sovereignty." You might place a small dish of fertile dirt in the north, seeds in the east, an image of the sun in the south, and a seashell in the west, all to honor the beauteous dance of the elements as the Wheel of the Year turns toward fruition. May your altar evoke a felt sense of possibility and infinite potential. These are the days of swelling purpose, weaving ancestral memory with long vision, and digging out the deep secrets, and your altar is a physical reminder of these fertile intentions. May you find what you seek.

CHAPTER 1

Season of Tender Roots

❖

Belonging

Surely you have never welcomed a wilder season than this. That journey out of winter might have meant death for a less bold version of you, or perhaps it did. Perhaps there is a heap of frozen flesh, a face with frost-webbed skin that looks much like yours, left behind in the snow, left to nourish the wolves and feed the loamy ground. Who you are now, a seeker having traveled through countless dreamlands of wintry snow-scapes and barren fallows, is not the wild one you used to be. Who you are now, a warmth-famished wanderer destined to better heal those deep but unknown wounds of the anguished dead, is not the same creature who dwelled in winter's darkness, who sought sanctuary at the hearthside and dreamed the smaller dreams.

Those final long moons of winter have been a birth, to be sure, and you have woken this brighter morning with a heart full of lusty Pagan po-etry and eyes that long for the reds of rose petals and ten thousand shades of green only a sprouting early-spring garden can show you. This moon cycle is the first of spring, running through the vernal equinox. Here you are, at long last, and the Garden Hag's been waiting with a bountiful table attended by an infinite number of spectral guests; you may not know them, but these ethereal ones most certainly remember you.

May this first moon of spring, this Season of Tender Roots, greet you as the Garden Hag does, with childlike curiosity and much, much joy. Her face is lined, her hair is gray, but her heart beats in the rhythm of the innocent erotic. You have come to her ivy-hugged house in search of some great, unnamed thing, and she is just the one to help you uncover that buried treasure, those invaluable golden depths of wild wisdom tucked away long ago, planted beneath the Elders' Altar for safekeeping.

Hag Lesson #11

Spring magick is lineage-mending witchery.

Our spring magick does the business of binding our dreams to those who came before us; our healing is their healing, and our longing is their longing.

Remind Me, Grandmother

A Whispered Lament

Remind me, Grandmother. I've forgotten my way again in this time-impoverished world where no one seems to know how to find that soul-well of patience you showed me when I was a babe. My blood remembers endless days spent tending resilient gardens, uninterrupted by those unsanctified screens and spirit-starved screams for immediate attention. And, in those rare still moments, my bones' marrow recalls retreat to the edges of waters fed by melting snows and into the yellow curls of budding daffodils.

Remind me, Grandmother. I fear I've misplaced the treasure map showing me where my ancestral inheritance was hidden. My spiraling double-helix sigils are stamped with the pain of famine, dead children, and betrayal. There is a persistent mourning in the ache of my joints, and day by day, they groan a little louder in a bone-on-bone keening for my forgotten dead.

Remind me, Grandmother. Without your perpetual hope, I'm in a dire place, precariously teetering on the precipice of feckless nostalgia and overromanticization of my haunted past. It's the mud-licking primal wild I'm after, you see, and I know you hear me.

Remind me of my tenderest roots, Grandmother, if only now, while I drift to sleep on these early-spring evenings.

———— ❧ ————

Sunrise Reflection: The Beloved Dead

The first moon of spring calls us to ask ourselves potent questions about lineage and legacy, about broken mother lines and misplaced myths. Witches lean toward intuitive understanding in these times of lost ancestries, rather than endless intellectual digging through records of birth and death, easily fabricated nonevidence and inaccurate reflections of the deep wells of passion and experience housed by the flesh of those who bore us. There is a rejuvenated purity to early spring, an air of wide-eyed, newborn innocence and electric possibility that pulls us closer to healing what seemed unhealable — that is, to integrating what once seemed so far outside us, too foreign and, perhaps, too revolting to possibly be part of us. Each spring we are blessed with what seems a newfound gift of grace, an invitation to encounter, if not hold in our shaking hands, the wealth of Earth-based traditions that our blood remembers and remembers well.

Those coming home to their Witchcraft, acknowledging the art of magick for the first time, perhaps, after sufficiently dismantling the walls of indoctrinated belief that blocked their way, often are met with yet another obstacle, one entirely unforeseen and seemingly insurmountable. If we are to embrace the rhythms of the earth, the Craft, and the land, we must feel into the beauteous fabric of which our soul threads are part. We must resist ignoring the scars we have inherited, yes, but we must also look to the wisdom of those who lived long before the dead ones we know by name. We must step back and broaden our vision, scrying our way from the intricate patterns of family and roots.

To do so, we must seek out the beloved dead. We must extend our reach beyond a century or two. We must cultivate the long vision that eludes these days, and we must take great care with our fragile psyches and questing spirits.

Tell me, how does it feel to set the intention to frame yourself as but a character in a larger story, without sacrificing your sovereignty? How does it feel, on the cusp of this fertile season of sensuality and abundance, to acknowledge that you were born, in part, to be the salve for the wounds of your kindred in spirit?

The wild-hearted are stronger in numbers, and your magick is that much more powerful when you acknowledge that it is sourced from legions of flame-tending altar keepers, masses of hearth holders and medicine people who, in their own way, still stand with you. Spring is the season of digging, but for now, we forsake the trowel for the pen, the dirt for dream visions. In your Book of Moon and Flame, free-write on the following prompts, if they feel true, changing the language as you see fit:

> *I come from a long line of flame tenders, and they remind me now of...*
> *In those wild dream visions, all my kindreds stand there, encircling a tree,*
>   *pressing foreheads to bark, and praying for...*
> *I am the living bloom sprouted from seeds planted by my great-great-grandmother in a lush land of greed and battle, and these resilient roots of*
>   *mine will never...*

Spring Equinox Celebration:
Twin Eggs of Birth and Renewal

Materials: Air-drying clay

To beckon warmer days, to breathe hot and melt those persistent morning frosts in the name of sheer and visceral desire, is a primal act. We find ourselves in the final stages of labor here, birthing something out of pure will and our human longing to create but not knowing, not yet, what our faithful efforts have yielded. The great paradox of spring is this: If we look to the creation myths across many cultures, we see that birth is nothing if not violent, a sudden and cataclysmic eruption of something epic out of a primordial dark womb. And yet, in spring, there is also a sense of lightness, possibility, and joy.

Our vernal equinox celebrations must weave these two seemingly opposing spring energies together, blending that soft-baby-animal creaturely and generative innocence with that bursting, disruptive force that brings all things new into being. Equinoxes are balance points between light and shadow, and on that first day of spring, we must welcome the sweet and sugary light along with the bold, bone-shaking dark.

At your altar, light your candle of sovereignty and welcome the spirits of your more ancient elders of good intent, those who have your best interest at heart, those who want you to remember the unique power that runs in your blood. Face the east, the direction of new beginnings and the spring season; then begin to mold two egg-shaped sculptures from clay by hand, honoring this season of renewed opportunities and endless chances, pondering the infinite potential found in nature, the sheer resilience of wild agency, and the peace that comes from knowing that all dies to begin again. What you failed to hatch last year, what stayed hidden behind your fragile eggshell walls, surely will emerge from the cosmic egg this go-around, vibrant, full of wonder, and poised for timely action.

Take care with these new creations, humble in appearance as they may be. Hold an egg in each hand, naming the one in your right the Egg of Morning, the one in your left the Egg of Evening. Begin to move now, as you feel called; these movements might be subtle and slow gestures or emphatic leaps and rhythmic pulses. Pray with your body. Become an embodied expression of possibility. Honor both the expanding light and the dwindling dark here, on the equinox. Imagine your beloved ancestors dancing with you, holding their own eggs and welcoming what comes. Invite your primal and long-gone dead, those who hold the deepest treasures, those who can initiate you better and more meaningfully into your Craft than any living human.

These delights are what our best times are made of, after all. These small revelries remind us why we have been born to flesh. Stay with this for as much time as you have, permitting your movements to perhaps find repetition; here is where we meet the body electric, when our dance becomes a sacred limb-and-spine offering. If you can stay in the dance until that blessed slightly altered state of consciousness comes, when the dance swallows the thoughts whole and there's little left but heartbeat and movement, you will encounter there a small piece of the Holy Wild sensual.

Your dance has charged your eggs with memory and feeling. Seal this ceremony by decorating them in whatever way seems right, perhaps with rose thorns penetrating the Egg of Evening or intricate symbols of blossom and root carved on the Egg of Morning. Drink something cool and sweet, and welcome all that comes, returning your eggs to your altar and thanking the ancestors in spirit who joined you in your celebration.

Adaptation for Families, Coven Groups, and Other Wild Circles:
A Dance of Light and Shadow

Communal celebration of our kinship with those quickening seeds and searching sprouts warms us when the chill in the air is persistent past its time. Consider adapting the aforementioned ritual to a wild circle of revelers by inviting everyone to dance and move. You might place a basket of premade eggs in the center, with all moving to bless these timeless symbols of gestation and new beginnings. You might have half the group represent the Egg of Evening, the waning darkness, and half represent the Egg of Morning, the expanding light of day, with each group moving through their own body prayer of becoming. Beat the drums. Howl. One of the greatest mottoes for spring witchery is this: *We must have joy in our Craft.* Resist taking yourself too seriously now — there's plenty of time for that later, after all — and honor what tribulations have come and gone during the winter season, what a welcome victory it is to have made it through to spring.

If you feel called, you might also make and decorate egg-shaped cookies or place small wishes and blessings inside eggs and hide them in that time-honored tradition with quite Pagan roots; the egg is hidden as a symbol of gestating the new, and uncovering it is a symbol of birth. With your wild circle, wear vine-wrapped flower crowns and call the days to swell toward fruition. Share stories of lineage healing and sweet remembrance, knowing that every belly laugh is as holy as any incantation could ever be.

Season of Tender Roots: New Moon

Grandmother Speaks:
Let's Get Some of This Blood in the Dirt

At long last, you have arrived. Something about this place sparks childhood memories of dewy forest floors and visitations by those mythic fair-folk, those thin-limbed creatures made of lightning that you were so sure were real — that is, until you were told you were dreaming. The Garden Hag's house is surrounded by blooms so bright they seem to hum, unable to live as such beauty and stay silent. You believe the house is made of stone, but those creeping ivy vines have wrapped every wall in deep emerald curls, and the door eludes you.

For a fleeting moment, you wonder if you are still alive, if perhaps you did indeed die on that winter mountain, and this is your afterlife, a lush place that has never known chill or famine. Even so, your heart beats loudly, and you smell the sweetness of wet dirt. Surely, in the ethers, the gods would never allow flowers to hold such potency, to be more glorious than the deities themselves.

"What are you waiting for, child?" Her voice startles you, and you can see nothing now but tall-growing sunflowers and rosy thickets. "Come, you must be hungry, and I daresay you look a fright." The garden becomes less forgiving now as you move thorny stems out of your path and make your way toward her voice, struggling to choose the right path. "That's it. Keep going; it will be worth it, I promise."

You're in the briars and brambles now. You question whether you took the hardest path, or perhaps all ways were fraught with such sharp-toothed obstacles. Your flesh is carved up by these wilds.

"You're nearly there. Just a little farther. Stay on the path you chose; don't second-guess yourself," she urges, and you think her voice sounds far too optimistic to belong to a hag. Blood runs in rivulets down your arms, and you taste iron on your tongue. She's really there now, though. You can see her thick gray curls through the brush, and you make one final push beyond these angry grasses and bladed branches. Erupting from the thicket, an aged blackthorn with low branches pierces the flesh of your legs and soft of your belly. You fall, bloodied but free, at the feet of the Garden Hag.

"You didn't think such beauty came without a price, did you?" She reaches to help you stand, and you blink the red from your eyelashes to see her better. She's a raw one, for sure, and the sun has loved her well for many years, but her rose-and-pentagram tattoo is still clear on her cracked-skin chest. She's dressed in sheer pastels, and you can see every sharp curve, every thick and raised scar, of her wise-woman body through her clothes. "Come, before you eat, let's get some of this blood in the dirt; the roots love it, and I have just the story to welcome you to my humble haunt."

The Garden Hag helps you to her bountiful table, lushly blanketed with all manner of homegrown fruit and root vegetable. Hiking her skirt between her legs, she sits at the garden's edge and leans close, smirking. When a hag such as this twists her mouth in that sly way before she tells a story, you can trust the tale will be a doozy. When the roses themselves seem to bend a bit closer to hear her words, you know you are about to learn much from this old one with a child's heart.

The Chicken-Witch of the Grove:
A Ceremonial Equinox Tale

To participate in this story ceremony, collect a single basket and eleven objects that can represent the passions, wounds, joys, art, memories, and great loves of your foremothers. These might be eggs, as they are in the story; crystals; flowers; or any other symbol of forgotten stories and hidden secrets. Scatter them around the room or in a natural setting, tucking them away as if you are hiding treasures for a curious babe, then begin to read aloud, setting the intention to symbolically recover lost pieces of your lineage.

Oh, child, you might want to cover your ears, for I'm about to tell you something that's sure to shock even the likes of you. Take a breath. Are you ready?

In all parts of the world, even that humble piece of green beauty you inhabit so well and with such grace, there exists a creature so wild, so beastly, no one dare speak her name. In truth, though, there are many reasons to go searching for her, this long-tongued mistress of all monsters, but only the bravest hearts ever do. They never have to look far, either; she's in the house around the corner, pushing the cart in the corner shop, and rocking the grandbaby on the park bench. Yes, she's fearsome, but she's hardly rare.

Do you know what she is yet? Can you tell by the lilt in my tone? My smirk? The spark in my eyes?

She's the lusty grandmother, low-breasted and sharp-tongued, compassionate in deed but obscene in humor. You might seek her out for advice; she's got years of wisdom tucked under her tunic. You might seek her out for a listening ear; she'll hear you like no one else can.

There is, however, one reason above all reasons why you might search for that mystery-keeping, hip-swaying hag — she's got the greatest stories.

She tells the stories no one else tells, those tales of unchaste-women-gone-warrioress and loose-lipped Witches who shared too much. She tells the stories others won't, and this is one she tells only the truest of hearts, only those who have expressed a longing for sacral wound healing that goes beyond talk and digs into the muck of it, into the fecund depths of shadow and rot, trusting that often there is, in the end, much growth to be born of disgrace.

Now, the lusty grandmothers all begin this tale like this, and I'm not one to part with their traditions:

Once, in a land where the mists remembered what people forgot, where the air was heavy with story and legend but those who lived there spoke in short bursts of arrogant rhetoric and one-size-suits-all maxims, there lived an ordinary woman who hungered for more. She yearned for poetry and passion, for those long-gone days of forbidden love and youthful rebellion. Where could she ever find her sisters-in-lawlessness who yearned to live as she lived, with an insatiable thirst for hedonistic ceremony, first-and-only kisses, blooming gardens, and sensual majesty?

This woman, this plain and simple chicken-witch who collected eggs at sunrise and tended to her garden until the evening skies glowed pink, woke each morning a little more ravenous for that particular secret that left unknown to her would continue to keep her from a more pleasure-filled life. She never kept a lover long, and her few friends maintained a careful distance. She boasted

sacred solitude and a love of the land to hide her loneliness, but, indeed, there was an egg-shaped hole in her
heart that she could never seem to fill.

Now, the lusty grandmothers who tell this tale disagree on many things, stubborn crones that they are.
Some say that this woman, this woman whom we'll call
Juniper, hailed from a long line of women who shared
her distaste for illusion, who yearned for something
greater and more mystical than this ordinary world was
showing them. Others say that Juniper was unique in her
particular quest for joyful community and magick making. In the end, who's to know? Isn't that precisely where
we all find ourselves, in that place of deep and debilitat-
ing uncertainty where our grandmothers are but black-
and-white photographs and our more primal ancestors
are mythic legends, at best? Juniper was much like we
all are these days: trusting in her belonging to something
greater than she had known but unsure of where to find
the medicine she needed.

The lusty hags agree on this next bit, though:

Against all odds and weighted by the heavy shroud
of mystery, Juniper had faith that she was the living incarnation of her ancestors' best-kept secret. One evening, just as that first new moon of spring was rising, she
set her mind to seek out that particular sustenance she
was craving. She left the warmth of her farmhouse bed,
called into the night by the silvery and spectral beams
of that milk-white sliver in the sky, passing through her
well-tended garden and by her many quiet chicken coops
and, before long, finding herself with mud-soaked feet
at the edge of a fog-filled grove. In this place, the grandmothers say, the trees had eyes. Juniper could sense the
wild all around her, mist-made fingers caressing her face
and hissing spirits singing softly into her ears.

Some of the trees watching her now were the kind

she was named for, the holy tree of cleansing and renewal to those ancestors she had never known. Others
were knotty oaks and naughty pines, holy ash trees with
spidery branches, and mourning willows, but all bent to
see the seemingly sure-footed maiden moving to stand at
the grove's center. Anyone who had been watching — if
anyone would have dared to watch such a clearly sacred
and solitary ritual — would have seen Juniper raise her
arms moonward, stand stone still at the center of that
place, and sprout shaggy greens from her head. They
would have seen her skin gray over into bark, her head
roll slightly to the side, and her eyes glaze over to become blueberry clusters. They would have seen her white
dress pierced through and through by branches, and they
would have seen a magick-starved woman turn into a
lush and full-grown juniper tree.

But no one was watching, and Juniper's experience
of that night was far different from what it might have
looked like to an outsider without the ethereal sight.

Yes, she did reach her arms toward the moon, but all
the while her roots were sinking deep, stretching low and
wide, meeting and intertwining beneath the soil with the
other trees' ancient memories. The other trees did not
look at all to her like bark-and-leaf, knot-and-needle forest dwellers, not any longer; she could see them for what
they were in that moment: mothers and grandmothers
come to meet her here, disguised as those earthly deities who were, like our foremothers, too often taken for
granted.

There were dozens of them, moving toward her now,
slowly and with much love in their eyes. She recognized
so few of them, though she saw her face in their faces. No
names had she for these matrilineal wisdom keepers, but
they indeed knew her. Juniper sensed, in that moment, that
each of these wild hearts held a piece of that secret that

eluded her, a particular line in the story that, until this very moment, she thought was hers and hers alone to know and to share, if she had anyone she cared to share it with.

A hooded and kind-faced crone stepped forward and pulled two small and spotted eggs from the thick woolen fabric she was draped in; one of the eggs smelled rotten and was dull in color, while the other was so vibrantly blue that it glowed with an otherworldly spirit.

"Take them both, child," the hag prompted. "This one is my grief over a babe lost too young, and this one is my love of the sea."

Move about the space now, and recover two objects that symbolize these ancestral pieces, placing them in your basket.

The chicken-witch took the gifts with great care, nodding in gratitude.

"And here," another grandmother stepped forward, dressed as a chaste and holy woman and holding two pink-marble eggs, one cracked and one whole. "This is my devout discipline that might have killed me sooner" — she handed Juniper the cracked egg — "had I not harbored such a wild lust beneath my overstarched skirts." Grinning, the old one handed her other egg, and it gave Juniper's hand the slightest shock when she touched it.

Recover two more objects that reflect these ancestral pieces, placing them in your basket.

"Don't dare forget these," offered another ancestor, a gender-fluid beloved wearing jewels of bone and shell. "This is my heartbreak when I left my land." They held a bleeding egg up to their cheek and christened it with their tears. "And this…" They paused, opened their mouth wide, and a blue-quartz egg rolled from their tongue. "This is the Witchcraft that healed me."

Again, recover two more objects, and name them what you like.

A seemingly faceless granny tapped her on the shoulder, and the chicken-witch gasped at the sight of her.

"Fear not, child," the shadow beneath the hood ordered. "I bring you the deep mysteries of your people." She handed her an egg made of bone with a skeletal hand. "The oldest medicine I have." She pulled another egg from up her sleeve. "And the long-vision." The spectral crone gave her still one more egg, a bark-skinned thing that seemed to be a seed, and then the whole of her vanished into thin air.

Recover three more objects, and name them what you like.

To Juniper, it seemed only a fateful, teary-eyed evening spent beneath a new moon, receiving long-kept wisdom and family knowledge, whispered slowly in her ear by one woman after another, handed to her as endless gifts of egg after egg. But to anyone living in the fast-paced world she had left, many moons would rise and set over this grove of mismatched trees set 'round the young, rebel juniper in the center.

"Such is the work of the spring," the last grandmother mused, handing the chicken-witch the last two of her gifts. Juniper's skirts were heavy now, weighted with a bounty of family secrets, cronely art, deep wounds and certain regrets, and hidden love affairs and, most of all, the wild inheritance that had been hers to claim all along. "This is a deep betrayal by those who claimed to love me." She held a humble and misshapen shell, the insides long leaked out, and soft whimpers and mewling sounds came from the pitiful thing as she handed it to Juniper. "That heart wound was mine, but it's yours to heal, my great-great-granddaughter. And this" — she pulled a large and spotted egg from her pocket — "this is my resilience, my refusal to stay down for too long; now it's all yours, as it's always been."

Recover the final two objects and rest your body now, humming softly with basket full and heart tender.

Now, some of the lusty grandmothers who tell this tale say that as soon as she took that last egg, the chicken-witch woke warm in her bed, laughing at the bizarre dream of treespeak and egg-bearing grandmothers, but that the very next day Juniper left her farm sanctuary and went into the world, celebrating the spring at a debaucherous garden party where she met a lover who would become friend, who would become partner.

The lusty grandmothers who harbor a love of the traditional fairy tale end the story like this:

The chicken-witch remained in that grove, a lovely young juniper tree to anyone who ventured to that hallowed ground, for many years, though to her it seemed only a single evening, until a sacred hunter with a warm heart saw her for what she was: a healing woman who spoke the language of the trees, who held a treasure trove of wisdom in her skirts, who needed no saving but rather to wake with a heart made more whole by blood and belonging.

◦━)✴(━◦

The Garden Hag goes quiet then, recovering from a story well told, and you ponder the treasures gifted you, on this fateful evening as this Season of Tender Roots opens itself to you like a wildflower beginning to bloom.

Opening Practice: Your Spring Initiation

There is much joy to be had under the first new moon of spring, to be sure; so, too, is there much healing to be done, much bleeding on the ground to feed the roots. You find yourself on a precipice of some great, unnamed thing here, and your inner hag is bidding you soften those hard psychic edges a bit. Surrender. Lay your winter-frozen flesh bare on the ground and welcome that annual melt.

Speak these words in a wild place, if you're able. Find yourself in those predawn hours when the house is asleep but the ghosts of the beloved dead are awake. Gaze into that swelling dusty-pink glow on the horizon, and know you are not, and indeed have never been, alone.

> This is my spring initiation, and I know now that the joyful hag is me. My heart beats in time with the drums of my forebears. My laugh is the cackle of every crone who came before me, and those mighty ones have surely dreamed me into being. Somewhere right now, in a time that is long gone but still is, there is a hopeful wanderer of my bloodline gazing at the sunrise, as I do in this moment, praying for the very wholeness and healing that I embody. I am the living incarnation of their secret spells, and somewhere, in a time that is yet-to-come, there is a hopeful creature connected to me through this silver-threaded cosmic web. Their breath is my breath, and they have woven the most beauteous tapestry out of these scars of mine.

Seal this ceremony by envisioning one of your most caring primal ancestors breathing in rhythm with you, in rhythm with the babes of the future who wonder about the wisdom of ancient altar keepers like you.

Waxing Moon Practice: Writing It Real

This first moon of spring is a soul-warming moon, and our magick is tasked with both manifestation and healing. As that moon of cleansing storms swells toward fruition, ask yourself what you are calling in that, if only in a small way, serves as a healing salve for the wounds of the wild, for the aches and pains endured by those who have come before us. We bridge the ancient with the new now, beneath these radically hopeful skies, and we bind the material to the embodied feeling.

Gather the signs you have been receiving from both dreams and the material world that seem to show you the way forward. Choose three life areas to inform your manifestation Craft as the moon waxes toward fullness; these might be sacred work, art, family, gender expression, romance, spiritual connection, communication, or any other aspect of your being that seems potent and pressing now. Certainly, we do not have such pieces of ourselves tucked away neatly in stacked boxes. Our work is hardly separate from our art or our communication. We are selecting certain puzzle pieces of our lives now as an act of discernment, of brave-hearted manifestation. We choose now to make the first mark on the blank canvas with hands shaking and brush dripping. We choose now because we feel those quickening energies sparking in our cells, and we choose now to claim the choice as ours.

Spend this waxing moon choosing the beginnings of what will be your spellwork in spring. Ask yourself what is in transition, what feels as if it is shifting underfoot, and what is teetering on some thin edge waiting for you to pull it close or push it away, once and for all. You might look to the creation myths of your ancestry, framing those tales of primordial darkness, violent deities, cosmic eggs, and ancient, long-rooted trees as telling metaphors for the magick of manifestation.

If it feels overly limiting to choose only three life areas, then choose more. If it feels best to work with only one area, then this is the path. Part of the Garden Hag's medicine is discernment born of vulnerable and honest reflection; we take stock, we choose the path, and we move forward, all the while listening to our inner crone for direction. Each morning as the moon waxes, set the intention to receive a sign from the wilds, and look to the ways in which nature itself is an oracle.

In your Book of Moon and Flame begin to describe the life areas as you want them to be, as if they were a snapshot of you in a future remembered into being. Write it real. This is not one-size-suits-all manifestation magick; this is word-witchery at its best. As you write, stay in touch with the embodied feeling of this moment you are describing, and be sure this is a feeling you can name as your own. As you see yourself there in that moment, is the feeling joy? Ease? Satisfaction? Release? Try to maintain that embodied sense of the moment while you write and describe nothing other than the actual moment of fruition, of vision realized.

All the While, They Were Writing It Real

Storm Moon Spells

––◄►––   ––◄►)(◄►––   ––◄►––

In their most epic moments, they were so still that ivy might have wrapped around their frozen flesh, that moss might have gathered beneath the once-soft swell of their thighs. The twitching of their right hand was the lone sign they lived on, pouring black-ink word-witchery onto the page like their very lifeblood was running out through the end of the pen and curling in dark, sanguine poetry, weaving and swirling about in aching words and lost stories. Spring storms raged outside their window, vicious battles between the lightning children and their low-rumbling hunter god, but they were unmoved. Were others to see them in such a state, they might think them a slow-breathing monument to a hunted witch-scribe, but they would never know their wildest secret. In those moments, they were writing it real, you see. They were breathing it all into being, one precious letter at a time, like a dream vision had by their great-grandbabes longing for their handwritten myths; in those moments, they were dreaming those holy innocents to life with the potent medicine scribbled and tossed about on the page. Yes, the harder-hearted ones wondered about them — pitied them, even — but, all the while, they were writing it real.

––◄►)(◄►––

Season of Tender Roots: Full Moon

Grandmother Speaks:
The Sweetest Fruit Is Only Fresh for So Long

The Garden Hag told you your scrapes would be worth it, and the bounty before you affirms her promise. A more beauteous tablescape you have never seen. Surely, you have come a long way since that first winter moon. Surely, some long-gone elder is blessing you from the ethers.

The Garden Hag is tending to your wounds now, blotting the blood and smearing bitter-smelling plant medicine on your bare back. Your belly is snarling, but the choices are so immense that you cannot decide what taste you'd like first on that overdry tongue of yours. Pitchers of pink liquid with golden flecks stand next to platters of fresh and glistening fruits and homegrown greens. The sweet scents are so overwhelming that you all but forget your wounds and scarcely feel the spittle running down your chin.

"Go on," she mutters. "If you dither in uncertainty too long, this bounty will fade. Already this arrogant sun threatens to brown the berries and wilt my roses. All of this is yours now; what stops you? Some distant memory of a mocking bully? Something said to a long-lost loved one, words you didn't even know were stuck to one of your bones like these thorns in your flesh? What stops you from claiming these gifts as yours? Eat now. Don't wait. The sweetest fruit is only fresh for so long."

Full Moon Practice: Cosmic Eggs of Creation and Will

Having described your dream visions, having written them real, gather three jars now, one for each of the life areas with which you are working; if you chose to have more or fewer life areas, then you'll need as many jars as dream visions. Each jar is a cosmic egg, a place to nest and gestate. Choose objects to place in the cosmic eggs that represent each vision, and be sure to include something you value in each jar. In manifestation spellwork beware of using objects that you care nothing about; this expresses your lack of commitment. This is not to say, however, that you must use objectively pricey items; these are small things that mean something to you. Inside each jar, place the objects along with a small piece of paper describing your dream vision that corresponds to that particular cosmic egg.

When ready, beneath the first full moon of spring, cast a circle or create sacred space in another way suited to your practice; then hold one jar at a time in your hands. See yourself in that vision you are calling in. Feel the feeling. Begin to move in small ways, and however you are moving, begin to see yourself moving that same way in the vision, breathing as you are now in the vision. Step into the flesh of the body that is *you* in that vision. This is your becoming, your holiest hour. You have already written it real; now embody it real.

Feel yourself surrounded by your beloved ancestors, and imagine them moving as you are moving, breathing as you are breathing. When each vision feels full, as if you cannot more powerfully be in that yet-to-come, already-here moment, place the jar on the ground and move on to the next vision. Move and breathe with each of your cosmic eggs, trusting that you are being held in this moment, that the moment itself is holding you, willing it real with you and for you.

After you have held each jar, stand in your circle now, feeling the energy you have raised through your vision, body, and breath. Stand in infinite trust, full of faith that you have rippled the cosmic fabric in that moment, and offer gratitude for what comes, for what is already here.

And so it is.

Season of Tender Roots: Waning Moon

Grandmother Speaks: The Strongest Medicine

You might have called yourself a glutton in your younger years, but you know better now. You know to eat when you're hungry and deprive yourself of nothing. You know not to apologize for having a feeling, creaturely body, and you know to sleep when the world has made you weary.

"I see you've eaten your fill, sweet child." The Garden Hag smiles. She sits across from you at the immense table, still covered in flowers and fruit despite your having had your ravenous way with nearly every food offered. The waning moon looms above, promising some great vibrant change. "I've prepared a room for you, but before you head for such comforts, I'd like to invite you to take the strongest medicine of all. Your stomach can handle it now."

You lean back in your chair and look her in her kind eyes, seeing no malice there.

"It's not a potent root or mushroom, this medicine." She pulls her silk scarf around her shoulders and leans closer, dipping a finger into some jam and licking it clean. "It's simply an understanding, a deep knowing of sorts."

You swallow, waiting.

The hag lets out a long breath and stands, holding her palms toward you, lifting her chin, and presenting her medicine like a grand entertainer.

"The strongest medicine is realizing you are but a single thread in the great galactic fabric. One little tug from you changes the design — reaches the ancients, even — and touches the yet-to-come. The strongest medicine is knowing that you are becoming the wild one you needed when you were younger; that you are healing inherited wounds just by breathing; and that you are a member of a near-infinite and ever-evolving community of sages, Priestesses, and holy ones, of imperfect seekers and flawed lovers."

She nods at the rosebushes that marked you well. "Those roses live now, but their petals will fall so others might bloom. This is the way of it. We are no different, and each spring we're reminded of our fleeting beauty, our interconnection with all that is."

She turns and walks toward the house. "Come, I'll show you to your room."

Waning Moon Practice: The Great Galactic Fabric

As a waning moon practice, consider making an offering to your ancestors. This might be a small gift, a flower laid beneath a tree or a poem written to those who came before you. There is no need to name these people unless you feel called to. You might make this offering just once as the moon wanes, or it might be a daily act of framing yourself as part of an unseen collective. As you make this offering, imagine some small child of the future making this same offering *to* you. See a world less wounded and a land left better by your hand, by the hands of those who act now to save what must be saved.

She Knows My Secrets Now

A Gift of Milk and Tongue to Mother Blackthorn

━━•◦❯(◦❮•◦━━

On an evening much like this one, I knelt and spilled milk on the roots of a stone-barked blackthorn tree in the name of the warrior-esses who came before me, who called that tree their mother god, who humbled themselves before those lightning children of Danu better than I ever could. She pricked my neck as I stood, and I wanted to spit at this tree called strife by the green-dwellers, but I gifted her my storyteller's tongue instead, leaving it as an ornament for her more beastly branches. She knows my secrets now, as I know hers, and I'll forever call this ferocious wolf-mother tree my kin, long after I lay my aching elder body down before her so my blood might feed her berries, long after her roots wrap around the curves of my bones, and long after the innocent babes come to her, spilling their own milk for the Fae and speaking prayers in a heathen tongue.

━•◦❯(◦❮•━

Season of Tender Roots: Dark Moon

Grandmother Speaks: Tomorrow, We Get Dirty

"All right, child. Tuck yourself in tight." The Garden Hag leaves a low-burning lantern at the bedside and opens the curtains. "Always sleep in moonlight when you can; it's good for your skin."

The bed is small, decorated with mismatched floral patterns, and the room smells of hyacinths and lavender.

"Dream deep, sweet one." She has an earnest look on her face now, taking the lily that was tucked in her hair and handing it to you. "Tonight, we sleep. Tomorrow, we get dirty."

Dark Moon Practice: Memories of Joy and Grace

Though we cast no spells beneath the dark moon, we can still do the work of preparing for what comes. As the first moon of spring wanes to dark, consider your cosmic eggs, those dream visions you are nesting now. Consider the feelings you have bound to each vision, and then call up a seed memory for each vision that resonates with the same feeling for you. If one of your dream visions is you in a new home, feeling both joyous and rooted, call to mind a memory when you felt that same, though perhaps less pronounced, feeling. Under the dark moon, find a memory of potent feeling that you can associate with each of your cosmic egg visions, then sleep well in this bright and blooming world you live in.

To the Season of Tender Roots, Farewell for Now

—▸✦◂—

Birth is violent, is it not? No wide-eyed babe enters the world with ease, covered in sweet-smelling perfumes, laughing and gleeful at the amusement of its mother's labor. This world is met for the first time with guttural screams, hot breath, and much, much blood. This world is met with primal eruption, with helplessness, and with an enduring trust that all is as it must be. We meet the spring with tender hearts thawing, with fragile roots seeking that particular nourishment they need from those who have come before.

To the Season of Tender Roots, farewell for now. We shall meet again next year, I a wiser Witch and you a growing garden tended well by the oldest gods.

—▸✦◂—

CHAPTER 2

Season of the Elders' Altar

---◆---

Heart Healing

The bounty of midspring restores our faith in ourselves, in our magick, in our place in this great and numinous story. Even so, there is a subtle melancholy to this second spring moon, an ache that persists despite these long-stretching days and our grand plans to not waste the warmth. This second moon of spring is a moon of challenge, and — though it emerges in many forms — the challenge we are faced with now, the challenge our inner hags want us to meet head-on and meet well, is to not leak our wild power, not to mistake separateness for sovereignty. In *These Wilds Beyond Our Fences*, Bayo Akomolafe writes: "The inside and the outside are not easily divided." We are part of all. All is part of us. We ourselves cannot be perfectly un-flawed and unmarred within a wounded world.

Hag Lesson #12

We can be fully sovereign and still be healing.

Those garden-tending crones teach us of balance, of old ways rooted in living slowly even on these brilliant mornings when the dawn comes early, when it seems we are drenched in the dews of infinite possibility.

We assure ourselves, day by day, that our time is well spent, that our art matters, and that, for all our grand technologies, we remain slow-moving creatures on a beauteous planet. In this chapter, the Garden Hag takes us to visit the Elders' Altar, a holy place where the best secrets are kept, and we are tasked with the fortification of our magick, with binding our spells to activism, with asking the hard questions about soul-deep experience and what it means to continually unlearn what we once called truth. Meet this moon with a brave heart and a poet's tongue, and surely it will be your wildest season yet.

Long May the Balefires Burn

A Bitter Beltane Prophecy

⊢—⊲⊩—————⊲⊩⟩◖⊲⊩—————⊲⊩—⊣

Tonight, these flames are kept alight by the sheer will of those rare, hopeful wild hearts who understand the meaning of rebellion. Numbered are the days of the corrupt powermongers who boast trust in a far-removed, vengeful sky god but believe in nothing. Their cog-and-gear hearts pump oversugared neon light through their veins by day and poison ink onto their tongues by night, leaving them riddled with the disease of moving much but doing little, planning it all but saving no one, speaking incessantly but sharing not one meaningful truth worth repeating. The cages are unlocked, the children are free, the walls are crumbling, the lives of these monsters are short, but long may the balefires burn.

⊢—⊲⊩⟩◖⊲⊩—⊣

Sunrise Reflection: Calling in the Stubborn Dreamers

Beneath the first moon of spring, you bound your cosmic eggs to seed memories of sensate mind and feeling flesh, to the prayers of your forebears, and to the budding greens of a well-kept garden. Now, as this mighty moon dawns, bind your cosmic eggs to one more force. Ask yourself: *How are my dream visions seated within the grander, global community? What meaning do my dreams have for the world of the future, for the legacy I leave behind?* Be a stubborn dreamer now, an outlaw with a bleeding heart. If, in your vision, you are joyously dancing, feeling unapologetic and wild in a way, perhaps, your grandmother never could, and you have bound this vision to a memory of you swaying softly to music last autumn, swelling with a similar lightness and liberation in your belly, and have left wildflowers for the ancestors beneath a tree as a humble offering, then now, my love, now you must connect even more intimately to the cosmic fabric. What does your openhearted dancing mean for others? Who are you dancing for? In your Book of Moon and Flame, reflect on these questions by the light of dawn, asking yourself how this vision of you is a conversation with the universe about how you hope the children of the future will live.

Beltane Celebration: A Fire of Demand

There comes a time when our longing, our subtler kinship with the mysteries, is simply not potent enough. At Beltane, we call in our fiercest fire magick, demanding that the world be rid of those long-standing obstacles to freedom. We condemn inequity, and we put it in the fire. We call out racism and white supremacy, and we put it in the fire. We shred the policies that fail to protect our precious planet, and we put them in the fire. We breathe contempt at misogyny in all its forms, and we give it to the flames. We do all of this in our spellwork, yes, and then we move beyond symbolic action and we vote, we donate, we march, and we make ourselves uncomfortable. We burn, so we can heal. We resist performing, and instead we act upon our worlds with as much zeal as our wild minds and feeling flesh can muster.

The fire element belongs to Beltane, to those heathen bonfire celebrations of both revelry and battle. On this holy day, the cross-quarter day precisely nested between the spring equinox and summer solstice and often celebrated on May 1 in the Northern Hemisphere, we must consider the bridge between the romance of this Pagan celebration and the pressing need to make change in our wounded world. Gather wood, and set a fire to burn, be it a humble one in a burn bowl or a great pyre by the sea.* Adorn yourself, if you like, painting your face with butterfly wings and gracing skin with glitter; then begin tossing into the flames sticks or twigs you've named as those things, those insidious forces, that do not belong

---

* Always be mindful of dry-climate fire safety regulations, and amend your rituals and ceremonies accordingly.

in this world. Toss it all into the fire, and watch it burn. Feel the heat of dying patriarchy on your face, then commit to taking in-the-community action in whatever way feels real and right to you, given your resources, privilege, and place.

We can delight in our activism, and we must have joy in our Craft. Beltane is an annual invitation to both honor and harness the power of the fire element, to make good use of a more righteous rage and not become stuck in apathy or immobilized by disdain. We, as Witches, can do all of this without sacrificing the heat and hedonism of a passion-filled Beltane because we understand that, in the end, our joy is radical. We need not choose between revelry and action; we can have both. If we are to survive, if we are to love this pleasure planet as she deserves to be loved, we must have both.

Adaptation for Families, Coven Groups, and Other Wild Circles: An Action Circle

In adapting this ritual for wild gatherings, consider letting this Beltane ceremony be an action circle. Perhaps gather small donations to be given to a collectively agreed-upon cause; decide on a plan for moving forward, for continuing the action beyond a single evening; then set the fire to burn. Witchcraft without activism dies quickly; it has no heat, no beating heart aligned with the planet's pulse. We cannot have joy in our Craft without the fire, and we cannot claim to be of the earth without working toward its preservation. Gather your people, strategize, act, love, and keep dancing, lest we forget what we are fighting for.

And so it is.

Season of the Elders' Altar: New Moon

Grandmother Speaks: Up and at 'Em, Lazy Bones

You awake with senses graced by birdsong and nectar, but it is the Garden Hag's words that pull you from sleep.

"The dawn has come and gone, child, and we have much to do before that mighty sun sets. Come on." She pulls the quilts back and extends her hand, garish enamel bracelets clanging together, and beckons you to stand. "Up and at 'em, lazy bones."

She tosses a sheer garment at you.

"Strip yourself of those heavy clothes that weigh you down. We move with a lightness today, with juice in our joints and a certain exquisite grace in our step. First, I have a morning story to share with you. Now, I know what you might be thinking…that it is bad luck to tell a good story when the sun is up. But, I assure you, this is one of the few tales that is daylight appropriate."

She takes your place on the bed, facing the night table — a creaky thing covered in nine candles, burned to the last of their wicks — and breathes deep, readying herself.

Temple of the Flame Tender:
A Ceremonial Tale of Wild Redemption

To participate in this ceremonial storytelling, have a fire source and nine candles before you on a small and humble altar, setting the intention to dream and be dreamed; then read these words aloud for you, for the elders, and for those yet-to-be-born babes who will someday look to you for your wisdom.

Even those bashful grannies — those rare and mild-tongued hags who, against all odds, have managed to retain the shyness of girlhood throughout their many years of silent rebellion, bathroom tears, and hidden joys — even those oh-so-quiet crones have stories to tell. In many ways, their tales are the best stories, for their words are never lost in the muddle of useless conversation or tiresome small talk. To be sure, all grandmothers are storytellers, though their story may be kept shackled to their ribs for decades until just the right moment unlocks its binds and sends it climbing their tongues. The stories these wise ones tell are not those with blatant meanings and hard-edged dialogue where all morals are laid out neatly like a well-set table.

No, these stories are those from which lessons must

be mined slowly, those that are never told the same way twice, and those that might make you weep during the first telling only to cackle like a Witch in autumn during each telling thereafter. These are the stories that must be earned, and only those seemingly timid and flame-tending elders can discern who is worthy of hearing such carefully woven tales, who is cunning enough to see those thin red threads of soulful understanding within the thick blue cross-hatching of lived experience and hard-earned arcane knowledge. I'd like to think this is one such tale — but, in the end, I cannot be sure, for I first heard it in one of those waking dreams that haunts you in early spring when the longing for the sun's grace is never greater and is all-consuming.

Those shy grannies say this story begins at precisely such a time, when Imbolc has passed and left a lonely-hearted creature thirsty for a better life than what she'd been given, when the shadows of Beltane are haunting even the most fervently guarded heart. Beneath that second spring moon, this wild one left the mountaintop house she had so carefully constructed, a brick-by-brick shrine to her discipline and achievements, a place where the wolves found her time and time again and where the wintry hags taught her well. She had developed a distaste for blind ambition, you see, and she set out searching for something truer, some wild place she remembered but had never seen.

Now, these slow-living grannies who tell this story have all the time in the world, and many of them would go into the trials and tribulations this wandering heart faced on her way east. Some will recount her nightmares and her many nights being hunted by spiritual predators. Others will dive deep into this wild one's backstory and wax poetic for hours around the fire, speaking of her wounds and wants. Alas, these grandmothers have far more patience than I do.

My story finds this seeking creature at the end of her

journey east, having arrived at the temple of the flame tender. This was a holy place, indeed, an ancient moss-stoned and hawthorn-flanked fortress that had lived through many incarnations. It had been sacrificial ground to the old hooded ones and a soldiers' sanctuary. It had been a craggy altar to the Cailleach, and it had been an abandoned ruin on which lost children played their out-lawed games. Even now, it is still all of these things and none of them, but that wandering heart whom we shall call Bride found this place at just the right time.

The breath of the moon was still cold in this Sea-son of the Elders' Altar, and were we to paint the pivotal scene of this beloved one's life and title it only with her name, our art would surely depict her right there, having journeyed long and well and found this sacred ground, falling to her knees, heart swelling with more gratitude than she had ever known.

This was how the old fire keeper found her; she was near frozen, bubbling with all the joy of a mad one who had forgotten the aches and pains of life, but the elder Priestess knew better than to send her away. Clearly, the old gods had led this wanderer here, and the altar keepers fed her homegrown leafy medicines and put her to bed.

In the morning, this fateful soul met with the High Priestess, an old stalwart grandmother who had a wild look about her. The two chatted for a time, though those shy hags who tell this story disagree on the topic of their conversation. The grannies do agree, however, on this: At the end of their meeting, the High Priestess left Bride with these harsh words:

"I see your journey here was a hard one, but it has not broken you of your lust for victory. If you stay here, my child, I assure you your time here will wear down that armor you wear, nipping away at your goals and your strategies bit by bit until you have no idea who you are or why you've come. Soon, you'll know nothing at all for sure, though you know much now. Even so, you must never lose hope, and you must keep opening every door — for you, for the elders, and for those yet-to-be-born babes who, someday, will look to you for wisdom."

Now, Bride was always up for a challenge, you see, so while the wise one's words might have scared a wildling with a weaker belly, they were precisely what that seeker needed to hear in order to stay put. Years and years went by after that fateful conversation. Bride became a Priestess of low degree, learning to tend the flames as the others did. There was a central fire in the holiest of holies that was perpetually burning, and the Priestesses were permitted to light three candles each day for their most precious desires. The ever-seeking and approval-hungry Bride thrived within this well-disciplined container. Each morning, she would wake, sip some tepid water, nibble on saltless bread, and light three candles of that central flame. One was for a lover with warm hands, one was for a poet's tongue, and the final flame was always for the Goddess — or, rather, a wish that the Goddess would find her and gift her with the answers to all spiritual mysteries and worldly delights.

Light three candles now: one each for a lover with warm hands, a poet's tongue, and the Goddess/God/Goddex.

By the light of day, Bride would hang on the elder's every word, taking furious notes and striving to be a star student of Witchcraft. After sunset, Bride would never lounge about with the others but would take to her room and ponder heady philosophies, ethics, and the merit of the Holy Wild.

Over time, the aging Priestess began staying inside the temple and refusing to leave. She would obsess over the altar, spending hours upon hours staring at the central flame and willing herself to learn its secrets. The others stopped inviting the Priestess into the garden or to share in their storytelling, and Bride again found herself quite lonely, chained tightly to spiritual discipline and self-imposed regimens that offered the illusion of predictability.

Alas, death even comes to sanctuaries such as these, despite our best efforts to stay safe, and twenty years to the day after the Priestess had arrived, the old flame-tending grandmother who kept the temple in order died. All the Priestesses mourned, of course, but none with more anguish than the lonely-hearted Bride, who wailed so loudly that none could sleep for weeks, and the others feared for the Priestess's health. A thick shroud of sadness she wore, and those days of good grief most certainly changed her.

Time dulls even the most biting of aches, of course, and by the following spring, the High Priestess could be spoken of with love and reverence and few tears. It happened, though, that the central candle on the altar was never quite as bright as it used to be, not really, and over the years the Priestesshood began to dwindle. Some of the women left for romance. Others left for art. In the end, only Bride remained.

Alone she was, but her routine kept her warm for a time. Each morning she woke; sipped her tepid water; nibbled her bread; then lit her candles for a lover that never came, a poetry that was never spoken, and a Goddess she never met. Her days were spent staring at the altar and willing it to share its secrets, and her nights were spent speaking to the dead High Priestess as if her heart were still beating. Over time, she started to see the ghost of the elder in her own face and hear her voice when she spoke.

The years flowed along like a slow-moving stream that wound about in a circle, always spinning 'round again to spring, unbothered by the unmet dreams of the flame-tending Priestess who never left the temple. Left alone with her thoughts, Bride began to wonder about the nature of time. She wondered if she had truly aged, or if she had merely remembered herself old. Her childhood memories seemed to be more fantasy these days, after all, and who was to say all of time wasn't an illusion? Without anyone to argue in defense of linear time and the value of those boxes labeled "past," "present," and "future," Bride slipped into a state of timelessness and grace, a holy void of sorts, that would have swallowed her whole were it not for her precious patterns.

One day, a day that began just like all the others, the Priestess woke, drank her water, and ate her bread, then began lighting her candles. Just as she lit the candle for her absent lover, a knock came at the door. Now, some of the shy storytelling grannies say that Bride heard the knock and ignored it, while others say that the Priestess, without any reference for what a knock sounded like after so many quiet years spent in solitude, could not hear the knock at all. She didn't answer the door, in any case, not then and not when the other two knocks came as she lit the candle for her poetry and another for the Goddess. The rest of her day dragged on as it always did, and the knocks never came again, not really.

Something had changed inside that temple, though. Some wild energy entered the place and refused to leave after that day when the knocks came. That central candle in the holiest of holies burned a bit brighter, nearly returning to the glory with which it glowed when the High Priestess was still living. Bride began dreaming the most fantastical dreams, waking in a cold sweat and calling out to the old grandmother's ghost. A year or more of these dreams went by, and the Priestess began to slip even more out of time without sleep to anchor her.

One such night, just at the Witching Hour, after a few hours of particularly fitful sleep, Bride began moving about the temple, as she often did. As she passed the hallway mirror, though, she stopped dead in her tracks, for there was most certainly the old High Priestess come back to life.

"What are you doing with yourself, child?" the reflection in the mirror said. "Day after day you light those candles for your wishes, then you don't even answer the door for a visitor? How will you know if a lover has come? Who will hear your poetry, and how will the Goddess find you?"

"A knock? Well, I — I don't recall —" she protested, but the grandmother interrupted her.

"Next time someone comes to the door, Priestess, let them in. Put your routine out for the dogs, and leave me in the ground where I belong."

The ghost kept looking back at her through the mirror but said no more, and the Priestess returned to bed. When she woke in the morning, she moved to sip her water but stopped herself. It was for mere moments that she stared at her glass recalling the spectral crone's orders, but that small window of time was space enough for her to hear a knocking. She recalled the grandmother's words and moved, not without caution, to the door.

Half her heart was expecting a lover, but what she found was a wild-hearted woman who had heard from her own mother about the holiness of this place. The Priestess was hesitant, but there was something about her way that made Bride invite her to stay. The next day, another wild heart arrived, and then another, then another. In only a few moons' time, the temple was full of Priestesses again. When early spring rolled around, the old Bride-Priestess found herself face-to-face with a strong-jawed creature who, she thought, seemed much like she used to be, chained to routine and ambition, fearful of all things unknown.

Like we all do, the elder had become the very teacher she had needed when she was younger, and she told the woman, this new seeker whom we'll call Brighid, in the most matter-of-fact tone she could muster, "Soon, you'll know nothing at all for sure, though you know much now. Even so, you must never lose hope, and you must keep opening every door — for you, for the elders, and for those yet-to-be-born babes who, someday, will look to you for wisdom."

In time, the newcomer fell into a ritual, lighting candles every morning for innocence, courage, and spiritual discernment. She was overly attached to Bride, that young one, always following after her like a loyal puppy and thirstily soaking up every bit of the elder's wisdom. Every morning, she lit her candles for innocence, courage, and spiritual discernment, and every night, she prayed to the old gods for the High Priestess's health.

Light three more candles now: one each for innocence, courage, and spiritual discernment.

Alas, death visited the holy place once more, as it always did, carrying Bride into the ether, where she joined those ghostly flame tenders who knew her best. The other altar keepers slowly left the temple for their many reasons, and Brighid found herself alone in the fire keeper's temple, waiting for knocks that, in time, did come. The lover with warm hands was first to arrive, followed by a poet's tongue, and the Goddess herself, and as time wound 'round like a circular stream, the Priestesses returned to the temple, the fire tender aged, and a wild heart who looked much like she used to look in her youth found herself there. "Soon, you'll know nothing at all for sure, though you know much now. Even so, you must never lose hope, and you must keep opening every door — for you, for the elders, and for those yet-to-be-born babes who, someday, will look to you for wisdom."

The budding Priestess, this new wild heart whom we shall call Bright, lit candles for the sacred trees, for good stories, and for those hearth-holding Witches who, when all is said and done, keep hope alive for those who have yet to know true belonging.

Light the final three candles now: one each for sacred trees, good stories, and hearth-holding Witches.

In time, it was innocence, courage, and spiritual discernment that came to the door, followed, of course, by more altar keepers and a wandering Priestess who would call in beauty, magick, and grace, only to be found by sacred trees, good stories, and the hearth holders.

Some of those bashful grannies who share this story end it with a song, others with a prayer, and some just a knowing nod that silently says, *Yes. Yes, you understand.* I, however, will end it with pertinent questions:

What have your forebears lit candles for that, at long last, has come to your door? Will you answer when the knock comes, and will you keep the fire burning for blessings destined only to find the yet-to-be-born?

⊶⊱✦⊰⊷

The Garden Hag does not wait for you to answer but stands, leaving you with the nine candles burning and these words: "Well, ponder these questions now. Meet me by the forsythias once you've dressed, and we'll go to the Elders' Altar, where nostalgia meets activism, where the deeper wounds meet the healer you've become."

Opening Practice: Flame Tending for the Yet-to-Be-Born

Materials: Three small, squat candles, one for each "cosmic egg" spell jar

As the new moon dawns at midspring, place your small candles on top of your cosmic egg jars. You might choose colors that correspond to your dream visions, or a simple tea light will suffice. When ready, affirm that you are in sacred space, feel into your body, and light these candles, one at a time, in the name of a less wounded, more whole world. As you light each candle, call to mind a vision of children in the future gifted with a dream similar to the dream you are calling in for yourself. If one of your cosmic eggs represents you rooted and secure in a new home, for instance, perhaps you envision future generations, the yet-to-be-born, swaddled and secure, as you light the candle. If you are calling in travel and spaciousness, perhaps you see young ones playing in wide-open spaces while you light the candle, affirming that what you are calling in for yourself is not for you and you alone.

Let the candles burn for a few minutes, holding your hands over the heat of each flame as you move between your visions. When it feels right, carefully pour some of the wax over the jar to seal it, then thank the elder ancestors for the flames they have tended for you. Open the circle and, ideally, allow the candles to burn out naturally, or snuff them if you must.

And so it is.

Waxing Moon Practice: The Wildness of Our Longing

As this potent moon waxes, consider that what you yearn for is also yearning for you, that you are more sensitive to the spiral dance of nonlinear time than you think, and that desire is memory. As the moon swells toward fullness, task yourself with this practice as often as possible. For each of your cosmic egg jars, move your thoughts between these four points:

1. Call to mind a seed memory — that is, a memory of you feeling the same feeling that is integral to your vision. While envisioning this moment, chant aloud: "Yes, thank you. More, please."

2. Now, come to the present moment. Chant: "Yes, thank you. More, please."

3. Call to mind the vision of you with dream fulfilled. "Yes, thank you. More, please."
4. Finally, picture the vision of future generations in a more sustainable world, feeling the same feeling that you yourself are calling in.

Do this strategically until it comes more easily, though it might seem difficult at first. If your vision is you joyously dancing in nature, the seed memory might be you softly swaying in your kitchen on the first warm spring day, and then the dream-world vision might be children dancing while bees buzz about and butterflies grace the skies. Envision these scenes in succession: first, you swaying softly, then you in the present moment as you are now, then the vision of you dancing in nature, then the dream-world vision, you in nature, present moment, softly swaying, present moment, nature vision, dream world, and continue. This is a psychic dance that makes for potent spellwork, binding what you want to what you already have to what you hope will bless the great-great-grandbabes of the future, be they your own blood or not.

Season of the Elders' Altar: Full Moon

Grandmother Speaks: Blessed by the Most Primal Rivers

The Elders' Altar is hardly as grand as you envisioned it to be. A lone and humble candle burns beside old, cracked antlers in the center of a flat slate stone veined with rose quartz and dappled with wax, set upon an immense tree stump, all nested well at the bottom of a steep hill. Morning-glory vines have overtaken it all, with blue and purple flowers spiderwebbing around even the candle, climbing the hill behind the holy place.

You are not far from the Garden Hag's house, and the journey seemed too easy, but you sense there is some battle in store for you.

"Not very impressive, is it?" The Garden Hag pokes at your arm, and you raise a brow in her direction. "I know. I thought the same thing the first time I came here." She pulls a lush bouquet from her long-flowing scarves and places it beside the candle. "Stand back."

The ground begins to tremble beneath your feet, just as a sudden white-blue streak of lightning cracks the sky and sends an immediate growl of thunder earthward. You want to ask what's happening, but you aren't given the time; the humble stump rattles, and loose dirt shakes at its roots, leaving an ever-widening hole beneath the quivering altar.

The rains are falling now, and the candle flame is sizzling with the relentless drops but somehow keeps burning. Your footing feels suddenly unstable on this quaking ground, and with no warning at all, a burst of rushing water erupts from the hole beneath the altar, coughing a river your way and drenching you and the Garden Hag in a salty splash.

"Hang on!" the crone shouts over the unrelenting sound of storm and flood. "This is what we have come here for."

You're on your knees now, clutching the hag's legs, and you can see that the waters are subtly pink in tone and smell faintly of iron. Even the rain tastes of seawater, and blush-colored droplets and darker red rivulets are running down your arms. More distant, the thunder growls, and the rain slows to intermittent drops as the stump's roots return to where they were when you arrived, dirt moving to refill the void and sky returning to a soft blue shade.

The chaos passed just as swiftly as it arrived.

The hag pulls you to stand, and you wipe the wet from your eyes.

"Well," she starts, "how do you feel?" She blots your face with one of her scarves. "You've been initiated now into a line longer than you can possibly imagine. You've been blessed by the most primal rivers of wild belonging. Such is the magick of this place."

Full Moon Practice: The Truest Healing

Materials: Cosmic eggs and offering to the ancestors

This full moon of midspring calls for high-fire magick, demands you muster up will and agency, and urges you to forge connections between all the potent reflections and small ceremonies you have done so far this season. For this ritual, you'll need your cosmic eggs, now sealed in wax from the new moon, and whatever offering you have been making to the foremothers since that first spring moon bade you examine more fully your ancestral lines.

Begin by casting a circle using the circle-as-story method, or create sacred space in whatever way you see fit. Feel into your body. Hum. Let your belly swell with breath. At the center of your circle, place your cosmic eggs and an offering to the ancestors. Choose one cosmic egg to work with first, holding it and facing north. Now, take a quarter turn to the east and call up your dream vision, what you first nested in the jar, what you want for yourself. Feel the feeling. See it. Know it as already happening. Turn and face the south, and call up the vision of the dream world, the children being gifted with the same blessing you are seeking. Feel the feeling. Turn west, and call up the seed memory now — your past experience of the same feeling you are calling in, in greater, more potent form. Face north, and come to the present moment, holding on to the same feeling.

Now, keep going, moving clockwise. Face east and call up the vision. Feel the feeling. Face south and call up the dream-world vision. Feel the feeling. Face west and call up the seed memory, again feeling into that moment in time, then returning to the present moment facing north.

The feeling is the glue, you see. The embodied feeling, the under-the-skin sensation, is the binding matter between all these moments. We add one more layer to this now. Stand at circle center, the point of sovereignty, and touch the offering you are making to the forebears. Speak gratitude, saying "thank you" or other words that seem appropriate. Now, move around the circle nine more times, coming back to center after each direction and repeating your words of gratitude. Come to the north, feeling the feeling of the present, then return to center. "Thank you." Turn east, feel the feeling and see the vision, then return to center. "Thank you." To the south, the feeling of future generations blessed and whole. At center, "thank you." Turning west, coming to the memory, feeling the feeling, returning to center. "Thank you."

Do this nine times before moving on to your second cosmic egg, going through the same process, adding gratitude to the ancestors after you have moved around the circle clockwise once, then continue for nine rounds returning to center four times each, before doing the same with the third and final egg.

This work is powerful, indeed. When you have finished working with all three jars, remain at center, at sovereignty, and speak a spontaneous prayer to your more primal ancestors, to those whose drums beat in your blood, whose prayers are stamped on your bones. Open the circle when it feels finished, trust the spell as complete, place your hands on the ground, return the cosmic eggs to your altar, and spend as much time out of doors as you did engaged in the spellwork.

And so it is.

Season of the Elders' Altar: Waning Moon

Grandmother Speaks: This Is Hardly a Day to Be Timid

The water runs cool around your ankles. You've stripped yourself of your garment, and you kneel in this fast-running stream, splashing your face clean and pouring handfuls of the pure stuff over your arms. The pink and red has dried in hard patches on your skin, and it's not coming off easily, even in this hard-moving bath.

"Just dive in," the Garden Hag says from behind you. "There's no turning back now, after all. You're changed. You're fearless. You've been tattooed by the blood of your own becoming, and this is hardly a day to be timid."

Waning Moon Practice: The Feeling Body

This is the season of deep sensory being, of the wild body. As the moon wanes toward dark and you buzz with the electricity of your full moon spellwork, begin to herald the senses as holy portals to the sacred. Take nothing for granted on these late-spring days. Breathe deeply and feel fully. Take a moment every morning to roll your tongue along the roof of your mouth, spiraling in and out in a mini-spell of sensual body blessing. Be lusty, as the best hags are, if only in that potent yearning for earthly belonging, and continue leaving offerings for the ancestors if you feel called. And so it is.

Season of the Elders' Altar: Dark Moon

Grandmother Speaks: Let's Dine Like It's Our Last Night

"The baskets are there." The Garden Hag bobs her head toward the immense, now-empty wooden table that held last night's luscious feast. "I think you should gather our food for dinner tonight. Let's dine like it's our last night here on this planet of passion and pleasure, like the oldest gods would want us to celebrate. Let's eat fruit so sweet that our great-great-grannies taste it in their graves, and let's know what it means to be a soft and fleshy human animal."

Dark Moon Practice: A Wild Walk

On the dark moon, take to the wilds during a liminal time, if you are able, at dusk or just before the sun rises. Even if you are simply gazing out a window at the skyline, spend a few precious moments in that rare state of being where you are at one with all that is. Look at what nature is showing you now, but do not be quick to name it. Feel yourself perfectly positioned here and now, and ask for the smallest sign of the yet-to-come.

To the Season of the Elders' Altar, Farewell for Now

Oh, you blissful season of balefire and jewel-orange dawns, how I'll miss you. Truly, I am wilder having been beneath your moons, and surely I'm a better Witch than I would have been if we'd not met. Until next year, you Season of the Elders' Altar. Farewell and merry do we part. All blessings be.

CHAPTER 3

Season of Mud-Caked Hands

---❦---

Gathering

Something in the air during late spring, on those cusp-of-summer late mornings when the scent of wet earth hangs heavy in the air, reminds us of the reverence our ancestors had for the intelligence of plants, for that greenspeak our blood remembers but our minds have forgotten. This last moon of spring tasks us with this remembering, begs us to get our hands dirty and commune with those allies who lived on this land long before we did. Our magick moves toward fruition now, as the sunlight swells to consume most of the day's hours, and we find ourselves making the most of what precious healing we have done during spring, integrating what we've learned since the equinox with a certain sense of youthful innocence, and, above all, enjoying all this majestic world has to offer, one sweet breath at a time.

The Garden Hag reminds us to take nothing for granted, to understand the romance between that slow build of spring and, straight across the Wheel of the Year's axis, that inevitable release of autumn. These are the liminal seasons, the 'twixt and the 'tween. Here is where our greatest work gets done, the work of transformation.

Hag Lesson #13:

In the end, we are all of the earth.

This chapter invites you to embrace the joy, to remember what it means to live on uncultivated land, to become an in-the-flesh heathen memory of ancient wisdom and a bright-eyed rebellious wish for a more whole world.

These Willows Owe Me Nothing
Dream-Wish Poetry at Dawn

If I were a wiser woman, I'd leave them be, these long-limbed willows who speak in whisper-hushed songs and divine my fragile future from nothing but the spiderweb patterns around my eyes. They know me better than I know myself, these trees. They've seen every woman I used to be, and though I so desperately ache to hear what they think of me, though I desire their approval more fervently than I've ever sought the validation of a king or holy man, these willows owe me nothing.

So desperately I wish to know what they know, to root my bones deep, twist my spine just so, and let the wind comb through my locks with the ease that graces their slim branches. Were I willow, surely I would hum with that under-bark pulse of otherworldly wisdom, with that rhythmic buzz I hear only when I press my ear to their lumped and knotted parts. These willows owe me nothing, but I, their loving dedicant, owe them much more than this Pagan poetry is worth. When this flesh of mine finally fails, my soul will run for these hills and spend eternity prancing about these mother trees, worshipping them more joyously in death than I ever could in life.

Sunrise Reflection:
The Love Language of Wild Queens

What would those wild queens of your ancestry tell you if they were here? What might they have to share about the nature of our green and growing medicines? What peace might come from letting their joy be your joy, permitting their stories of longing and lust to live themselves out through your skin and blood? Approach this practice with levity, using the prompts I offer here or changing them if you prefer. This is the wildest story you have to share this morning, so untether your words and refuse to tame or edit that love language of yours.

I woke with a song in my heart, wild queen that I am, and I vowed...
Communing with the dawn, I believed myself to be...
In that moment, I decided to seek out the ancestral tree, that holy place of...
Pressing cheek to bark, I saw visions of...
Pressing tongue to bark, I tasted memories of...
This tree held potent medicine indeed, and I knelt before it like...
I might have believed myself to be dreaming, had I not felt...
The scent of these leaves would be forever imprinted on my soul now, as if...
Tomorrow might be a different story, but for now, I know for sure...

Season of Mud-Caked Hands: New Moon

Grandmother Speaks: You Belong Here, Too

The garden is daunting indeed, stretching on and on before you for what seems like miles, and your baskets are still empty. The wounds from these thorns and the raised bumps from the more vicious leaves still mark your skin, and you're hesitant to venture into those bountiful wilds again. What if you don't return? What if those raging vines overtake you, and your flesh becomes food for the worms?

"You're different now, Witch. Are you not?" The Garden Hag startles you, pressing her hand to the back of your heart and nudging you forward. "You didn't respect these plants before, and they knew that, wise and sensitive things that they are. Go on. Go in, but be sure to ask for their gifts before you take them. Be prepared to be refused, but be open to receive. This is their house, their holiest of holies, but you belong here, too."

You hesitate, and she sees your fear.

"Ugh! You are taking yourself far too seriously." She shakes her head. "I've just the story for you to set your mind in the right place and soften you up a bit. Relax. Shake your shoulders. Breathe, and listen to this perfectly distasteful tale of an old friend of mine called Bawdy Betty." The hag begins, caressing a gardenia while she speaks.

Bawdy Betty and the Lady in Beige: A Late-Spring Tale

You're sure to know one if you see one — those grannies who seem to live outside of time, those wild elders who seem to pop in and out of existence as if they know of some secret snag in the space-time fabric that permits such ghostly travel. I've wondered myself if there's something of the other-folk to them, but their origins are hardly my business. What I do know is that they — these funky hags who dress in colors so garish, who clash their florals with their stripes with an optimism that could power the world if we could harness it — have the most hilarious stories housed within their rainbow-bright hearts.

Their stories are best shared in the late spring and with a good deal of chocolate, on one of those peculiar days when the air is so warm you toss your obligations in the bin and take to the woods. Their stories, like this one I'm about to share, might make you blush just a bit, might make you wonder what you've gotten yourself into, or maybe, gods willing, make you stop taking yourself so seriously and remember what it means to let laughter be prayer, to let a giggle be the best ritual.

Those bright and carefree grannies aren't generally fans of the once-upon-a-times, so they tend to begin their stories with a bit of rhyming nonsense:

Spring is here, but times are tough
So here's a tale of fun and fluff.

Or:

Enough with all the tears and frowns
On these, the days of flower crowns,
Save your whimp'ring, keep your pout
It's your joy I cannot live without.

Those grannies brush your face with their feather boas then, sip something strong, and bid you lean close so you can feel the heat of their breath while they tell the story of Bawdy Betty.

Now, Bawdy Betty didn't start out bawdy at all, not in this version of the story, anyway. She had lived most of her life with pursed lips, wrapped up tight in the tethers of judgment and etiquette, thoroughly disgusted with those who lived out loud, who spoke their minds, ate sugary things, owned fat and long-tongued dogs with childish names, and painted their skin with glitter for no good reason at all.

Bawdy Betty would suck her teeth in disgust at these fools, at those very giggling grannies who might tell this story. "Just who do they think they are?" she'd say. "Who raised these fops? Has no one ever taught them of good taste or ladylike manners?"

Her deep disdain for these wild-souled and hard-loving creatures, these wicked ones she considered so far below her own station, what with their tacky wallpaper and time-wasting ways, festered and swelled to consume poor Betty until, bless her straight-laced heart, she stopped leaving her house. At least she could be sure that she wouldn't run into one of those rainbow-clad hags behind her thrice-locked doors and barred windows; she was a frightened one, you see, this Betty, and she even started keeping the curtains closed for fear she might see one of the bright and bubbly ones bouncing down her street, so carefree and in want of a girdle.

Betty just couldn't bear the thought of their feckless and whimsical ways, and she locked herself away from their world.

Years went by with Betty locked — quite contentedly locked, I might add — inside her white and sterile house. She spent her days eating unspiced food and ironing her beige suits. She spent her nights playing chess all by her lonesome, standing and moving to the other side of the table in between each turn. She won every game that way, but she lost just as often.

There was one dark shadow in that pristine life of hers, though, like a single droplet of red sauce on a bleach-white tablecloth, and — what was worse — there was nothing she could do about it. Bawdy Betty was dreaming, you see. Night after night, she dreamed of those vile monsters she detested. By day, her house was silent but for her own lonely voice, but by night, the cackles and filthy humor of loudmouthed ones filled her fragile mind. Her home was blissfully without busy patterns or bright shades, but her dreams were full of peace-marring paisley and neon-sequined plaid. Their overblushed and too-highlighted faces haunted her even by the light of day, and none of her pills or prayers would dull the nightmares.

These dreams were getting worse, too. On the worst nights, Betty would even dream of herself as one of these monstrous mavens she hated. She'd dream of looking into the mirror and seeing her eyes coated in violet cream shadow and a plastic jeweled tiara on her head. She'd dream of her own voice being so loud it made even the other boisterous crones cover their ears, and she'd dream of her well-patterned routine melting into an iridescent sea of wildness and rebellion, naked and low-breasted dancing, reckless tree climbing and bare-handed cake eating.

After one particularly restless night, Bawdy Betty crept bleary-eyed into her kitchen craving something hot and bitter, but even with eyes squinting from sleeplessness, she could see something was quite amiss. Her mouth dropped at the sight. Her stomach wrenched. There, on her spotless white marble countertop, was a hot-pink silk scarf.

Oh, and the thing was revolting, positively insulting to Betty's decency with its vile hibiscus flowers and phallic vines. It reeked of perfume, too, so much so that Betty didn't dare touch it, so she backed out of the kitchen slowly, her eyes glued to the thing the whole time, ran up to her room, locked the door, and hid under the covers.

She prayed for hours. "Please, please save me from these demons that are hunting me! Banish them from my home! Rid these rooms of their garish ways, and protect my weak and weary heart from their obscenities!"

Those flower-loving grannies who tell this story disagree on precisely how this next bit happened. Some say Betty drifted to sleep and dreamed of a great battle between the prim and proper women and those freewheeling wildlings. Others say she simply grew bored; some say nature was calling, and even the most stubborn and prudent queens will be pulled from their pomp and circumstance when their bladders are full and their bowels are twisting.

In any case, the grandmothers agree that, in time, a boldness returned to Betty's thoughts, and she timidly crawled from her bed, opened the door, and peered into the hallway.

"Hello?" She swallowed. "Listen, this is my house, and if there's anyone here, I demand you leave at once!"

Two things happened then: Betty's eyes were shocked to life again by another flash of color, this time in the form of two fluorescent orange high-heeled sneakers, and before she could faint and save herself from such vulgarity, a voice interrupted her loss of consciousness.

"Oh? Or you'll *what*?"

Now, Betty knew that voice, and knew it well. She'd tried to forget it for many years, to no avail.

"Do you remember me?"

Betty crushed her eyes shut and refused to turn around. She screamed, slammed the bedroom door closed, turned the lock, and leaped back into bed, burrowing beneath her overbleached pillows.

Her thoughts sent her back in time for a moment, to her childhood years when faeries were real and the lines between fantasy and truth were quite blurred. This voice was from those years. She remembered a night, a night she had convinced herself was a dream, when that voice urged her to be wild, to climb trees, to walk on forbidden land and swim in secret rivers where water sprites would whisper stories of crone mermaids and the heathens who loved them.

"What are you hiding for?" That voice was in the room now, rough and raspy with its years of hysterical laughter and hard partying, or so Betty thought.

"You're not real!" Betty managed. "Be gone with you! You don't belong here!"

The pillows were being pulled from her sanctuary one at a time, and Betty readied herself for a fight.

"It's you who doesn't belong here, doll," the voice scoffed. "No one belongs here, except maybe one of those white show cats with a diamond collar. It's time to live, baby. Get up."

The last pillow was pulled from Bawdy Betty's face, and she saw that shadow creature from her childhood again in all her over-the-top glamour and glory.

It was her own face, to be sure. Her own lips, though adorned with neon-pink gloss. Her own eyes, though hidden by red sunglasses with heart-shaped rims.

In that moment, she realized that this monster who had visited her that night when she was younger, this bizarre ghost whom she had first called her fairy godmother and then a dream altogether, was but a glimpse of who she might have been had the world been kinder and the bullies less loathsome, had she not been told to stay quiet and keep her knees clean.

"We've all got a demure and controlled side, but we've all got an outlaw side, too, you see," the flashy femme said. "Even you." She waved her hand around the colorless room. "If this place hasn't killed your wild, nothing will. Now wake up and go see how much fun you've got left in you."

Some of the lighthearted hags who tell this tale say the loudmouthed one pinched Betty. Others say she started to sing show tunes, but they agree that the very next thing Betty knew, she was back in her bed, but not wrapped in those sterile sheets and hiding.

She tossed the tattered stuffed animals out of her way and opened the bright, imperfectly handsewn curtains. Checking to make sure her hair was properly mussed, Betty sighed with relief, looking around the room at her lovely green-and-pink checkered wallpaper then down at her mismatched socks. Her sloppy-tongued dog lumbered into the room, sat at her feet, and looked up at her, hungry and curious.

"Oh, Nipples, thank gods. I had the worst nightmare that I'd become boring. I dreamed I turned into that frightful overstarched ghoul I saw once when I was young. I thought it was a dream, but...I don't know. I used to call her the Sad Lady in the White House." Nipples made a concerned sound, and Bawdy Betty shrugged off her nightmares. "Come, let's go do something crazy. What do you say? Life's too short to be beige."

◄─►≬◄─►

The Garden Hag repeats the last line of the story and then nods toward the garden, prompting you onward, adding, "I'll wait here."

Opening Practice: A Helper Tree Found

As this last moon of spring dawns, venture into the wild. You might go into a green space if you live in an urban area, or you might already have the wealth of a fertile expanse of forest stretching out before you; it matters not, for all you search for is a single tree, a lone and beautiful ally whom you can invite to be a part of your magick. May this tree be a living altar for you on these warmer days, a bark-and-root reminder of your belonging to this blessed planet and this sacred cycle of birth and death. Much like working with deities in our Craft, we must resist *using* our plant allies; we honor them as citizens of the global community, held with much reverence.

In *Celtic Tree Magic*, Danu Forest writes: "Regardless of religion or culture, humanity has long held trees to be beloved kin." Set the intention to find this tree that longs for you as much as you long for it, then press your palm to bark when it shows itself to you. Ask if it would like to work with you, if only with your energy, but "be prepared to be refused," as the hag says. When you find a tree that feels, in the subtlest way, as if it leans toward you as you lean toward it, as if there is a quiet magnetism between your energy and its energy, give an offering of only three breaths; the tree breathes in what you breathe out, and vice versa. The pact is complete. And so it is.

Waxing Moon Practice: Humble Offerings by Morning's Light

Materials: A gift for the helper tree

Summer is the season of gratitude, passion, and desire fulfilled. As we move closer to that sacred season of nature's abundance, we are called to acknowledge the gifts we have been granted. As this powerful moon waxes, review your spellwork from the spring season and ask yourself what has been gained, what prayers have been answered, and what nods have been given from the ethers that tell you, *Yes. Yes, your magick is real.* Whenever possible, in the mornings during the waxing moon, give a humble offering to your helper tree. If you are unable to physically visit the tree often, take a moment to psychically visit and make your offering, envisioning yourself there, leaving some small thank-you of stone, water, moon blood, eggshell, bone, or berry. Be sure that your gift is environmentally sound, that it will nourish the tree; better, ask the tree if this is the offering it wants. Forge a connection between what you have been gifted of late and gratitude to this wild earth that is your home. All blessings be.

Season of Mud-Caked Hands: Full Moon

Grandmother Speaks: You're on Your Own Now

You're deep in the garden, spurred on by the promptings of the Garden Hag, but you still haven't picked so much as a berry from these sweet-smelling bushes and fruit-heavy trees. Some small and wild voice inside your head tells you to kneel right where you are and dig for ginger root, but you ignore it, continuing your timid walk through the bounty. The voice tells you to reach high and pluck the low-hanging peaches, but some unknown in-the-belly fear stops you short.

"I can't see you, but I can tell you're wavering," the hag hollers from behind you. "I'm not helping you. You're on your own now, Witch, but remember who you are, a wild heathen baptized by her ancestral inheritance, a warm incarnation of every primal crone's prayer, and a bold and brave heathen whose blood remembers these fine, growing things."

Just then, you feel the ground humming below you, and a forgotten hymn in a mother tongue you don't speak begins playing on repeat inside your mind. Your eyes fix on the ripest jewel-bright strawberries you've ever seen, and they call to you from the earth in a hushed but persistent tone. In that moment, you remember. You remember how to hear them, these medicines that were the magick of the old ones, potent and plump with the healers' juices, with the witches' elixirs. In that moment, you remember them, and they remember you.

Full Moon Practice: Sweet Reward

This full moon practice is a celebration, a reward for work well done, and a congratulatory prayer on the final full moon of the spring season. These are the beginnings of gratitude magick, our most potent practice in summer, and here we gift ourselves with what we ourselves desire.

As the contents of your cosmic eggs gestate on your altar, nourished well by these milk-silver beams, ask yourself what three gifts you can give yourself now that, if only in a small way, endow you with the very feeling you are calling in. For example, if one of your cosmic eggs is gestating new love, perhaps reward yourself with a ritual bath full of rose oil and calendula flowers, a luscious ode to the worthy Witch that is you. If you are gestating freedom or travel, perhaps walk to a wide-open space and sense the infinite possibilities that surround you. Reward yourself with the very things you want, this full moon — and, for the love of all things wild and holy, do not take yourself too seriously.

And so it is.

Season of Mud-Caked Hands: Waning Moon

Grandmother Speaks: There's So Much Joy to Be Had

You would surely be lying if you said you weren't pleased with yourself; this grand table has been set by your own mud-caked hands, after all. Every piece of fruit was picked by you; every sprig of mint and basil leaf that graces the glasses of hand-squeezed juices gifted themselves to you and you alone. Your plate is full, and this is sure to be the sweetest meal you've ever eaten.

"A well-deserved reward, this." The Garden Hag nods with approval. She's bare-breasted tonight, wearing nothing but a violet-rimmed bonnet. "Eat up. I suppose tomorrow you'll be on your way, and you'll need your strength to reach that southern hag's house."

You bite into an overripe peach, letting the juice run down your chin in the most unladylike fashion, hearing the hag's words and resisting grieving too soon. The night birds are singing, and the air is heavy with a rain that's yet to be unleashed, making the intense floral scents surrounding you so potent that they threaten to overwhelm. You will miss this place, and this place will miss you.

"Don't you go being sad now, child," the Garden Hag orders, gnawing on a carrot. "There's so much joy to be had in those summerlands where you're headed. In any case, you'll be back again next spring, and I'll barely recognize you, dripping with another winter's worth of wisdom and demanding nourishment."

Waning Moon Practice: Grieving Spring

Permit yourself the chance to grieve this mist-heavy season of storm and bloom, holding a poignant death ritual at your altar or leaving flowers on the roots of your helper tree. Speak freely of the most potent moments you had under these spring moons, as if you were speaking a eulogy at the funeral for that wild season, then begin the work of opening to that hot, heathen season that waits for you on the horizon. Stare long out the window at this perfect sky, and sing the names that were not given but claimed. Call out to those wanton and wicked ones who came before you, and let them know you're still here, still tending the flames for them, as they are for you.

Spring's Eulogy

She found me so dried out, that old hag of spring. She pulled me from the snows, thawed my bones atop her woodstove, and asked me to share my stories of shame and pride, of guilt and grace. I obliged her, that kind-faced one, and I told her of every wound I could. I rattled off the midnight aches, the lovers who left me, and the babes I never bore, and — gods help me — she listened. She listened while I retched out my pain, while such unpoetic and unromantic histories spilled from my lips. She bade me dig into the secret treasure troves of my aunts and my grannies, to claw into phantom graves and sift through my own psychic soil to find a bit of gold, to finally inherit what's been coming to me since I chose this body, this earth.

I'll be damned if that old hag wasn't onto something, and I'll miss her terribly now that she's gone, now that the warmest days have come for me. That winter hag's hardened into a crag, like she always does, and now this spring crone has laid her rotten flesh upon that altar. By the time this summer sun's had its way with her, there will be only bones and jewels left. Even so, I wish her well, for she heard my story, listened with her whole heart, and bowed in gratitude like I'd shared an eloquent monologue with perfect rhythm and immaculate intonation, not the simple biography of a woman worn down to the nub and reborn into a fuller, fleshier shape.

⊷✦⊶

Season of Mud-Caked Hands: Dark Moon

Grandmother Speaks: This Place Has Been Good

"You look well, child." The Garden Hag is dressed for your departure, swimming in full and billowing silks, hair braided with white lilies. "This place has been good for you."

She hands you what looks to be a treasure map, bows demurely, and turns her back to you.

"Walk south. Just when you start to get overwhelmed with thirst, right when you think you'll never feel cool water again, that's when you're nearly there. Check the map; you might miss it." The Garden Hag keeps talking behind you as you make your way fearlessly into the flowers and trees. "That Desert Hag likes to stay hidden, but she'll let you in if you find her. Tell her I said hello and ask her to tell you the story about the lightning tree. She loves that one. A trickster mind, she has."

Dark Moon Practice: The Purge before the Fruition

Beneath the dark moon, release the materials left by your spring spellwork. The clay eggs might be planted or repurposed, perhaps blessed with saltwater and cleared. The cosmic egg jars, if it feels time to let them go, can be ceremoniously emptied, their contents burned or sustainably released. The summer solstice is a time of intense fruition, the peak of the Wheel of the Year, and our magick needs all the room it can get. The work of Witches on the cusp of summer is to honor the bounty they have been given, to revel in gratitude and abundance, and to connect their will to their wants.

All blessings be, this dark moon. All blessings be.

To the Season of Mud-Caked Hands, Farewell for Now

―◆―❖―◆―

Begone with you, spring. I'm on to the longest days, and I've decided to let this wild sun have its way with me. To the season of long-rolling storms and mud-caked hands, farewell for now. We're sure to meet again, unless this wicked world takes me too soon, unless those ghosts I miss so dearly pull me from my body in autumn and take me home. Even then, I'll return to you a garden-haunting specter who lusts for wildflowers and creeping vines. Even then, I'll write you poetry from beyond the grave about tender roots and slow-budding altars. Even then, you'll be my most treasured time. And so it is.

―❖―

WILD SPRING PRACTICES AND SACRED REMEMBRANCES

- Connect the visions you long for to "seed memories"; this allows for your perspective of linear time to curve, to bend, to slowly shift into a spiral.
- Thoughtfully bind your magick to both your own ancient and compassionate ancestors and the yet-to-be-born babes of the future. Make regular offerings to them. Remind yourself you are a bridge line in the cosmic web of being.
- Check in with your small collectives, covens, families, and councils of friends. Share the deep dreams. Cocreate the vision for the next chapter in the group's story.
- Acknowledge, respect, and donate to the indigenous people on whose land you live and work.
- Consider having an accountability partner who can rein you in with respect to your spiritual pursuits, keep you from taking yourself too seriously, and ground you in the here and now.
- Know that your sensuality is radical, and plan micro-retreats for yourself that prioritize embodied joy.
- Make (at least) one single, conscious effort to care for the land you live on every day; pick up plastic, give to the indigenous,

ask questions, end support of environmentally unconscious corporations, plant seeds.

- Ground yourself in your body often. Dance, breathe slowly and in the belly rather than the chest, feel the bones of your feet press into ground, and feel your heartbeat.

- Remember that what we might call "healing" is actually more about awareness and integration than about fixing, sewing up, or neatly naming aspects of our complex, chaotic, and beautifully grotesque stories.

House of the
DESERT HAG

Opening Summer's Portal

Invocation to the

Crone of the South

—◆—◆—◆—

Mighty Witch of Sun and Oak

Smite the hearth and drop your cloak

Sky clad we'll walk. In love we'll be

The longest day spent raw and free

So often, the sacred levity of summer is lost on us, swallowed whole by the modern struggle to live the best life, to plan the epic extended holiday that will surely be our salvation from our cages of time poverty, to retreat from the complexities of our many-layered schedules and intricate, ever-expanding webs of work and consumption. Were we to have elders to gift us with their stories, to hold us and teach us their sweet-living ways, surely they would urge us to slow our pace on these longest days. Surely those old ones would ask us where our greatest joy comes from and for what, in this moment, we are most grateful.

Many of our ancestors honored respite and revelry on the shortest night, letting the indoor fires die out and gifting the senses with all manner of intrigue, the grotesque and the beautiful, the birth and the decay. Summer is a season of fruition, of pulling together our resources and finding solace in the small moments. This is our annual afternoon spent dancing, spent fattening ourselves up on the well-tended bounty. Here, we must face the challenge of embracing that embodied enjoyment of all we have without rushing to purge, cast out, or grieve too soon for summer's end.

That beloved Desert Hag knows the merit of an open heart and the feeling flesh, and the stories she keeps and shares are those of many-bodied moving prayer, full moons, and long-vision. That desert-dwelling crone is in love with the land and all its creatures, with those fierce canyons and wide-eyed, scaly creepers, with those thin-thorned and tough-skinned plants that know what it means to do battle with the sun gods. If we listen closely, that deep-loving woman will tell us her secrets, and she will surely leave us changed before the Harvest Moon rises.

Overview of the Summer Journey

Season of Wild Delights

Nourishment: Activating
Story Medicine: The Faerie Doctor's Daughter

Season of Holy Thunder

Challenge: Reaping
Story Medicine: The Witch and the Lightning Tree

Season of Midday Grace

Wisdom: Softening
Story Medicine: Biddy's Retreat

The Summer Altar, Handmade from Song, Fire, and Joy

May your summer altar be an ode to cosmic heat, to the god-stars, to the flames of inspiration as they come to only you, only in your dreams. Gather sacred relics born of fire: burned wood, volcanic glass, or images of lightning or solar deities. Name your central candle "Heartbeat," and position the elements around this pillar. Perhaps choose objects that have been graced by their elements for a length of time, like sea glass for the water element in the west or wind-worn fabric for the air element in the east. Your altar should speak the language of the apex, the climax, and the high-fire full moon. These are the long days of the Holy Wild, and our altars are nothing if not shrines to our undying rebellion.

CHAPTER 4

Season of Wild Delights

Activating

Such swiftness there is to summer's arrival. We find ourselves there, beneath that low-hanging and arrogant sun, just when our tamer stories have all but run out, just when we begin to wonder why we chose to be born into these soft and feeling bodies. Our hearts are overfull here, on this intense moon cycle that runs through the summer solstice, thumping and pregnant and pulsing, rhythmically drumming the same tune of adamant rebellion our more recent dead knew so well but played only in secret. This first moon of summer finds us baptizing ourselves in the nectar of heathen revelry, sharing tales around the campfire of forbidden love and battle iron. Surely, these stories are not suited to those with the more delicate sensibilities, for their language alone will suck the innocence right out of even the purest and most youthful soul.

Hag Lesson #14

Summer magick is born of activism and gratitude.

Summer stories are marked by unbridled passion and the pleasure-filled ache of a Witch's becoming, and so, too, is summer magick born of fire, conviction, and the rawest gratitude we know. The Desert Hag urges us to peel back the tougher skin from our own hearts, to lay bare the desires we might hide beneath colder moons. Hers is not a Craft of secret keeping and mystery work. Hers is a Craft of open-armed sharing and communal fire tending.

You find that wild one just in time, you see, just when the loneliness of spring threatens to swallow you whole, and she has been brewing precisely the medicine you need to quench your thirst.

Teach Me, You Old-Boned and Diamond-Eyed Deity

Oh, my hard-loving lightning god, my dreams have been of giants and green women of late, and I've waked swollen with a pulsing desire to share stories in a language I do not speak. These nights are too short for my haunted heart, and I am missing the dark and deep, the cool and creeping. I am missing the ghost stories and the warmth of wool, and I fear I'm in danger of sleeping through these brightest days of wild delights yet again. Teach me, you old-boned and diamond-eyed deity. Teach me how to suck that savory marrow from these overfull days. Teach me how to heal the wounds of my grannies just by breathing, and teach me to dig up the undead poetry even here, even in these gardens spilling their curling and hungry vines all over this hallowed ground, even here in this overmined place. In the deep below, I can hear the summer stories hissing, and I know they want to be told by a Witch as wanton as me.

Noonday Reflection: Lit by a Lone Star Come Too Close

The intensity of our early-summer magick is born of the ancestral work we've done in spring, of the digging we've done into the wounds of the forebears and lessons of the lands whose maps are stamped on our very bodies, whose rivers branch and fork like our veins, and whose mountains mirror the curves of our ivory, spiraling bones. We reflect now, with immense gratitude, on our inherited gifts, and we welcome what we might call the impossible into our lives.

Tell a story of miracles now. Tell a story of belonging to place. Tell a tale of a Witch come fully home to themselves, arrived at a place of complete dancing-in-the-moonlight bliss, graced with some great miracle they never saw coming and laughing with their whole body at their unexpected good fortune. Tell a story of bright-blooming fruition. Weave the familiar with the fantastical, and in the story, become the warrior who has broken some familial pattern that might have otherwise kept them small. As always, you may use the prompts I offer here or write your own.

This summer solstice holds it all for me, and I can scarcely believe...
My face is lit by a lone star come too close, and even now I know...
I might say it was impossible, that great blessing that graced me when...
Tomorrow, I'll find myself right where some part of my soul has always been,
    in love with...
For today, I will stay right here, singing songs of...

Summer Solstice Celebration:
Rejoining the Band of Storytelling Heathens

Materials: Outdoor firepit or burn bowl and candle

Those ever-warmer days that bridge the Beltane cross-quarter day and summer solstice beckon us to leave the comfort of our homes and venture out beneath those vast and ancient skies we so often take for granted. There is a call to break the rules, to taste the forbidden fruit, to put to bed the indoor fires that kept us warm throughout the colder months, and to gather with those wild ones who know us best. On that longest day, prepare to revel in celebration, song, and story.

Ideally, this ritual is done with a small group, but should you choose to move through this ritual on your own, invite those soft-whispering summer ghosts to walk with you, to remind you why you were born into this feeling body of yours.

Late in the day and as close to dusk as possible, light your central altar candle, breathe, and call to mind all the magick work you have done from Yule until this moment, during the half of the year when the days are growing subtly longer. Permit your memories to rise and fall, and notice the feelings that grace your body as you recall those moments of somber ceremony, beneath-the-moon spell casting, and joyous dance that have colored the moons when the light of day slowly overtook the dark of night. Imagine your great-great-grandparents moving through similar rituals, perhaps in secret, and speak "thank you" in the tongue of your ancestors. When you feel ready, walk slowly with your candle, leaving the quiet shelter of your house and heading outside, where a readied but yet-to-be-born fire awaits you. While you walk, ask these ghosts who walk with you to grant you a story to tell, to gift you with some piece of an in-the-blood secret you've yet to resurrect from the dark and deep.

"Sing your songs through me, you heathen elders," you say. Bid the stories rise. When ready, light your summer solstice fire, your Litha* flame, be it large or humble, from your central altar candle, and stand before this beacon of vitality, of enduring transformation and fierce-crackling delights. Snuff the altar candle out once the fire is lit, symbolizing the transition from a quieter indoor Craft to a more raucous and joyous out-of-doors witchery.

Speak to the directions now, first finding the north and asking for your story to be heard and heard well: "Elders of the North, hear my story. Elders of the East, hear my story. Elders of the South, hear my story. Elders of the West, hear my story."

The greatest stories are told around the fire as the sun goes down, after all, and you have a loving spectral audience with you now, this holy evening. When ready, let the ancestors grant you a story, speaking freely into the flames, describing any images that come, allowing your voice to blossom into song if you feel called, shouting loudly, or whispering so softly that only the spirits can hear you.

Feel the story in your whole body. What sensations come to you as you speak these words? What deep feelings rise from within, beginning so close to the spine and rippling out through the bones and the blood? Become the story as you speak it. Tell it true. Story-tell your way through some ancestral portal you didn't realize was right there for you, and rejoin that band of loudmouthed heathens to which you've always belonged.

---

*   *Litha* is the traditional name for the summer solstice Sabbat, originating from an eighth-century manuscript entitled *The Reckoning of Time*; the word is believed to mean "gentle" or "calm."

Stay here for as long as you have. Tell as many stories as the most beloved ghosts will grant you, ideally letting the fire die naturally. Speak gratitude when finished and, if possible, wake early to see the sunrise the next morning, already a beacon of the slow-creeping dark.

Adaptation for Families, Coven Groups, and Other Wild Circles: *Blessed Be the Story Makers*

Storytelling is infused by the spirit of community, and this summer solstice ritual is ideally done in a group. Begin indoors if you are able, everyone with their own candle that symbolizes their Craft during the half of the year when the days grew ever longer. Ask participants to walk ceremoniously toward the outdoor circle, where the fire will give light and warmth to everyone's tale, where the scent of smoke will infuse each storyteller's words with a primal aliveness that is undeniable, that permeated every Earth-based tradition and grants any story a sort of of-the-land wildness. Have everyone light a piece of kindling from their own candle to ignite the communal fire, then honor the directions, affirming this gathering's place in the world. All will snuff their candles out when ready, and the storytelling will begin.

Move clockwise around the circle, with everyone sharing whatever story rises to roll from their tongues. There will be tears and giggles, shock and belly laughter. Whatever stories arise, however fragmented or nonsensical, are the perfect solstice stories. If song and dance erupt, such is the way of these fireside gatherings. Our summer Witchcraft must make room for levity and rebellion, after all, and we do well to not be rigid about our ways beneath this wildest moon.

Season of Wild Delights: New Moon

Grandmother Speaks: If Your Heart Is True

The desert sky is indigo velvet above, fading to the palest blue and peach-pink at the horizon, so dotted with diamond pinprick stars that you scarcely notice the first new moon of summer as it rises, a pale gray beacon of hope above the humble clay and red rock house of the Desert Hag. You wonder how you'll find her once inside. Will there be some intense labyrinth to weave through like in the spring hag's garden, or does an even more harrowing experience await you?

The air is quiet and still, moved only by your panting breath, and you would give up all you know for just a sip of something cool.

"Hello?" you call, voice hoarse from dryness, while you trek through what you hope are the last sands of this journey. The clay hut seems dug straight out of the ground, and you cannot tell its size. Should a strong wind blow, surely this hag's house would drown in these jewel-orange sands, and you're awash with gratitude that the weather is calm here.

A rustling inside the hut tells you that, just maybe, you were heard. Just maybe, your thirst will be quenched before the last of the sunlight sinks below the dunes, before your body dries out and this desert becomes your final resting place. A door you'd swear had not been there before swings open, sending a slow trickle of sand raining down atop the hag's head as she, this majestic woman, leans into the night from her hovel.

"Ah! I've been waiting for you! Come!" She beckons, shaking the sand from her short curls and waving you forward. "You must be thirsty, child."

It's true, as you can scarcely swallow, but you muster enough energy to answer her. "Yes! Thank you! I feel I've been walking across this desert for days, and the scaly creatures are hardly good company."

"Ha!" she booms. "You don't know them very well, then."

You move to go inside, feeling a blissfully cool breeze come from the open door, but she blocks you, holding up a steady hand. This woman is a presence, indeed.

"I'm afraid I can't let you inside just yet, love."

Your heart sinks.

"Oh, don't look so sullen. I can't let just anyone inside, you see, but I do promise it's an easy task I have for you, if your heart is true."

"All right," you concede, having no choice at all.

"Before you come inside, before I serve you some of my homemade brew and let the shadows of this place soothe your skin, I must know…for what are you most grateful in this moment?"

Her dark eyes are full of earnest, and her skin glows as if she had sunbeams running through her veins and starlight for bone. There is an otherworldly quality to this strong-jawed hag, and you are certain that she means business.

"Gratitude…well, I must think for a moment." You feel speechless. The hag looks disappointed, so you keep talking. "I'm sorry, it's just that I've been so worried about not finding you, about being lost and alone…I haven't really had time to be grateful."

The hag clicks her tongue and purses her lips.

"Well, I did think for a moment about how happy I was that there was no strong wind, as it might have covered your house in sand, and I wouldn't have found it."

Her eyes soften just a bit.

"And I'm, of course, very grateful for the cool breeze blowing on my skin now, even if I'm not permitted inside, and the sky is just dazzling here, and the moon is so eerie and perfect, and your skin is just so enchanting, if I may say so, and, well, I suppose my heart feels quite happy."

The hag smiles, claps once, and hands you a tall glass of precious water. "Yes, wonderful. Speak gratitude and you will surely be my most honored guest. Drink this. I've just the shortest story to share before I let you in." She begins, transforming into an otherworldly storyteller.

The Faerie Doctor's Daughter: A Ceremonial Solstice Tale

This is a ritual storytelling ceremony. If you choose, you might participate in this tale, setting up a central altar reflective of holy blackthorn branches and raven feathers and, when prompted, moving to a different position and envisioning one of your foremothers, as directed, and freely speaking a story to her. Begin reading, knelt at your central altar, and welcome what comes.

Though only the rarest few, only the wildest of heathen hearts, come to know those crusty crones of winter or those shy grannies who quietly rule over early spring — and, indeed, rarer still are those strange creatures we might call the lusty grandmothers — most souls blessed with a long life do, at some point, come to know that beloved hag we might call the forgetful grandmother.

She lives in that liminal place between knowing and not knowing, graced with one blissful moment of memory as she inhales, then already mourning its loss on the out-breath. The once-strong fabric of her life's story, so meticulously woven together from white-hot youthful passion and red-bleeding motherhood, from violet altar tending and indigo prayer, from emerald-colored grief and silver-threaded solitude, is precariously breathing now in a state of eternal undoing and coming together, her entire existence being stretched thin, then pushed together again, the integrity of the strands tested day by day until those sharper dreams slice through the more distant memories, leaving homes and daughters and grandbabes as naught more than frayed ends of a broken thread by morning.

I wonder about that pulling apart and coming together that happens to the forgetful grannies' stories. I wonder if, like the swelling babe grows too big for its warm womb and must be born into the cold and bright at long last, the stories lived out loud by those old ones grow too big, too long, too full of characters and places and feeling, to be held by any one body, to be told by any single voice. I wonder if the stories themselves struggle and stretch, then surrender to their small containers only when a familiar face assures them of their identity: *Yes, yes. This is who you are. This is where you came from. This is why you're here.* The story succumbs to such certainty for a time but, in the end, when that familiar face tilts itself to the side in pity and demurely takes its leave, then the story says, *No, no, this is not who I am. I am bigger than this body, this name, and this place,* and that's what I think those forgetful grannies are pondering when they stare long from the window.

We think them lost, you see. We think they float in a hopeless, misty realm where the past seems to be present, but I wonder if it is only a soulful learning they are feeling then, with their bodies still and their eyes wet, if they are quite ceremoniously reordering their relationship to time, making room for a story that has stretched too big for any one mind we might call sound or sane to hold it.

I wonder — in my loneliest moments I wonder — if these grannies are not forgetful at all but rather the greatest story keepers, laden by a language insufficient to share the immensity of their elder wisdom.

The elder story keepers might just share this ritual tale with you if they could, if they were so inclined, if they thought you worthy, if they cared enough to hard-mine the hidden words from their frozen graves. This isn't a myth with a clear beginning and climactic center, nor is it a story where the listener is a passive recipient of humor and understanding, occasionally offering a giggle or a knowing nod. No, as a listener to this tale, you must move. You must permit your whole body to respond, and you must inhale to stretch the story and exhale to wrap its longest threads around your ribs.

Ours is a Craft of poetry and questing, ceremony and resting. Our Craft is fueled by an embodied kinship with heathen lands and our spectral foremothers who still surround us, who still smother the hearth fire by night and rekindle its flames by day, and this tale begins in a place where moss-covered land meets gray waves that, in turn, meet stormy sky. Here, in this wild and Pagan place, forgotten myths claw their way up from the wet ground, hissing and howling like fleshless and undead myths seeking a home on some wanton Witch's tongue. Here, our story begins.

The women who live in this place of land, sea, and sky are thin-limbed but hardy-boned. Their stomachs are often empty, but their hearts are full of love songs and battle hymns. Their clothes are ragged and thin in places, but they wear a soul armor forged from ancestral myth and the inherited priceless jewels of truly belonging to a place. These women do not live outside of time; they live in and of time. Time is their long-tongued lover. Time is their precious elder-teacher, and they've learned much from its spiral-dancing ways.

Most of these strong-backed women know better than anyone else that stories matter, that fairy tales passed down from great-granny to babe matter, and that there is no greater tragedy than a story lost. The story keepers who share this particular myth, this tale of the Faerie Doctor's daughter, all begin by saying that the land itself was a story, that every low-groaning oak was a god-hero and every patch of moss was an enchanted once-upon-a-time and happily-ever-after. And, for all their apparent forgetfulness, the grannies who tell this tale always remember this invocation:

Once upon the land and sea
Where stony sand was blessed by Sidhe
A seal woman lost, forgot her way
A poor soul found by loudmouthed Fae

Where the story goes from here depends on who is doing the telling, but most of the elders say the Faerie Doctor's daughter had lived too much for her own good, had collected too many wounds to count, had packed so much joy and so much grief and so much prayer beneath her freckled flesh that she was ready to burst apart into a heap of shredded emotion, unable to cook up anything worth hearing from that raw rabble of wild, feminine experience. It was just as summer solstice approached, on one of those aching nights when spring's death rattle sounds like a woman's desperate heart drum as she runs northward from her house, like breath panting and the deep sobs that jostle the bones apart at the joint.

The Faerie Doctor's daughter had forgotten who she was, you see. She had forgotten that her story mattered, and she had forgotten what patchworked wisdom had once kept her warm. When one forgets the merit of one's myth, one becomes lost in the unforgiving sea of ennui and sinks straight to the bottom, unable to muster the will to rise, to breathe. When this happens, the old ones say, it is up to the otherworld to remind one.

The Faerie Doctor's daughter found herself on her knees now, her arms bloodied and wrapped tightly around a blackthorn tree. She was willing that embattled wolf-mother wood to take her, to turn her body into a sacrifice to the tree gods, to wrap its roots around her ankles and pull her under, to stretch her tongue long toward the waning moon; at least then, she thought, she would have a story. At least then, she'd leave an epic tale of martyrdom behind, and the children would sing sad songs about the Faerie Doctor's daughter whose body had turned into blackthorn shrine.

Some of the grannies who tell this story say she spent an entire year and a day here begging to be swallowed whole by the hallowed ground. Others say it was only moments before she laid eyes on her messenger — a loudmouthed Raven in a crowd of quiet crows it was, come to balance its black feet on the lowest branch and spit thorns at the weeping woman.

"Oh, Raven, I beg of you, speak to this tree called Strife in that dark-winged language you both know so well. Tell her to take me under. Tell her I've forgotten all my stories, and I've lost my poet's tongue. Tell her my flesh is wasted unless it be food for her roots."

The Raven cocked its head to the side, the old grannies say, and spit another thorn her way, pricking the fat of her cheek and squawking.

"Please, Raven. I am a desperate woman. Can't you see that I'm a boring, loverless hag? There's much woe in a storyless life, is there not? Do you wish me to continue living like this, a doll hung on a tree with nothing but tears to keep her warm?"

It all happened at once then, say the grannies. The Raven was fed up with her sniveling and swooped down to peck out her eyes, just as the blackthorn tree groaned and stretched its branches higher and roots longer. The Faerie Doctor's daughter surrendered, pulling herself from the tree and lying on the earth while the Raven danced upon her face.

"Yes, yes." She laughed. "Yes, of course. This is how it should happen. Take me, Raven. Let me be your meal, for surely I do not deserve to see the dawn."

The Raven stopped then, satisfied the woman was blind, and stood at her side with wide wings. "You are a Faerie Doctor's daughter who came to sacrifice herself at a blackthorn tree, only to meet a talking Raven who pecked out your eyes. Now, you say you are storyless, but I might point out that this night's events are hardly mundane and, in fact, have the beginnings of what might just be the greatest story ever told."

Her breath caught in her throat then, not only because there was truth in the Raven's words but also because, though her sight had most certainly left her, she could see with the faerie vision now. The Raven looked more black-feather-caped sorcerer than bird, and the tree was an immense, full-breasted, and thorny crowned crone-god.

"Keep walking north now, child," the Raven-man urged, reaching out a long-clawed hand and helping her to stand. "Walk northward to the house of the Grove Maiden, for surely she shall help you remember your myths."

Move slowly now, walking just a few steps northward.

She wanted to protest, but walk she did, unsure at first, with arms outstretched, but eventually seeing with that second sight her Faerie Doctor mother had but she never did, not since she was a babe. Along the way, she gathered offerings for the Grove Maiden, offerings of bone and antler, and her humility swelled as she wandered the way only a woman stripped bare of her sense of belonging wanders. Some of the grannies say it was many moons she walked, that she was an old hag herself before she reached the Maiden of Moss, Holly, and Yew, but all the elders agree that she did, in fact, reach this faerie ruler of the northern lands, laying her offering at her feet and saying, "I've come here, feet firm on ground, to remember what it means to belong to land."

The Grove Maiden stretched her arms long then, and they split at the ends like twigs. Her flesh pulled back from her face, and her eyes and mouth became knots on bark. But, even so, she spoke to the Faerie Doctor's daughter, saying, "Tell me, love. Tell me a tale of a young one in a wild place, of learning from land and tending that infant spirit of belonging with dedication and much, much faith."

Close your eyes now, and begin to see an ancestor's face before you. Your blood remembers this face, this steward of the land. Let her pull the stories from you. Speak freely now until it feels finished.

And she spoke her stories of the land, looking into the eyes of an ancestral maiden whose roots grew deep while rattles shook and altar candles burned. When the Faerie Doctor's daughter was finished speaking, finished harvesting tales long buried that contained that potent medicine of wonder and whimsy, finished letting words drip from her tongue like pomegranate juice from an underworld Goddess's lips, the Grove Maiden asked her a poignant question:

"If your most sacred work in this world were a tree, tell me, what would it look like? What color paints its leaves, and what scent graces its bark in spring?"

Close your eyes once more, and answer this question, still speaking to your ancestor.

The grannies say that the Grove Maiden was so moved by the Faerie Doctor's daughter's answer that she turned all the trees in the grove into the one described by the woman, then bowed demurely and left the newly heartened storyteller with nothing to do except return to the blackthorn.

Say "thank you" in the language of your ancestors, then return to the central altar.

On her journey back, she pondered the merit of her stories, of the unique taste of her home-brewed words. They had spilled from her lips so easily, inspired by nothing more than the land itself, calling up precisely the memories she needed in order to tell a story well, and she was suddenly, epically aware of the sweet taste of her storyteller's tongue. She found the Raven-Sorcerer sleeping in the shadow of the blackthorn, but that giantess heard her coming and bent her branches to greet her.

"Ah, you've returned! I'll bet that Grove Maiden sucked the stories out of you, girl. Go and see the Lightning Mother now. Walk southeast and straight into the storm."

The Faerie Doctor's daughter protested, "But I've no eyes, and I've just returned from such a long journey. I'm sure I've no stories left. I'm all dried out from the talking."

"Well," the blackthorn snorted. "Yes, land stories will do that to you. This is why you need the Lightning Mother and her jolt of cosmic star stuff. This is why you need to keep going, lest this place surely become your grave."

The Raven-Sorcerer stirred awake then and spit a thorn in her direction, and the Faerie Doctor's daughter did as she was told.

Begin walking slowly southeast, setting the intention to meet a "mother" ancestor.

The journey, say the grannies, was a painful one of bare feet on craggy stone and sleeping in pools of saltwater. The woman gathered offerings of glass and lightning-struck wood while she walked, and in time, she did find the Lightning Mother dancing atop a cliff and humming hymns of battle and dying the good death. The Faerie Doctor's daughter could not look upon her even with her second sight, for this old god was made of white fire. She kept her gaze cast low on the ground while she lay her offering at the Lightning Mother's feet, whispering, "I've come here, wings dripping wet, to remember what it means to belong to sky."

The Mother sparked her awake then, a shock of story running through her like a river of diamond-bright stellar fusion, and she said, "Tell me, child. Tell me a story of a great storm, of raging spirit and passion. Share with me your tales of temptation and rainwater, of thunder and war."

Close your eyes, seeing this ancestor before you, and speak freely this new story.

And she spoke her stories of sky, spirit, and storm, bowing before their ancestral mothers while bones rattled and altar candles burned.

The grannies say that the Lightning Mother was so taken with the Faerie Doctor's daughter's stories of sky and storm that she emblazoned her words upon her fiery wings and took to the sky, inspired to cast a spell upon the land that would break all chains forged by religion and greed. Before she did, though, before that Lightning Mother left the Faerie Doctor's daughter, she asked her this:

"What old gods comfort you in your most trying moments? What faces do you see only in your dreams, and for whom do you build your shrines?"

Again, close your eyes and answer this question, speaking to your ancestor.

The old grannies say that the Faerie Doctor's daughter left the lightning-charred place after answering, windswept and primal growls swelling in her throat like thunder, inspiration sparking bright in her blood.

Bow in gratitude to this ancestor of yours who listened to your stories, her stories; then move back to the central altar.

She journeyed back to the blackthorn tree to find the Raven-Sorcerer wide-awake now, perched on the thorniest branch and singing a dirge without harmony.

"I've returned from the stormy place," said the Faerie Doctor's daughter, "and I think I'm ready to go home now. Thank you, Priestess Blackthorn, for urging me to visit that Lightning Mother, for now I remember why I'm here."

The Raven went quiet and side-eyed her. "Liar. You don't remember anything at all."

"I do!" the Faerie Doctor's daughter protested. "I do remember. Let me go home so I can calm these visions of stormy skies. I must pray away this longing and show my devotion to the old gods, lest they forget my name."

The Raven laughed. "Yes, nothing will set you alight like the stories of the sky. You think yourself a Goddess now, I know, but you've only met land and storm; their lessons are nothing without those of the sea." He spit a thorn at her. "Walk southwest now, princess. Walk to the house of the Sea Hag, and tell her the Raven said hello."

"But — but I've no stories left to tell. I've been burned to bits."

The Raven started singing again, blending his final direction into his song: "That's why you need the hag of the sea. The wildest of all, the grandmother Sidhe."

Trusting now that she was choiceless in the matter, the Faerie Doctor's daughter walked west toward the land of gushing gray waves, seals, and sea monsters.

Begin moving southwest now, intending to find a crone ancestor who will hear your stories.

She gathered shells and freshwater while she walked so she might have an offering for this hag, this hag who would surely be disappointed in what few stories she had to share.

The land went low and wet while she walked, and the sky fell into dusk. She heard the hissing of elementals all around her, and for the first time since she'd left her home, this wild one was afraid. The roar of the sea was no comfort, either, for it whispered its own stories of shattered dreams and sunk boats, of lost loves and haunted depths. At long last, the Faerie Doctor's daughter found herself standing on a rocky beach facing west, staring into the eyes of a long-whiskered grandmother seal whom she knew to be her immortal foremother.

"I've come here, with salt-streaked cheeks, to remember what it means to belong to the sea," said the seeker, laying her offering down before the seal hag.

"Tell me, child," the hag spoke low and gruff. "Tell me a story of the underworld, of faraway travel and water in the eyes. Tell me a tale of rough oceans and deep mysteries, for surely you know such stories."

Close your eyes and speak your stories now, seeing an elder whose blood is your blood.

And she shared her tales, pulling straight up from the well of feminine mysteries, while bones rattled and altar candles burned.

The grannies say the old seal was so thrilled to hear such tales of mermaids and water horses that she bade all the selkie women come out of their sea caves and sing for the Faerie Doctor's daughter. The otherworldlings did just that, swaying and crooning melodious verses that awoke something in the woman's blood, something long forgotten, something so painfully missed, something she'd lived without for a long, long time.

"Before you go," said the Sea Hag, "do tell me why you're here. Why have you come seeking the counsel of an old seal? What medicine do you keep — do you know that you keep, though it be hidden beneath the waves?"

Close your eyes once more and answer her.

The Faerie Doctor's daughter took her leave then, soaked in the stories of not just the sea but also the sky and the land, returning to the blackthorn tree to find the Raven-Sorcerer gone and the blackthorn tree covered in ice.

Bow in gratitude, then return to the central altar.

"I've returned," she declared, but no one answered her. "Mother Blackthorn? Why do you not speak?" She rushed to kneel at the foot of the old god tree, but the ice-coated thorns were no longer sharp as she wrapped her arms around its bark. She pressed her face against the frozen trunk and spoke into the melting frost: "I remember now.

I remember. I remember my stories of land, sky, and sea, and I have never known such belonging."

The grannies who tell this story always seal it with their own tears now, for they, too, understand the treasure that is a story told right, the precious gem that is a memory sparked to life in a sea of shadow. Many of those elder story keepers say that the Faerie Doctor's daughter woke then, whole and unmarked, two eyes still bright and rooted in their sockets, skin chilled but unstuck by thorns where she slept at the foot of the blackthorn.

The grannies never end this story with tie-it-up-in-a-bow promises like "and she never forgot again," for we all forget from time to time. The forgetting, the loss, is part of the magick, for it makes space for the new stories to be told, after all. When we forget too long, though, when the darkness threatens to take us under, it is up to the otherworld to help us remember. We need only listen. We need only walk to those thin places where land meets sky meets sea.

Over time and bit by bit, even stories like this one, the stories told by the elder-crones whom we might call forgetful if we didn't know better, stretch and break, too, leaving nothing but a few fragile threads of innocence, grace, and the purest unconditional presence.

⊶⊱✢⊰⊷

The Desert Hag concludes, bows with a feigned demureness, and bids you enter the blissful shadows of her home.

Opening Practice: Your Summer Initiation

Materials: Three small bowls, at least nine strips of old light-colored cloth, fabric marker

The epic task of this first moon of summer is to make peace with the practice of fierce and intentional gratitude. Mind you, this is not a call to be decidedly content and refuse to strive, or to rush past rage, or to accept the unacceptable. There is much wrong with our wounded world, after all — and, by extension, there is much that we cannot, that we *should* not, force ourselves to be grateful for. This is not an oversugared practice of skirting around the magick and hoping our thank-yous and our well-wishes are sufficient to bring about change; rather, gratitude is a true and often overlooked Witch's skill.

When we practice gratitude beneath the summer moons, we are inviting what we already love to bloom. We are welcoming greater boons into our world by using the grateful heart as fertile soil, and we are opening ourselves up to receive all that is ours, all that our foremothers prayed for on their many fire-tending evenings left alone with the flames.

In his book *Consolations*, David Whyte writes that "gratitude is the understanding that many millions of things come together and live together and mesh together and breathe together in order for us to take even one more breath of air, that the underlying gift of life and incarnation as a living, participating human being is a privilege; that we are miraculously part of something, rather than nothing." Even in seemingly dire moments, we are not alone; we are part of the great, pulsing heart of life.

As the first new moon of summer dawns, begin this gratitude-bowl practice. Consecrate three small bowls in the elements, using those already on your summer altar if you are able; then choose three life areas with which to work your gratitude magick. These might be the same life areas as the cosmic egg work from spring, but they need not be. You might choose romance, parenting, and art making, or you might choose money, home, and travel; any life area that you feel shifting right now will work, so long as it holds meaning for you.

You might look to the writing from the noonday reflection practice for inspiration, but be sure to choose three life areas you truly care about right now, in this moment. When you feel ready, cast a circle, welcoming the beloved ancestors, then hold the first bowl as you face north. Ask yourself what life area this particular vessel represents, then ask yourself for what you are most grateful with respect to this particular part of your life right now. This might be a recent memory or a more permanent feeling state of gratitude, but call to mind at least three things pertaining to this one life area for which you are most grateful right now, as you are, a Witch facing north and honoring their place here on this earth. For example, if the life area you choose to work with is love and partnership, you might call to mind gratitude for a heartfelt and fleeting moment of intimacy, a sudden realization of what you truly want out of a relationship, and an understanding of your renewed wholeness that allows you to authentically be in a loving partnership with another human being.

When you feel ready, synthesize these three gratitude points into three single words or three short phrases, writing them on the strips of fabric and placing them in the bowl. Return this bowl to the altar and choose another, now facing southeast and repeating the practice: Ask yourself which of the two remaining life areas this vessel will represent, call up three points of gratitude, write them on the fabric, then return the bowl to the altar before doing the same practice a third time, working the last bowl and facing southwest. You will now have three bowls on your altar dedicated to three different life areas, each containing at least three strips of fabric on which separate expressions of gratitude pertaining to that particular life area are written.

Before opening the circle, return to the altar and hold each bowl again, one at a time, calling up all points of gratitude and, importantly, feeling the in-the-heart sensation, that subtle warming that swells within the ribs when you are fully in that state of embodied fruition. Try to remain in that state, if you are able, while you speak these words:

This is my summer initiation, and I am truly a most thankful sprite. On my grave will be written nothing but the poetry of moments, rhyming and rhythmic thank-yous to no one in particular, only those holy crossroads of time and space, those sacred and fleeting points of becoming when I was nothing but a flesh-and-blood shrine to sheer heart-born grace, when I wanted for nothing if only for that small space between the inhale and exhale, when the world was made of emerald-green gratitude, tiny sparking building blocks of thank-yous. My life was built from these moments, after all, and from the ethers I shall watch the world go on without me, warmed by those many ephemeral glimpses of who I truly was, those embodied reminders that I was living well. Surely I made the most of my time housed in this soft, feeling flesh.

Seal this ceremony by chanting "thank you," practicing feeling the true, under-the-skin sensation in response to the words. Open the circle when ready, and welcome what comes.

And so it is.

Waxing Moon Practice: A Practiced Thanks

As the first moon of summer waxes toward full, continue the practices from the initiation ceremony. Working with those three life areas, when you are met with a moment that sparks gratitude, make a note, mentally or literally; speak or think *thank you*, being sure to feel the feeling; then add a strip of fabric, one for each moment, to the bowls each evening if you are able. There is an art to this, you see — a repatterning, of sorts, that requires a commitment to noticing the small moments. Of course, there are many forces that understandably and sometimes necessarily block the feeling of gratitude. The skill is spotting the moments that seem as though they somehow found you, somehow graced your day with precisely the medicine you needed, then succumbing, in only a few short breaths, to the embodied sensation of pure, unadulterated *thank you*, without rushing past this feeling.

We are not replacing any other emotion with gratitude. We are not naming gratitude superior to grief or rage or melancholy; we are simply noticing the fleeting points in time that already exist, attending to them and filling them with a natural thankfulness. Much of our time-impoverished world encourages us to not lose control, to not sink into the space of the heart because it forces us to descend from the rigid intellect that knows everything for sure. If a Witch rewires themselves enough to just take a breath and notice those moments when their magick is speaking to them, saying *Yes, yes, I am real*, then they are well positioned to wield their spell-work and wield it well.

This Witch Is a Time Traveler
Poetry of the Ungrateful Heart Made Whole

———⊪——— ⊪❭❬⊪ ———⊪———

This Witch is a time traveler, and she's returned to those few and far-between childhood moments, those taken-for-granted breaths when a warm morning was medicine enough to heal the bleeding cuts left from the sharper nightmares, when sweet corn nibbled at a wooden

*table was prayer enough. She's made the journey back to those wild
teenage days when riverside chitchat and smoke swirls were ritual
and long stares at the full moon were sacred, solitary ceremony.*

*This Witch is a time traveler, and she's gone back to give thanks,
not to a vengeful god but to the spirit of these moments, to those
holy crisscrossing strands of time and place where pure presence met
heartfelt joy. It's not too late, after all. There's no past fully left
behind, and as much as that Witch remembers the future into being,
she has pulled the past forward to collect all the gratitude she can
pack in her bag.*

*This Witch is a time traveler, and she has infinite moments to
visit, all woven into that holy cosmic fabric, all waiting to be seen,
heard, and known.*

❧❦❧

Season of Wild Delights: Full Moon

Grandmother Speaks: You've Got Stories, Child

The beneath-the-dunes hut is blissfully cool and a welcome delight
for the senses. The walls are brilliantly painted murals and glittering
mosaics, an otherworldly breeze spirals about the room and sparks
countless wind chimes to life, and the place smells so strongly of those
chilly scents of sage and eucalyptus that your lungs and breath thank
you for introducing them to this wild place.

Your thirst has nearly abated now, though at first you all but guz-
zled three pitchers full of water, and you're able to truly taste this light
and lemony brew the hag has served you.

"Tell me a story now, Witch," the hag urges, her back to you while
she prepares something sweet smelling in her humble kitchen. "I'd
love to hear a story while I cook. These walls contain many stories,
but I'm always ready for another."

Your eyes settle on a dried bird wing — a hawk's, you think — and you're sure that this creature's ghost contains more stories in a single striped feather than you do in the whole of your body.

"Well?" The hag turns to face you. "Don't tell me you're one of those wanderers who claims to have no story." She shakes a wooden spoon in your direction. "You've got stories, child. Everyone does."

Full Moon Practice: The Three Stories

Materials: Journal, writing utensil, gratitude bowls

Beneath the first full moon of summer, take an inventory of your rag words, those sentiments of gratitude you wrote on your strips of fabric while the moon waxed. In your Book of Moon and Flame, write each bowl's words on its own page. Look to the first page now. Look to the words you have written, and ask yourself to write a brief story describing your transition from right now, this moment, into the total moment of fruition you are moving toward. Use your own gratitude words as puzzle pieces for the story. Ask yourself what you want most in your life with respect to that one life area, see yourself there living that dream vision, then use these gratitude words to describe your journey from this moment, beneath the full Litha moon, to that moment of complete vision realized. You may use the prompts I offer here or write your own:

> *Once upon a summer moon, I left my safer haunts to wander...*
> *Deep in the ancestral forest, I encountered...*
> *Gifted with that wisdom, I moved swiftly toward...*
> *Little did I know, there was an ancient prophecy foretelling of my...*
> *The healing came from...*
> *Now, heart swelling with gratitude, I am...*
> *I've come a long way since summer solstice, but here I am now, fully...*

In preparation for the ritual, write this story three times, once for each gratitude bowl, using the words you yourself wrote as reflections of gratitude. As close to the full moon as possible now, carry your three stories along with your three bowls outside to an ancestral tree — that is, a tree that was sacred to your ancestors.

When you feel ready, imagine yourself surrounded by both your beloved dead and the yet-to-be-born babes. Ask them to join you here. Tell them that your healing is their healing. Tell them you have leaned toward the familial ache, and tell them they still breathe through you. Choose which story to begin with, then read it to them, to the elements, to all future generations. When you are finished, tie the rags to the tree loosely, being careful not to damage this beloved ally.[*] You will be returning to the tree the next day, so the gratitude rags need only remain overnight. Move on to the second and third story when ready, speaking to the grandmothers, ceremonially tying the rags to the tree for them, for their healing, for your healing, and using great care. Tend to the spirit of this moment. When you finish, call up as many memories of gratitude as you are able, watching the fabric sway in the summer breeze. Cultivate the feeling state of gratitude; then feel — do not just see but *feel* — yourself living your dream visions, all three of them fully realized.

Invite this moment to exist outside of linear time. There is an essence to this fleeting intersection of time and space, and you are simply one of the elements of that essence. This ritual is not about you, as some separate animal, in a specific place. There is no separation between every piece of this moment and you, between every rag on the tree and you, between every ancestor around you and every cell in your blood, between the lifeblood of this tree and what runs in your veins. Become the infinite fabric of connecting threads, spun with wisdom and blessed by a grateful heart.

Return to the tree the next day, and be sure to remove all rags. You may repurpose them, tying them together in a "gratitude garland," or release them in another sustainable way.

And so it is.

---

[*] The "rag tree" tradition runs strong in the Irish and British Celtic lands, though traditionally the rags are torn from an ailing person's clothes or belongings and tied to a tree, often a hawthorn, as a prayer for their healing. A lack of environmental consciousness has, unfortunately, tainted the tradition and caused significant harm to many trees, an outcome precisely the opposite of affirming a kinship with a sacred tree in order to foster human healing.

Season of Wild Delights: Waning Moon

Grandmother Speaks: Of Honest Contentment

An evening of folk tales and storytelling it has surely been, and your voice tires of sharing so much truth. This hag has already taught you much about the merit of your voice and that authentic currency that is heart-born gratitude, but now you need to rest. It's long past the Witching Hour, and the sun shall be rising in the east soon. You wonder when the hag will lead you to a soft place where you might rest, and you wonder how long your manners will keep you from admitting that your body is too tired to carry on this revelry.

"Ah, well, I've heard enough for tonight, I think." She senses your fatigue. "Let's take to our beds. In the morning, I shall pose a potent question to you, dear heart. For now, let us rest well in a state of honest contentment. Tell me, child, have you ever known such total and complete acceptance of who you are and where you find yourself?"

You want to ask if that's your potent question come early, but she continues.

"Have you ever rested in complete grace without looking for the world to betray your joy?"

She doesn't need you to answer, for she can read the confusion in your eyes, empathic creature that she is.

"No need to say more, love, but you really do need to learn to ask for what you need. Let's ask for some dream medicine and wake more whole women than we've put to bed."

Waning Moon Practice: A Moment of Pause

Solstices are stopping points, places of pause. At Yule, we pause in the void, in that primordial swirl of infinite creative potential. At summer solstice, at Litha, we pause in fruition, in that full-belly moment of brightness and love. As a waning moon practice before midsummer, find small moments of pause. This can simply mean continuing the gratitude practice but extending those embodied feelings of thanks for as long as possible. Importantly, they will still be fleeting. They will still sweep in and out of your heart space, and this is as it must be, for our lives will always call us away from an embodied, inner solstice. Even so, gift yourself with just three long breaths of pause when gratitude finds you or when you receive a cosmic message that all is as it should be.

To Such Hard-Woven Stories, Surely We Belong

Musings of the Heathen Storyteller

———◆◆———

What if we write not to instruct, not to dictate immutable spiritual truths or wrench stony, one-size-suits-all maxims from overdry lips? What if we write to offer up the stories of our eternal becoming, if only to ourselves, if only to the ghosts of our foremothers who lean over us while we scratch away on tear-soaked pages long past our deep-summer bedtimes? What if we write because those busy-handed hags couldn't? What if we write to weave together the ruddy threads of our most willful longing with our fragile sovereignty and deep regret, with our long-buried ancestral inheritance and our modern rebellion, crafting a more beautiful and brazen fabric from the mundane strands of what is, at best, only ache and awe, wound and wonder?

What if we tell stories not to entertain, not to dazzle and disgust, but to encounter something of the fierce-mystical-monstrous there on the invisible line between what is offered up through word and gesture and what is heard, embraced, and digested into many individual belly cauldrons of experience? What if our stories are ceremonies of meaning making and integration, paradoxical candlelit shrines to who we were before the story was told and hopeful fantasies of who we might be when the story ends and silence swallows us whole?

What if we tell stories because we simply must? We simply must push our language beyond post and page from time to time, and we must let the story speak our soft-clay souls into being, humbling us into ephemeral moments of rhythmic words meeting bone, new myth meeting blood, and sharp poetry meeting the hunted flesh. Here, there are no storytellers and no audience; there are only the old ones who speak through us, our lithe tongues animated by witch-ghosts and our eyes haunted by those long-gone crones who knew us well in life but even better in death. To such hard-woven stories, surely we belong.

—⟶⊷✦⊶⟵—

Season of Wild Delights: Dark Moon

Grandmother Speaks: With Feeling Flesh and Low-Drumming Hearts

"There's nothing like sleeping in the heat of summer, with sand behind your ears and sweat tickling your neck, to remind you that you're alive — am I right?" The hag tosses you a thin sheet before disappearing into the shadows, and you are already sinking blissfully into sleep. "There's nothing like a cool floor beneath you and ancient sand all around you to remind you that no one has escaped death yet, but we are surely blessed to be here now, with feeling flesh and low-drumming hearts."

Dark Moon Practice: The Spirit of the Moment

Recall the full moon practice now, as the moon goes dark. Recall the practice of tending to the spirit of the moment like an altar keeper tends that physical expression of the sacred. Under the dark moon, having worked with those points of pause, now begin to feel into each moment as if it has its own ghostly energy. Let the moments of pause be windows into this practice, and consider now, before the new moon dawns, just how every moment in time can be met and met well, just as a creature or soul can be encountered.

To the Season of Wild Delights, Farewell for Now

I've never known such gratitude as I do in this moment, ye Season of Wild Delights, for you taught me how to love the small times. I know more of linear time's illusion now. I've peeled back its mask and seen the great galactic orbs spiraling under its grim face, and I've whispered "thank you" to the otherworld for granting me that second sight. To the Season of Wild Delights, farewell for now. We'll meet again after one more great turning, and I'll have many thankful moments packed under my skin. And so it is.

CHAPTER 5

Season of Holy Thunder

---✦---

Reaping

Welling over with slow-spilling abundance, the midsummer moon is a time of subtle unrest, of nights that are growing ever so slightly longer moon by moon, of precarious equanimity, blessing, and harvest. We look to our elders to guide us toward balance now on these long days when autumn is already looming, already sending ghosts to haunt us in the night, and we seek solace in the archetypal wild feminine, in those deities who still spark in our blood despite the efforts of the wicked ones to snuff their flames.

Our magick shifts here, turning infinitesimally toward the dark and the deep, toward shadow and the unseen. Here, we continue the magick of gratitude and the craft of pausing, of enjoying, of intentional being-ness, but we do so with one eye fixed upon the boneyard. Here, we face the challenge of wielding the fire to drive change in our worlds, without sacrificing the power of intimacy and a thankful spirit.

Call to mind the image of a wild hag's heart set alight, slow burning with diamond-bright heat sourced straight from that sacred compassion only an elder knows; this is the sigil of the midsummer moon, the inner altar we are all tasked to keep and keep well.

Hag Lesson #15

The integrity of magick depends upon cocreation.

Where Do the Churchless Go to Sing?

———◄►◄►―――――◄►◄—►◄►―――――◄►―――

Again, I find myself kneeling here at your altar, lightning keeper, praying to a faceless Priestess who has no name other than Wild. A longing for the ancestral righteous runs in my blood even now, even when I've forgotten the mother-tongue language and have only pieces of the old ceremonies still stitched to my robes. My Craft is an imperfect patchwork garment sewn up sloppily, shredded, then hand-tied together again, but I'm wearing it well, I think, these sea-blue prayers of my grandmothers, these golden and somber ceremonies given me by my most treasured teachers, and these hot-pink and forbidden dances I've harvested from some unknown cemetery where the neglected ways go to die.

So tell me, Wild, where do the churchless ones go to sing? Where do the wayward witch-mothers go to light their altar candles for their poor babes who may never know the belonging I feel right now, right here, beneath this summer moon. Tell me, lightning keeper, for whom do you pray, and on whom do you cast your more potent enchantments? During my most indulgent moments such as this, I think you just might pray for me, and this is the only supplication I shall accept beneath the summer moons.

———►◄—◄►―――

Noonday Reflection: The Gift Giver's Breath

We ponder now, as the darkness begins to swallow the light day by day, the nature of our vulnerability, the power had by a truly humble heart, and the beauty of our very breath. Reflect now on the merit of gifting and receiving, on the ebb and flow of reward, joy, and sacrifice. In your Book of Moon and Flame, ponder three realms of your life, perhaps the same life dimensions you worked with during the gratitude practices of the Season of Wild Delights, and ask yourself what you are giving in those areas and what you are receiving. The gifting may be as simple as attention, devotion, or presence; it need not be a resource-consuming action. Similarly, the receiving may not necessarily be a climactic or sudden windfall, though it certainly can be. Take an inventory now of this natural exchange, this rise and fall of your truest currencies. If your life areas are abundance, art, and partnership, for example, choose one to begin with and ask yourself to describe the flow of energy in that one area in terms of giving and receiving.

. We must let every part of our lives breathe, after all. All is an exchange. All is interaction; this is the crux of magick. We are a part of it all, and the all is part of us. Though our capitalistic economy would certainly have us believe that we should always be consuming, that we should gorge ourselves all we can, that our businesses should be in a permanent state of swell and our self-worth should be tied to our finances, the wild will tell us *no*. No, we are not meant to swallow all we can until we burst. We are meant to sustain ourselves and our world, gifting the outbreath, coming to a place of void and rest at the bottom of the exhale before inhaling again.

If you choose art, for example, ask yourself how you are receiving art, and in what form. How are you gifting art to the world? This is, importantly, not an exercise in self-admonishment but rather a way of identifying potential imbalances as they exist in practice, before casting spells for some grand vision that may exacerbate an already-unsustainable state. As we approach the time of banishing, purging, and release in autumn, we lay the groundwork for discernment, for truly choosing what needs to go in order to make space for what comes. In what ways do these three life areas make you feel full, and where do you feel in a place of lack, if at all? Ponder these questions now, beneath the Blessing Moon.

Lughnasadh Celebration: The Bread of Life and Death

Lughnasadh is a cross-quarter day, nested midway between the summer solstice and the autumnal equinox and often celebrated on August 1 in the Northern Hemisphere.* This is a time of early harvest, of gathering,

---

* In Irish Gaelic, the word is derived from *Lugh*, the lightning god and member of the Tuatha Dé Danann, and *nasadh*, meaning assembly.

kinship, and Holy Wild nourishment. We find ourselves fully in touch with the cycle of death-birth-death here, sensing the slow-creeping days of mourning and ghostly storytelling but all the while with a brilliant sun in our eyes. Our celebrations are homecomings here, felt and in-the-blood ceremonies of food, dance, and drums. We honor the light without turning from the shadow, and we welcome what comes without severing the future from the past.

As a simple celebration that honors the first harvest, bake a small loaf of bread with great care. Use a recipe that feels right, perhaps one inherited or that speaks to your ancestry. As you work, as you stir and knead, ponder the nature of the great wheel's turning, and call in the letting go. Ponder the nature of gifting and receiving, of these small rituals that speak to the holiness of our humanity. When the loaf is finished, place it on your altar overnight if you are able, from dusk on the evening before Lughnasadh to dusk on the evening of Lughnasadh. Speak prayers of gratitude to the oldest gods you know, to your grandmothers, and to the land you find yourself on. Go into the wild on the night of the cross-quarter day, and leave your bread somewhere it may serve to nourish the creatures of this world or those spirits who dwell in the realm of the Wild Unseen. Offer a final blessing, then act. Do three deeds that you might call *good*, three somethings truly born of the heart, for a loved one, for your community, and for yourself. And so it is.

Adaptation for Families, Coven Groups, and Other Wild Circles: Ancestral Thanksgiving

In adapting this ritual for a small group, you might ask everyone to bring an offering of food to the gathering that all might share in community. Let the offering somehow represent an inherited gift, something passed down from a time long gone or yet-to-be that seems like potent medicine right now, during these trying times. What lessons run in your blood? What practices might you have forgotten but, somehow, still remember, despite the heavy blades of colonization and capitalism? Bring the food of belonging to this feast. Bring the sustenance of knowing that we all come from a rich, Earth-based tradition if we trace the lines far enough back through the muck, through the ash. Permit this feast to be a commitment to remembering, to both receiving what is yours and becoming the gift.

Season of Holy Thunder: New Moon

Grandmother Speaks:
Rough Places Show You What You're Made Of

You feel you invoked it, this looming storm, for your eyes could not stand the sun for one more moment, and the Desert Hag warned that you had a long way to walk before you would come to that hallowed ground. The light has grown dimmer, the air cooler, and your breath comes more easily now, though your trek through the sands does not. Your legs are heavy and wanting rest.

"We're nearly there," the hag promises, unbothered by the challenge of this journey. "You didn't think this little wander would be an easy one, did you?"

You shake your head, certain that this walk has been an easy one for the Desert Hag, who seems to float above the windblown curves of rock and sand rather than trudge heavily through the rough terrain, as you do.

"Rough places show you what you're made of, child." She twirls her long knotted walking stick like a featherlight baton. "Rough places ask you who you wish to become, stripped raw and bare. Rough places force you to come to grips with what you truly want in your most trying moments. Do you believe me?"

Words escape you, and she side-eyes your insecurity.

"Well, then." The hag smirks. "Here's a story to embolden you."

The Witch and the Lightning Tree: A Midsummer Tale

Those forgetful grandmothers, those story-keeping elders whose tales grew too big for their bodies, have much to share with us about time and loss, but what of those prayerful grandmothers?

The devoted crones who bid you speak rhymes before a hearty supper, who wave their arm about in a one-limbed blessing, a moving sigil that means far more to them than to any holy man who might do the same, surely they have their own stories, too, do they not? Surely they have the holiest stories to tell, should we be granted just a few minutes with them. Surely the prayerful grandmothers have much to share with our lost generations about what it means to belong to a place.

If we lean close and listen, for they often speak quietly so as not to offend any vengeful god, we might just be granted the very medicine we seek, for they have much to say about the sacred. To be sure, we may have to sift through some outmoded language that denotes a certainty unsuited to our times, or we may have to dig under verses we don't believe in and rules we were born to break. But, if we can tune in to the deeper, more guttural voice that runs like a gray and wild river beneath that rigid rock of religion, even the most rebellious Witch can glean some wisdom from those prayerful elders who live close to death, who walk alongside the holy, and who understand the desire to belong better than most.

This is a story these prayerful grannies tell, a myth of finding the very thing we seek right where we stand, of resisting the urge to snatch up what is not ours to take, and of recovering the treasure that is our inherited and most soulful place. Now, these grandmothers are dedicants, true and sworn believers in naming what's right and what's wrong, so we must forgive the dryness of their words from time to time. We must hear their stories while drinking something cool and wash the sand from our tongues when they are finished. These hags know things that we don't, and they know they know things that we don't. In the absence of any deity who chose us, we might kneel before these crones and call them god, but they wouldn't want us to waste our spiritual currencies — our hymns and our ceremonies and our prayers — on them, you see. They wouldn't want us to forget that the land holds us and holds us well, and their stories remind us of precisely these things, precisely what it means to belong to this joyous and wicked world.

Their stories are slow-cooked, these old mothers', passed down through the generations, changed by the tongue that's doing the telling, tucked away in dusty attics, then pulled out again when the time is right, when some lonely heart has lost her way and asks for direction; to those instances, this story is well suited, indeed. These stories are made for those times, for those liminal, fog-filled points on a soulful journey when the route forward is forward no longer. These grannies aren't ones for indecisiveness, you see, for they always know precisely which way to go, exactly which myth to pull from the shadows, and exactly the poetic brew needed to soothe the worried heart.

"Come, child," they might begin. "Come and face the southeast, the direction of the Lightning Mother from where the winds of spirit and wildness blow. Breathe deep, like every rush of air through your lungs is a thankful and whispered prayer all its own, and let's come to know the Witch and the lightning tree together; she's much like you, I think."

The Witch lived in a stone house, and she had always lived in a stone house. The walls were made from quartz streaked pearlescent and dug from the land by her long-dead great-grandmother. The house pulsed with memory, sat square to the north of her ancestral ground. There was a rich and abundant garden nested in the east and well tended by the Witch each day, as her granny had shown her how to make the onions sweet and the carrots grow long to fruition. To the south stood a burned-black lightning tree, leafless with charred bark and severed branches, and between the garden and the tree stood her grandmother's grave. To the west ran a quiet and unassuming creek, sourced from where the Witch did not know.

The prayerful grannies make a point here, at this early juncture just after the story's birth, to speak to the sanctity of that lightning tree. "A holy tree, indeed," they say, nodding with that expression those old crones get when they're wondering if you're worthy of knowing something they know quite well. To any listener they might deem ready to hear such a deep piece of the wild mystery, they might then speak to one of the many traditions that hold a lightning tree to be a sacred shrine, kith and kin to the gods, some might say.

But the Witch had no memory of the lightning tree's power. The Witch had forgotten the stories passed to her by her grandmothers and through her dreams, and to her, that lightning tree was shabby, gnarled at the edges, the hungry ghost of a once-mighty hazel, and far too mundane to be mystical. Over time, the Witch grew to hate that lightning tree. She would dream of it coming to life and swallowing her whole. She would watch it walk in birdlike jerks, dragging its ripped-up roots behind, casting shadows on her garden and coming toward the house. She'd wake in a cold sweat, breathless and haunted. She'd look out her window then, seeing the moon lighting the tree in the ghastliest places, and she'd fall to her knees and pray to a god she didn't believe in to save her, to strike the tree again with a storm and burn it to ash for good.

Night after night this happened, until one summer came when the dreams were truly wretched, truly the stuff of nightmares and blood-filled horror. She struggled so much to sleep that her days seemed more dream than reality, and she started to live in that liminal place where the Others, those spirits and those elementals, can find you quite easily — too easily, some might say. She still tended her garden by day but could scarcely eat, her appetite all but lost for fear of the lightning tree.

She started to wonder if she was praying to the wrong god, if there was some other blue-skinned warrior or bearded being that would answer her prayer, so she took on new rituals, new chants, new ceremonies that were not her own. The lightning tree still stood, no matter to whom she dedicated her incantations.

She decided it must be a Goddess, then. Surely, there was some hooded Priestess, some well tender, some full-hipped mother god who could answer her prayers, and she threw herself onto another path entirely. Even so, the dreams kept coming and the lightning tree kept standing.

Summer began to wane now, and the nights were longer. The nightmares were more brutal than ever before, and the Witch was starved for her own savior spirit, tormented by the tree's terrible presence. On one fateful evening, a storm was brewing in the west. Thunder rolled strong and true, rattling the walls of the Witch's quartz house and charging it with a wild electrostatic energy that weighed heavy on her head like a burdensome crown.

She had to get out, you see, so she walked straight into the storm, straight toward her grandmother's grave. Lightning flashed on the horizon, streaking across the sky behind that wicked tree, and the Witch pounded her fists upon her granny's mossed-over grave.

"Why?" she wailed. "Why won't any of the gods answer me, Grandmother? This evil tree still stands, still creeps into my dreams at night, and I can bear it no longer!"

Now, the prayerful grannies who tell this story sometimes disagree on this next bit, and I've seen them fight for hours about the right way to tell the end of this story. Some of them stop for a moment and say a short and breathy verse to themselves before going on, and others will also pause, looking into the distance as if they were seeing the story play out in the corner of the room. Those who pray before continuing tend to say that the Witch's grandmother appeared to her then, a full-body apparition returned to the material plane just to scold her grandchild. "A worthy reason to come back," they would laugh. Those who simply pause and look to the shadows tend to leave that part out, neglecting the grandmother's ghost altogether and jumping to the next piece of the story.

What the grannies agree on is that the Witch turned fearless then; made bold by either her grandmother's ghost or the spirit of the storm itself, she walked straight to that lightning tree, spit on its roots, and started to climb.

Branch by branch, she cursed the thing, stomping hard with her feet and pulling down on the thinnest branches with all her might, but the lightning tree did not budge, made sturdy by its years, by its burn, and by some indefinable thing of which the woman was not aware but would soon come to know and know well.

Just as she reached the top, just when she'd spoken her last hex and called on the storm to take them both down, a curious thing happened. The storm hushed, and the charred bark turned softer under the Witch's hands. Stranger still, the Witch's hands were small like a child's, and there were sudden sunbeams streaming through lush hazel leaves above where she sat, nestled between two branches like a little bird. She was still herself but many, many years younger, before life had started to sting and time had started to tug on her skin.

Some of the grannies who tell this story say that it was the grandmother's ghost who was suddenly there in the tree with her, while others say it was the tree itself who spoke, but they agree that the Witch heard these words, whether from hazel or specter:

"Don't you remember? These branches were your god once, and your whole religion was this, climbing higher and higher. Play was your prayer, and you knew in your small bones that you belonged right here."

Lightning struck then, all the crone storytellers agree. The Witch was cast out from the tree, sent flying like she was spit out like an oversize hazelnut, and she woke at dawn the next day with a renewed sense of certainty. She repented prayers spoken to gods that weren't hers, and she went about the business of simply remembering. Much more energy was wasted on acquisition, after all, than simply appreciating what was already hers, and the lightning tree no longer haunted her.

She left offerings to the wild hazel each day and spoke gratitude to it by night. She had much to learn from this holy thing, much to remember, and much to pass on, for there is the particular flavor of the sacred that runs in our blood and assures us we belong. There are the ceremonies stamped on our bones, and there are the beloved ways so familiar they get neglected, dismissed as boring or insufficient when, in fact, they are the very medicine we need.

"Amen! Seá!" say the grannies.

⊶⊶)(⊶⊶

The Desert Hag stops then, punctuating her story with only her breath and a low, telling hum. You feel you are nearly there, nearly to some magick place that will most certainly change you, and you wonder if you are ready for summer's greatest lesson.

Opening Practice: Our Web of Being

The midsummer moon is the Blessing Moon, a time of heart centeredness and much, much story sharing. This moon is a portal for coming home to the sanctity of our own stories, of standing on the imagined bridge between them and the holiness of those old, forgotten traditions. As an opening practice for this moon, call into question the rigid timeline of past, present, and future; break the past and the future out of the cages we tend to lock both our memories and our hopes in, those entirely fabricated prisons that permit us to dismiss both past and future as simultaneously, and quite contrastingly, unchangeable and nonexistent.

Make good use of your quiet moments beneath this new moon, and consider that all is happening at once, with your more ancient ancestors still building their stone altars and your great-great-grandparents still on their knees praying and you right here and the babes twenty generations from now already creating their art, whatever their art might be, whatever state their world might be in. Consider, further, that you are a microcosm of all that is, with the many systems of your body pulsing as one, yes, but also with your own soft flesh and wild soul a reflection of how beauteous an entire human community can be.

Our magick works only when we see ourselves as an aspect of the whole, as a coven of cells singing the same Pagan hymn of cohesion and belonging. We all long to belong, and we are all integral bridge lines in the cosmic web of being.

Waxing Moon Practice: To Make Peace with the Mystery

Witches make peace with the Mystery, time and time again. We grapple with questions about the nature of deity, the merit of our magick, the neutrality of energy, whether we are good, whether anything or anyone is good, then we decide we know some concrete truth, uncovering some part of the secret, before tossing it out and beginning again. The Mystery is a force with which we hold hands — a loyal lover, of sorts, who is always with us, who teaches us to not become too sure of anything at all, including our own position in this wounded world.

While the moon waxes, as often as possible if you feel so inclined, free-write using the following prompts and reflect on your words. Welcome the contradictions as evidence that we are ever-changing and integral parts of a greater, cyclical whole.

Love is…
Love is not…
God/dess/dex is…
God/dess/dex is not…
My place is…
My place is not…
My ancestors are…
My ancestors are not…
I am…

I am not…
The greatest Mystery is…

Season of Holy Thunder: Full Moon

Grandmother Speaks:
Initiation into the Priestesshood of the Lightning Keepers

There are those who are skilled storytellers, there are those who are skilled listeners, and then there are those who are masters of both the genuine telling and the deep listening. This Desert Hag is surely the latter, and you've spent this long walk hearing her well-told tales of the bone stealers and the trickster gods, hanging on her every word like a toddler clings to her mother's skirts. She tells a story as if every listener is a pivotal character in the plot. And since you happen to be the only one here in a heavy body, every story she told was about you.

She listened, too, though. She heard you speak of your many adventures, your travels east to the hungry vines of the Garden Hag and your trek south to this wild place. You told her of the Elders' Altar, and you spoke of the wounds of your foremothers in a way you hadn't before, flavoring their stories with your story, their passions with your particular purpose in this life.

"Ah, you see! Stories help us make sense of this wicked world. Should we lose our stories, surely we would lose ourselves."

You nod, then nearly trip over a charred piece of wood buried deep in the sand. Perhaps it was a fallen tree, but only a piece of the trunk and a lone blackened branch stretch up from the otherwise-barren earth.

"Welcome to the lightning tree, child." The hag waves her hand over the pitiful thing, and the sky turns the color of soot.

You're sure your face isn't hiding your confusion well. This is why you came all this way? The sight of this poor bit of wood is what your sweat has paid for?

"Tell me, what do you think the story of this wild relic might be?"

You shrug, having no memory of this place.

"Has the sun dried out your imagination?" The hag shakes her head, then lifts her chin toward the storm. "Well, it's going to get watered now. Go on."

You start to speak then, feeling foolish, weaving a feeble tale about a Witch who lost their gods and forgot their way, but the hag looks pleased by your words, nodding and clapping in just the right places. Her already-luminescent skin starts to glow a bit brighter while you speak, as if the story itself feeds her, and just as you finish, just as the rain begins to pour, the hag holds her hands out to you, bidding you dance with her.

Before you know it, you are twirling around the log, laughing and singing with this wild one who somehow knows you so well, and the storm is blessing you both with its winds and its waters.

"The grandmothers of this desert say this tree was the first tree, that it was born and burned right here in this holy place just for those who long for a missing god in order to have something to worship."

You want to ask if her words are true, but you know better.

"They say if you touch its bark during a lightning storm, you'll see your future, and they say your initiation into the Priestesshood of the Lightning Keepers will be swift and sure."

Full Moon Practice: Held by the Long Arms of Time

Beneath the full midsummer moon, consider yourself held by something both greater than your single body *and* made all the greater by you, by your holy hands and your beating heart. Go into a wild place if you are able. Stand with feet firm on ground facing south, the direction of fire, and open your palms to the energies that surround you as if you are poised to hold hands with some immense but unseen force. In this moment, permit yourself to feel small, to feel as though you are but a sparking electric instant within a grand, sparking sea. Breathe as part of this far-spreading and waving cosmic web now.

Invite all those who came before you and those who will come after you to stand here with you now in a way that denies the before or after, that welcomes the folding of that web so your most primal ancestors are here and now. The babes of the future are here and now. Beneath this full moon, every one of these sparks is held by the long arms of time. Every one of these diamond-bright pulsing stories is an integral strand in the broader tapestry, and those beautiful crossroads where your sparking story meets another are holy jolts of love and pain if you look close, lightning strikes of conversation, birth, sex, death, laughter, and knowing nods; these human ceremonies are anything but mundane. They are the very electricity we are made of, the life force that runs through us, that feeds us, that keeps us warm and keeps us going. Be here for as long as you can, feeling into this state of complete connection, though you are alone, and welcome what comes.

Season of Holy Thunder: Waning Moon

Grandmother Speaks: It Shall Heal

Your hand is shaking, the fat of your fingertip brushing the wood as if it holds some terrible poison, but it happens then, just as the old hag said. You see yourself as a crone even older than this desert keeper who has brought you here. You see your hands touching this lightning tree just as they are now but covered in paper-thin skin, spotted in places and wearing rings you do not recognize. There is a young one with you here and a storm overhead that throbs in your joints as much as it does in the sky. This is you as elder, you are sure. This is you as a teacher of the old ways, as a dedicant, as a lover of the old gods and the very incarnation of who you needed when you were younger, when you stood as this babe does right now, looking to that Desert Hag for direction, thirsty for so much more than water, looking for her to show you the way.

You pull back, startled, and the Desert Hag helps you to stand, looking to your hand with great interest and modest concern.

"It's a bit burned now, but it shall heal." She drops your hand and bobs her head homeward. "Come, and I know you know I love a good story, but don't dare tell me what you saw. There are some things best kept secret, best left to gestate a bit before they're born to words."

Waning Moon Practice: The Made and Maker

Much has been questioned beneath this Blessing Moon. You've asked yourself to consider beliefs about love and time, connection and separateness. As the moon wanes, consider that your sovereignty, your individual belly-born power, need not be sacrificed for the sake of intimacy. Your unique magick need not be diminished by your practiced humility. These are hard truths.

Our Craft is our art, so we consider our relationship to our witchery much like a painter's relationship to a painting or a baker's relationship to bread. We are the maker, yes, and the art is made, yes, but what of that third, less definable force that is the practice of the making? In Celtic spirituality this is the "shaping." There is the shape, the shaper, and the shaping in a holy trinity of artistry; it is in that third piece where the magick sits.

As the moon wanes, ponder that trinity in terms of your individuality, the cosmic web of all things, and then that third, less definable thing that mediates this relationship, that facilitates your sovereignty and your intimacy with all things.

How is your sacred work in this world made stronger by relationships?

How is your Witchcraft made stronger by your relationship to your ancestors, your loved ones in this life, or the yet-to-be-born?

How can you tend to the making, to the shaping, as much as you tend to the shape?

Season of Holy Thunder: Dark Moon

Grandmother Speaks: Wanderers Such as Us

"We've made it home, soaked but in one piece. We've lived a story out loud from last dusk to this one, and the sunset is the most glorious one I believe I've ever seen." The hag is listing the objects of her thankfulness now, and you are reliving the vision shown you by the lightning tree.

"I can see you have much on your mind, child, and rightly so. Why don't you go and have a nap while I prepare a supper worthy of wanderers such as us?"

Dark Moon Practice: Calling On a Dream

On the eve of the dark moon, ask for a dream. As you drift to sleep, just before you fall off the edge of consciousness, ask for an ancient and beloved guide to greet you, to show you just what you need to know right now. So soon, the autumn will dawn, and we shall require the support of those hearth holders of our souls we can only come to know in this before-dream state. Ask for them to come and come they will.

To the Season of Holy Thunder, Farewell for Now

Wildest season of heart and storm, to you I am forever grateful. These are the nights of the lightning keepers, and I know myself as one. These are the dawns of the bone collectors, and I know myself as one. These are the days of the garden tenders full of faith, and I know myself as one, and these are the dusks of the knowing hags, and I know myself as one.

And so it is.

CHAPTER 6

Season of Midday Grace

❖

Softening

Perhaps there is no time of greater liminality than the last moon of summer. The wild winds of change blow from all directions, and we sense some undefinable thing slipping through our fingers. We befriend our grief, and we hone our ability to savor the warmth of these still-golden days. Beneath this last moon of summer, our dreams turn toward the haunted and the spectral. The yearly Witching Hour is nearly upon us, and our magick begins to lean toward the shadows.

We begin to ask ourselves now what needs to go, what needs to be thinned out, and how we can release such things with both intention and grace. The Desert Hag has taught us the merit of story and the wildness of our own untamed hearts, and now we ask ourselves how that wisdom might best inform the season of banishing. What has gratitude taught us on the longest days, and what will grief teach us now? The hag urges us to not run away too quickly from these potent questions, to not run toward resolution. We don't know until we know, after all, and a good story cannot be rushed.

Hag Lesson #16:

Gratitude becomes grief.

A Good Story Cannot Be Rushed

A Fever-Dream Encounter with the Innocent I Once Was

A late-summer fever took me once, and my blood grew thick with lava. My skin blistered, and my heartbeat lulled to a slowness that gifted me with a time traveler's patience. Swallowed whole at midnight by heat and shadow, I found my aging flesh standing tall and whole in the cluttered bedroom of my childhood, my grandmother snoring at my side and spiders weaving webs between the clotheslines outside the window.

That young one I used to be woke frightened, seeing this tattooed and sag-jawed hag that would be her destiny, and I raised a lone finger to my lips to bid her stay quiet. We stared at one another for a long while, and I thought of all the warnings I might give her. "Do not go home with that man," I might say, or "Best not trust that beastly woman in the pink house." So overwhelmed with all I might tell her was I that, in the end, I said nothing, not until the sun started pinkening the light behind the mulberry tree and the birds began busying themselves with song. Only then did I smile at the little one's freckled, fat cheeks and tell her to keep writing the slow tales that never end, to keep scribbling in the margins of every book, and to remember that a good story cannot be rushed or it dries out too soon and crumbles into dust.

Noonday Reflection:
Just between You and Those Old Crows

Let us consider now, as summer wanes, those wild demons we might call secrets. What secrets have you kept, and for whom? What secrets do you keep still, and why? Ponder the relationship between boundaries born of self-love and secret keeping.

In *Eastern Body, Western Mind*, Anodea Judith writes: "All action is communication. When we keep a secret, we not only have to monitor what comes out of our mouths, but also what we might say with our body, eyes, or facial expression. We become vigilant of our own being — separate from it rather than a part of it. We are then separate from the spontaneous, streaming vibration that marks true aliveness." Where are secrets in your body, and are there any begging to be set free? You may use the prompts I offer here or create your own, but write a brief reflection from the perspective of a secret; this secret can be specific or general, something hidden on the individual level or within the collective.

I am a secret, so I'm told, and that means...
If I could be known, I would want to be known as...
There are some who I hope never come to know me, though, and they are...
I think I was tucked away tightly because...
Though I remain hidden, I think now that...
My name is...

Season of Midday Grace: New Moon

Grandmother Speaks: Now's Not the Time to Look Up to Heaven

The canyon seems to lie miles and miles below you now, as you faithfully follow the Desert Hag on a treacherous climb. Yesterday's journey to the lightning tree was arduous enough, but this new adventure is testing your many phobias. Your breath feels shallow, and you fear you might fall, but surely the hag has you even now, even as she walks ahead of you and leads you onward.

"Every footstep anchors you, child," she calls back to you over her shoulder. "Now's not the time to look up to heaven. Look down to your feet. Feel your foot bones on ground, and know you were made for these times."

You are skeptical, and she senses it, cunning one that she is.

"Here's a story for you, to keep your mind on what matters." The hag slows her pace to match yours. "You'll only fall if you think too much."

Biddy's Retreat: A Late-Summer Love Story

This has been a wild year indeed, has it not? You've met many, many storytelling grandmothers who want you to know what they know. The forgetful grannies taught you that memory was an illusion, and the lusty grannies taught you that sensuality and pleasure are fundamental human rights that are ageless. In late summer, though, as the light shifts ever so slowly and the shadows are sharper, we might encounter one of the wisest grannies of all, the healer-grandmother. She's got a remedy for anything that ails you, that old crone, but whatever stinking salve or bitter brew she gifts you, the true medicine is in the stories she tells.

These healer-grandmothers are honest folk, and their words are few but true. When they lean close and tell you a secret, you have no choice but to listen and listen well. This particular tale is a shorty but goody, an age-old myth of nature's protectors and their hiding places, and the healer-hags who share it while they serve you strong tea all begin by testing the listener's loyalty.

"Tell me," they might say. "What do you think about the state of this world?"

Now, any answer along the lines of a disgusted expression and downcast gaze that shows you are hurting, that you are burdened by these trying times, will earn you the story. Only those who smile and ask for clarity or, worse, laugh and wave the question away are refused the tale. You see, the healer-grandmothers walk close to the earth, and they love the whole of nature more than they love any single human. The loyalty they require is not to them, nor to any elder being, for that matter; it is to the holy planet mother that bore us all. When they are satisfied that you love this wild world as they do, they might begin the story by introducing you to Biddy Cloda.

A woman after their own hearts, Biddy Cloda shares much with the healer-grannies who tell this story. She would spend her days among the medicines that grow, gathering blackthorn branches for protection, honey-suckles to call up an embodied joy, and vines of ivy to weave the baskets that will contain it all. She lived alone but was never lonely, held well by the elements whenever she needed nourishment and loved well by many friends who would come to visit and visit often.

One day just before the Harvest Moon dawned, one of Biddy's closest friends came to bring her a gift of grain, but Biddy was nowhere to be found. Soon all Biddy's friends were searching high and low for their missing companion. Well into the night they scavenged through the forest and around the riverbanks, carrying lanterns and searching deep into the enchanted cave where she was known to find sanctuary.

It was near the Witching Hour when one of Biddy's beloved friends, Dot McGee — a heathen who con-formed to nothing at all let alone traditional gender la-beling and had, incidentally, been Biddy's first and only love — thought they heard their dear friend calling to them as if she were there in the flesh. The voice was so loud that it startled poor Dot when it pealed, "I'm right here!" But, alas, only they had heard the scream, and the other searchers thought them mad. Most of those search-ing, dear as Biddy had been to them, gave up within the week and assumed their beloved friend dead.

Dot was the only one who refused to give up. All through autumn and into winter, Dot would go to Biddy's house, tending her precious garden and keeping a fire burning in the hearth in case their friend came home. On the one-year anniversary of Biddy's disappearance, Dot sat all night long in the place where they had heard Biddy's voice, but they heard nothing but night birds and a spectral wind. Several years went by, and Dot continued to tend Biddy's home so it would not fall into disrepair. They fought the town council when they wanted to sell dear Biddy's house, and they began to leave sacred relics in the place where they had heard Biddy's voice so long ago. On the fourth anniversary of Biddy's disappearance, Dot was sitting on the hallowed ground near the river, surrounded by the gifts they had left there for Biddy over the years.

"Say something, Biddy!" Dot called. "I know you can hear me!"

Their words were met only with silence, and Dot lay back on the ground to stare at the swelling moon. Sleep had nearly taken them when they heard rustling and sprang to stand.

"Biddy?"

The hairs on the back of Dot's neck stood on end, and they began to back away from the noise. From out of the trees' shadows lumbered a Pooka, an ominous otherworldly spirit with a long face and eyes full of mischief. Dot was aghast.

"Shoo, Pooka!" they ordered. "I'll not be getting on your back, no matter your promises."

Dot knew Pookas had an affinity for taking humans for violent rides, and in that moment, they had to wonder if that's what became of dear Biddy.

"Go 'way with you," the Pooka said, rolling its eyes. "Who says I want you to get on my back? I've only come to deliver a message from your friend."

"From...from who?" Dot was cautious.

"Biddy, of course, you old git!" The Pooka turned away from them and was heading back into the shadows.

"Wait!" Dot called. "What's the message?"

"She thanks you dearly for tending to her home, and she says she'll return in three years' time, right here, to this very place."

"Three years? Why...?" Dot started to protest,

wanting to inquire further, but it was too late. The Pooka had disappeared.

Though Dot wanted so much for their encounter with the Pooka to have been a dream, they knew it was as real as anything was. For three years, they continued to care for Biddy's home, but they stopped leaving totems for her, trusting that she was, indeed, returning. For weeks leading up to the seventh anniversary of Biddy's disappearance, Dot could barely contain their excitement. They had managed to gather some of Biddy's old friends, though none believed Biddy to still be alive; they were humoring poor old Dot, you see.

From dusk until midnight, Dot and Biddy's old friends sat on the hallowed ground.

"Dot…" some would begin, wanting to take their leave and urge Dot to do the same, but they did not have the heart to break old Dot's heart again.

"Yes?" Dot would answer.

"Oh, never mind," they'd concede; this went on for hours.

Just as midnight approached, just when Biddy's friends were standing and preparing to leave Dot all by their lonesome, the air went still and warm. Even the river seemed to go quiet, and an eerie mist began to gather in the shadows from where the Pooka had emerged.

"She's coming," Dot whispered with much certainty. And, sure enough, from out of the mist emerged Biddy, looking as though she hadn't aged a day.

The people gasped, knowing that dear Biddy had been with the fair-folk these last long years.

"Don't touch her!" one of the more superstitious crones ordered. "She might be a changeling. We'll have to throw her into the fire to be sure she's really Biddy."

Dot and Biddy were already locked in that hug that only happens between long-lost friends, though. Until the sun rose the next day, Biddy told stories of her life among the Fae, of how she was living right on top of this world, being shown how to better love the growing things and the flowing waters. She spoke about how the faerie-folk are waiting to come home, waiting until the human community can cease its degradation of the elements before they materialize into heavier bodies.

The healer-grannies who tell the story always end it by claiming that Dot was a relative of theirs, a great-great-auntie or cousin thrice removed, and that they tell this story to provide hope where there sometimes is none. They say Dot and Biddy lived out the rest of their days together, of course, both carried into the otherworld by the Pooka when the time of their deaths was nearing so they might oversee the faerie-folk's return someday, should such a great day come.

The Desert Hag's eyes are full of hope in this moment as she ends the story, and she stares off into the distance as if she sees angels in the canyon.

Opening Practice: Pondering the Fractal

We are surrounded by reminders that magick is, indeed, everywhere. We are fractals of a greater whole, and we need only look to our planet's orbit, our star system, our galaxy — to the cosmic infinite — to see that separation is an illusion. In *Emergent Strategy*, Adrienne Maree Brown defines fractals as "infinitely complex patterns that are self-similar across different scales," explaining that becoming a fractal is an "invitation to practice the world we wish to see in the current landscape." This last moon of summer calls us to shore up our reserves of compassion and interconnectivity before the Witching Moons shroud us in shadow.

Ponder the fractal now, as the new moon dawns. Ask yourself this

potent question: *If the world was no utopia but rather a soulful collective of crea-*
tures living, working, making art, dancing, praying, and tending to the planet right
alongside one another, what deep-seated truths are rooted in this place? What force
pumps the blood through this global community, and from where does its
commitment stem? Make a list of such holy things. What practices do the
children in this new world do each day? What have they learned, and who
are their teachers?

Now, look to this list and ask yourself to what extent your life, right
now, in this moment, embodies these core truths. Are you a living and
breathing fractal of the world you want? If there are gaps between these
truths and the life you live, what forces have created these gaps? In the life
areas where you are wholly living as a core fractal in the world with which
you hope future generations will be blessed, what allowed you to do so?
Who helped you? From where has your resilience to a society that benefits
from your isolation and rigidity been born? Can you use the same resources, internal or external, to cultivate more strength in the areas where
you are lacking wholeness? If you ask yourself right now, *Where do I feel*
broken? is it in these very same places that your living practice is divested
of your most holy longings for the world at large?

Waxing Moon Practice: The Witch's Retreat

As this last moon of summer waxes toward fullness, task yourself with
planning a mini-retreat wherein you become a living fractal of the world
you want, not just for yourself but for the children of the future. Afford
particular attention to the gaps, to the places where you feel your fractal
might be frail or cracked, an imperfect mirror of the whole. This can be
as simple as an hour spent in nature pondering the hard questions, or you
might call in other wildlings to be with you, to cocreate a day of activism
and joy, or poetry and sacred swimming. Spend time as an intentional
fractal and make note of the magick you see ripple out from these seemingly small and humble hours.

Reframe what it means to retreat. Run from nothing, not today. Come
home to the truth of how to best spend these precious days if the systems
within which we lived permitted us the freedom to do so. And, just maybe,
touch those forbidden places where there is only the illusion of pressures,
schedules, and timeliness.

Season of Midday Grace: Full Moon

Grandmother Speaks: Lightning-Struck Skin

The canyon's lowest points look like infinitesimal shadows, and sun's rays are casting bright sigil-like shapes across the cliffs. You have never been so high, never so all-seeing. The Desert Hag holds your hand to soothe your anxious heart, and you stand awestruck at the sheer beauty of all that is. This is a perfect and holy ritual. This is the essence of beingness. Together, you and this hag are a living prayer, a wild and unsung song with only a single lyric: *We two were here.*

"Look there." The hag nods to the west. "You'll walk that way when you go."

Your breath catches now, refusing her words. Never do you want to leave this place.

"Do you see those dark stretches of shadow running east to west? They look a bit like red veins or rusty tree branches?"

You nod. Yes, you see them, these slow-thinning twig-like lines, as if the desert itself has webs of nerve ganglia.

"Those are fractal patterns of a river long dried, and lightning-struck skin looks just the same. Flesh charred by storm has the same ever-repeating pattern as a river's ghost. Now, just how can a human animal deny its debt to this land?"

Full Moon Practice: An Offering to the Broken

This is a potent moon, indeed, and we ask ourselves now to find a place that feels wounded or broken in the way we ourselves, as a fractal, feel a similar ache or that is marked by a similar scar. You need not be in an epically wild and isolated place. Built and urban areas are just as much a part of nature as the lush and green; they are simply more shaped by their least humble inhabitants. Find a place that mirrors your own longing to heal, or your own bitterness or rage, or your own apathy or stubbornness. Whatever the gaps between your deepest truths and your lived-out-loud life, whatever bridge your new moon practice sought to build, find a place that reflects that back to you, and make it an offering. It may be a song, a poem, a bit of water, your own candlelit presence. Become the medicine for your own ailment now, and bless the spirit of this moment, of this moon, with your very breath.

Season of Midday Grace: Waning Moon

Grandmother Speaks: I Wish to Speak Only of Such Love

Every joint in your body throbs from the journey, and you feel as though some of your oldest wounds have been reopened somehow, their makeshift stitches shredded by your time spent in the purest and most unconditional presence, high above the world. A knot in your belly burns hot for some unnamed thing. Speech eludes you, and you sip water seasoned with sweet mint in the cool shadows of the Desert Hag's home.

"You don't owe me your feelings, child," the hag started, rocking slow in her chair and lighting a pipe. "But I might offer you this: Whatever enrages you, whatever curls your hands into fists and sends you spiraling into a fit of action, is born of a deep love for something else. So, I might ask, what is it that you love so much that your wounds are aching in this way right now? Is it your wholeness? The planet? Those fleeting moments of being that come and go too soon? Let's not have any other conversation unless it's about the love of some great thing that, when threatened or taken too soon, sparks that world-changing ire. Tonight, I wish to speak only of such love."

Waning Moon Practice: Grieving Summer

Build yourself a shrine now, Witch, a memorial for the wildest summer you've ever spent. Let it be a fractal reflection of the past three moons as you lived them, and there is no need to shun the lessons. You might write letters to those who taught you well, even the difficult lesson keepers who would deserve no kind words were you to meet them again. On this shrine you might place mementos of trips spent well or spent poorly, along with photographs or art. Grieve summer now for all that it was and was not, for the Witching Moons of autumn are nearly upon us.

Summer's Eulogy

———❦———

In all other seasons, truth be told, age has taught me to restrain my wilder expectations to protect my fragile heart from disappointment. Alas, summer defies such constriction, and year after year, this sunniest season shows me how strong the shadows are in the brightest light. Year by blessed year, this Witch wonders how she always becomes a babe on those hot days, again seated at her grandmother's kitchen table spreading fresh butter on homemade bread, watching the woodpecker busy himself and planning for a future full of infinite possibility. Year by exquisite year, I welcome the cooler winds that come. I salt my autumn hunger with a potent mourning for those longest days, and I whisper-pray to the freckle-faced child I used to be, "All is well. Even now, all is well."

———❦———

Season of Midday Grace: Dark Moon

Grandmother Speaks: Walk West, Beloved

Eyeing the hag, you are unsure how you can bear to leave her. This desert has become your home. These dunes, these canyons, these dried rivers all live within you as much as you do within them, and her grandmotherly grin now, in this moment, will surely be the memory you cling to during your darker hours.

"Walk west, beloved. Follow the branches of dried-up currents, those ancient and prayerful designs that are map to your becoming." The hag hugs you now, a proper embrace that does what every hug is meant to do, born of genuine compassion and human-to-human heat. "Do tell the Sea Hag I said hello, and remember to mourn for your dead."

Dark Moon Practice: Welcoming the Great Letting Go

When the final moon of summer wanes to dark, welcome the great letting go with much intention. Affirm that you are in sacred space and free-speak a prayer of greeting to this season. Envision the Sea Hag in all her glory, moving toward you with shells in her hair and many, many stories in her heart. You might share a tale or two with her as well, offering up some home-brewed memories of fireside revelry or ghostly encounters. Hold summer in your right hand and autumn in your left now on this hallowed evening. Rest in perfect love and perfect trust. And so it is.

To the Season of Midday Grace, Farewell for Now

Deep bows to you, dear summer, for you have indeed taught me all I know about sunburn and sweet tea. To the seasons of stories and storm, farewell for now. Surely we will meet again when I, a wiser Witch, come to find you on that shortest night next year. I'll have learned new songs and become bolder, I think — but, until then, you are the greatest hymn I know.

WILD SUMMER PRACTICES AND SACRED REMEMBRANCES

- Connect the visions you manifest to seed memories with the feeling of embodied gratitude — the heart-born, energetic resource that attunes you to what you love, and the glue that binds the past to the yet-to-come.
- Know that you are constantly being cocreated by a number of forces, seen and unseen. You are in an eternal dance with not only who you were and who you will become but those around you; the environment; our culture; and all that was, is, and will be.
- Celebrate often, indulge in the beauty of the natural world, and leave no trace on those hallowed grounds that bear witness to your joy for a time.

- Physical heart opening is an embodied expression of generosity, empathy, and gratitude; reach the arms long, arch the back, lift the chin, and welcome what comes. Once physical heart opening is comfortable, practice pulling the sensation of gratitude down toward the ground. Wrap gratitude around the leg bones, and feel it radiate out from the bottoms of your feet.

- Check in with the collectives, covens, and families to which you belong, and discuss the big visions, the most potent dreams, that bind you together.

- Look to your loved ones and ask them: "What do we want most out of this bizarre life we are creating together?"

- Trust in those fleeting moments when gratitude shows you that the future of our planet, of our global community, is worth fighting for.

- Affirm that your story is important, that life is change.

- Surround yourself with those who will hear you when you say *I am changing*, and tell them you are grateful for their acceptance of your wild seasons; be accepting of theirs in return.

House of the
SEA HAG

Opening Autumn's Portal

Invocation to the

Crone of the West

—◆➤❋◄◆—

Keeper of the autumn moons

Teach me how to read these runes

Brew me steaming broth of bone

Tell me tales, you skull-faced crone.

We stand on the cusp of the autumn season as if atop a great craggy cliff, gazing westward across the sea, tasting mystery on our tongues and welcoming the cooler and more haunted nights. Our magick in these months turns to release, to banishing, and to protection, and our fireside stories speak of ghostly wanderers and spectral companions. These are the days of the good grief, of honoring our ancestral inheritance and building altars for our beloved dead. These are the quieter nights of disembodied whispers and honing our second sight, and we begin, yet again, to make space in our worlds for all that may come.

The Sea Hag lives on the edge of the world, grandmother to the selkies and lover to spirits only she can see. Her lessons are those of feeling into the wild ache of not knowing, of sitting in the mist without deciding too quickly which direction is the right one, and her poetry drips with rain and brine. There is an otherworldly quality to this aged one, for certain, and her thoughts slip so easily away from the material and toward the unseen. Befriending the Sea Hag means befriending the dark and looking our own deaths right in the eye — but, surely, there is no one better to guide us through the shadows.

Overview of the Autumn Journey

Season of Orphaned Dreams

Nourishment: Grieving
Story Medicine: The Selkie-Hag's Pelt

Season of the Haunted Heart

Challenge: Shadowing
Story Medicine: Goldie's Shadow

Season of Spice and Hearth

Wisdom: Dying
Story Medicine: The Soul Cages

Season of the Thirteenth Moon

Becoming
Story Medicine: The Unburnable Beloved

The Autumn Altar, Built from Bones of Our Forebears

Prepare to build the holiest altar of the year. Take a breath, clear and clean the space with juniper smoke and oils of rosemary or clove, then gather the belongings and pictures of your ancestors. Represent them well. Build them shrines. Ask yourself what was sacred to your people, and place it on the altar along with creaturely bones or skulls. Let your altar speak of a kinship with death, with shadow, and with the unseen. Name the central candle "Beloved." Holding hands with death permits us to live better, and loving our ghosts nourishes our grieving heart in a world where grief is something to be shunned or rushed through. Build an altar that speaks to your wholeness as a creature of this earth, dancing from birth to death and back again, encircled by your many, many hearth holders of soul.

CHAPTER 7

Season of Orphaned Dreams

❦

Grieving

We wed our grief beneath the first moon of autumn, befriending the marrow of loss and opening ourselves to the grotesque beauty of rot, death, and dark. This is shadow season. This is the annual keening, and we must hold our orphaned dreams a little closer to our hearts on these haunted nights. Grief itself is never an obstacle; rather, it is the unacknowledged grief that will block any and all dream visions from coming to fruition on this, the moon cycle that runs through the autumnal equinox. Autumn's dawn glows with an ethereal and otherworldly light, whispering to us as we fall asleep that not all is as it seems — that, for all our intellect and reason, there is much the human animal must relearn about what it means to mourn.

Hag Lesson #17
Our wholeness demands we mourn.

The elders teach us to not run from our own demise, not shed the weight of grief too quickly, and to resurrect a holier death ritual than those we have been taught to attend, wearing black for but a day then going about our lives, orbiting around the unspoken absence of a loved one, a lost dream, or a dead and buried part of ourselves.

Stories of the west are born of the softest mystery and quiet grace.

They do not seek to penetrate or ignite but rather converse in whispers and with much compassion — such is the way of the Sea Hag; such is the way of autumn.

The Wild Unseen

A Fateful Keening for Our Winters That Will Never Be

━━◄▮►━━━━◄▮►◗◖◄▮►━━━━◄▮►━━

A midnight fit, it was. A touch of early-spring fatigue salted with a good deal of extrasensory indulgence sent me straight to a well-attended grief ritual for this, our most beloved world. Here, I came upon an ominous spirit with black-mirror eyes and much to say about the watery fate of this planet. I refused her at first, curling into a mewling ball beside the slow-lapping waves on a stony shore, cupping my ears lest I hear a nightmarish prophecy that spiral me deeper into the mouth of madness. But there was something so graceful about her long-limbed gestures and gentle manner that I was spellbound in love.

Even as she said, "Best teach your babes to swim and swim well," her voice was a soothing swaddle in some otherworldly shadow rhythm that hugged my heart just so, that dripped with a certain enchantment with which I was not familiar, that seemed like the only poetry that mattered or would ever matter.

I couldn't protest, you see. I had no words of objection, and we two began weaving a raft out of gull bones and hair. So soon we were surrounded by changeling children made of lightning and old gods whose names have been forgotten by even the most scholarly Pagan storytellers. Curious these ancient earth protectors were, befuddled by this strange partnership and wondering whether they should bless or curse a union built on that holy fault line between hope and apathy, birthed in that liminal place where wounded land meets swelling sea meets impending storm, where an aching dream meets a telling augury.

Signaled by a western wind, it seemed, the lightning children began wailing, an ancient keening that bathed us all in the wildest sounds of pure, blood-deep mourning. The seals slipped from their rocks and swam to join us onshore, and black red-eyed dogs lined the cliffside above us, backed by a slow-swirling sky and howling with the old magick. Even the mist grieved. Even the scent of brine was an invisible death shroud cloaking us all in the great letting go.

We were death harmony. We were potent lament. Ours was a living story of bewailed longing for a future that would never be.

Still, my thin-bodied cocreator and I kept weaving, kept stitching and sucking the blood from our pricked fingers, kept stubbornly crafting that humble raft while the sea crept closer and more otherlings gathered to become part of this unraveling secret I hoped I might live to tell. Those shrill and sad sounds hummed forth by the lightning babes were met by rough-voiced battle hymns more spoken than sung, growled into the wind by the old gods with painted faces and the hooded giantesses who now stood on the horizon, waist deep in the surging sea.

The shadows grew sharper on the ground, and a pitiful sun edged out from behind the thickest layer of clouds. My inhuman friend whispered some words of comfort, though I cannot recall her intonation, and the epic gathering turned into a wake for all winters. The lightning children rode atop seals, squealing and singing songs of pirates and sea hags, while the old gods beat rebel drums and danced the way those knowing mourners dance, the way those who know the merit of a soul returned celebrate even the most fearsome of changes. We reveled well into the night, if I remember, and I snuggled to sleep on my friend's lap, nested on a raft and lulled by the pulse of new ocean currents beneath me, cheeks stained with tears for the colder world I was born to and skin cracked from compassion for the coming of the waters, for the stronger webs woven in these dire times, for the resilience of the soft human animal, and for the companionship of the wild unseen.

—◆—)(—◆—

Dusk Reflection: Once Upon an Ending

Our harvest magick demands we attend to our own reaping, come closer to our raw and tender places, and hold ourselves kindly while we confront our shadows. Open to this season with all that you are, considering grief to be gratitude for what you love so dearly that you mourn its loss. Consider that we love life more fully when we live close to death and trust in the magick of the wild unseen.

Tell a tale now, a tale that defies linear time. You may use the prompts I offer here or create your own. This is a story of life after death, of potent possibility, and of ancestral remembrance.

This story begins with a death, the death of…
On a somber autumn evening, I built a shrine to…
On this Harvest Moon, I shall welcome the Mystery with…
I shall sing songs of…
I shall know the birth that follows death, and I shall know it as…
Here, on this hallowed ground, I am…

Autumnal Equinox Celebration:
The Best and Last of Their Names

Materials: A basket or bag for gathering, an offering for the land, photographs of loved ones gone

Nested between the first harvest cross-quarter day, Lughnasadh, and Samhain, the holy day that marks "summer's end," the autumnal equinox is a balance point of light and dark, of hope and shadow, and of thinning veils. We welcome our ancestors of good intent, those who were connected to land and understood the merit of belonging, and we welcome them to stand with us on these nights when all spirits walk heavier than they do on brighter days.

As close to dusk as possible, go into the wild and set your mind to gathering. Hold close to the knowing that this time is full of both light and shadow, both wound and healing, and ask for your loving ancestors to walk with you while you gather small, dying things; these might be fallen branches, browning grass, or bones. Ask each object for permission to bring it home with you, and remember that rot feeds the ground. Know ·that even these seemingly lifeless things have a spirit, pulse with the same star stuff that bore you. Hear your ancestors whisper while you gather, telling you, *Yes, that seedpod there*, or, *Look to your feet, child, or you'll miss it!* Take nothing that grows, and leave an offering on the land before you go, thanking the spirit of the place.

When you return home, build a humble altar out of these objects, placing them in a spontaneous symmetrical pattern while you speak prayers to the world to which you belong. Let it be a somber ritual of honoring the death time, and feel as though each object represents a spirit, one of the ghosts who stand with you now. Speak love to them. Speak grief. Weep for their orphaned dreams as well as your own. Feel into the heartache that says you are alive and well, that you are capable of this beauteous act called gratitude. Bewail your grandmothers, knowing that the tears you shed for them are also tears shed for parts of you, and build a shrine to them, to you, and to the wounded world.

Adaptation for Families, Coven Groups, and Other Wild Circles: A Witnessed Grief

In adapting this ritual for a group, invite all participating souls to bring an offering to the land on which you will walk; this might be water, eggshells, some hallowed object that was sacred to the indigenous people of the place where you will gather. Encourage humility, and ensure all individuals ask for permission before collecting their brown leaves, twigs, or whatever seems to be inhabited by the spirit of death. When the time comes, cocreate the shrine in the same wild place, returning the objects to ground. You might invite drummers and song. You might ask the participants to free-speak poetry or stories of their forebears. To seal the ritual, however, do invite silence. Bid all wild souls encircle the shrine, hold hands, breathe together in deep grief, in deep gratitude.

Season of Orphaned Dreams: New Moon

Grandmother Speaks:
We Are Blessed by These Changing Tides

The wind has been thick with salt for hours, but only now do you begin to hear the intermittent hushed crashing of waves onshore. Yes, you are close. The sun is pitiful here in this place where cloud gods seem to rule, where all things green and growing are coated with the thinnest layer of frost, and where the air itself seems haunted by trickster spirits.

The land comes to an abrupt end now, and you stand high above the sea, high above that wild and infinite expanse. Truly, there is no better expression of the wild unseen nature than the sea. A stony beach is below you, brine-kissed rocks glistening like sealskin, at the foot of these cliffs. Unsure of how to reach the sea but knowing you must, you whisper a prayer into the wind, half fiery incantation and half heartfelt plea bidding your grandmothers come to your aid.

You cannot know whether you lifted your own arms or if they were raised for you by spectral hands, but you feel yourself float easily now down, down, and downward still. You are a raptor seabird diving for soul-food. You are ravenous for deeper belonging. You are a featherlight prayer for all humankind, for all wildness from now until forever.

She, the Sea Hag, finds you in midair. She is more specter than flesh, this long-haired crone, and she joins you on your descent to the gray waters below. Her eyes are kind, and she sees trepidation in your expression. This was an angry sea, after all. The waters are full of drowned souls; you can feel it, and the Sea Hag wraps a cool skeletal hand around your wrist.

"Don't fear, my child. We are blessed by these changing tides."

You seem to drift downward for an eternity, and the Sea Hag offers you a spectral story to pass the time.

The Selkie-Hag's Pelt: A Harvest Moon Tale

So merrily, child, have you met the grandmothers of spring and summer, those beloved hags who house the stories of altar keeping, laughter, and ritual in their hearts. And yet, only in autumn, only when the ghosts walk heavier than the human animals, do we encounter the spirit-crones, those dead grandmothers who knew us well in life but even better in death. Their stories warn of wasting the feeling flesh, of taking for granted this precious soul's incarnation. They speak from love but with a bitter tongue, and even the most selfish among us have no choice but to listen to their disembodied voices when they come in the night, gracing our dreams just at the Witching Hour and bidding us heed their direction.

This story is a timeworn tale, to be sure, passed down through generations of famine and loss, of spiritual wounding and doomed sea voyages. The dead grandmothers who choose to tell this story do so because they see something of themselves in the way of those they haunt. A quiet tendency to twitch curtains and look longingly toward the west, perhaps, or a subtle way of walking through the world that says, *I know things. I am bigger than this life*, draws the ghost down to be teacher and friend, protector and confidant, keeper of the secret whispers spoken only in apparent solitude, though the spirits are indeed all around.

The ghostly grannies begin this story wordlessly, hissing softly through their teeth to echo the sounds of the sea. If you go into the night on a mist-filled evening and face westward, you just might hear their hushed incantation, their homage to the gray waves, to the fisherfolk, and to the slippery-skinned otherlings who live between worlds.

The story begins with a wayward seal-woman, a mischievous selkie who had grown to loathe her faerie blood. This wanton soul, half woman and half seal, was a shape-shifter, an orphan, and a loner. The dead crones who share this tale all say she kept a bitter disdain for her own kind nested close to her spine, this poor selkie creature, and with every passing winter, she grew more desperate for a life spent on land.

The elder selkies were wary of this wildling's haunted heart, knowing a rebel when they saw one. One fog-filled autumn morning, they caught the outlaw seal-woman staring at the beach wild-eyed and craving trouble. Together, the old seal-people warned her to stop longing for the legged life, to enjoy her softer skin only while resting on the rocks safely distanced from the shore, and to never venture onto the beach where the lusty pirates gathered.

"Even if those lechers leave you be," the eldest selkie said, "you would certainly meet your doom in the long caves."

"Yes, most certainly," the others echoed their Priestess.

"In those thick shadows, you cannot help but see your future, and there's not a selkie alive who wasn't driven mad by knowing her fate."

The land-loving selkie clicked her tongue and retorted, "That's it? Surely, to see one's future is a great gift. Surely, I wish to know what will become of me."

The old seals eyed each other.

In that moment, she was uncertain whether the elder selkies were conspiring to send her away or truly trying to protect her. But, in any case, it mattered not, for her mind was well made up.

"You must consider this, child. Do you really, truly wish to know your destiny?"

Something in the elder's tone did give her pause, but she was a stubborn creature. Without saying goodbye to any of her beloved kin, without so much as a nod to the old seals, she slipped into the sea and headed for the stony shore.

"Don't let those pirates steal your pelt!" one of the old seals howled after her, but she barely heard her beneath the gray waves.

"Or your jewels!" said another.

"And don't dare let yourself dry out!" another elder said lastly.

Before dusk, she was shoreside, stretching her human limbs long, naked and shivering. Never before had she felt cold like this, a chill that ran bone-deep, but she had only her pelt to keep her warm. Alas, the rules of the otherlings were quite strict, and if she were to stretch that tough skin thin around her shoulders or pull it long to warm her feet, she would again be seal and her time here on the beach would come to an end. If she were to strip herself of the frigid woven seaweed-and-shell jewels that she wore around her neck, she would lose the medicine of her people forever.

Decidedly, she befriended the cold, tucking her pelt under her arm, willing her jewels to dry, and walking north. There were no pirates to speak of, and she was a bit disappointed by their absence, truth be told. The caves would be close, though, and the wind was easing its bite. She pondered the elders' words while she walked, but there was no hesitation in her step.

Yes, this was the right thing. She would find the cave, see her future, and get on with living it as a whole human woman, legs and all. Weary she was of her patchworked sea-and-land life. So exhausting were the nights spent listening to old ones' myths of salmon and merrow. She hungered for stories of wolves and wild mountain people, and she longed to commune with these things called trees.

Midnight came and went. The rebel selkie's jewels had iced over, but the pelt was giving off a lovely heat. She switched arms every so often so both sides could taste some warmth, then she'd pause her walk and stand on it to warm her feet. She could feel the pelt's desire to be stretched around her, as if the skin was the very essence of her otherlingness, and she wondered if she would ever be able to let it go forever.

Shortly before dawn and just as the sky was pinkening, the selkie came upon the cave. The beach had ended abruptly, the tide was low, and the shadowy entrance was the only thing before her on her path except the high-stretching cliffs that surrounded her. Taking a breath and looking west to the sea, the selkie-woman sensed an elder seal watching her, praying she would return to the waves and leave this hallowed place be, but she had come too far to give up now.

She was here, and she was staying.

The cave reeked of brine and death. The walls were streaked white with salt, and an eerie gurgling bubbled from deeper in the darkness. Looking over her shoulder, she checked to ensure the entrance was still there, and the cool beam of moonlight told her yes — yes, she could still get out if she had to.

Such craggy ground was her lair when she was in seal form, but her human feet were soft and aching from a night spent walking. She could not go any deeper without rest, and she wished, with all that she was, that she had learned how to make this warm and wild thing the old ones called fire.

Curled into a ball with her pelt wrapped tight in the curve of space between her hip and her low ribs, the selkie fell into a deep sleep. Never before had she slept in her human form, and her dreams seemed to understand what shape her body had taken. Her dreams were so often of shipwrecks and great whales, of sea serpents and water horses, but these human dreams were of hearth fire and hot meals, ivy-blanketed walls and chimney smoke, fat-cheeked toddlers and bearded warrior men.

She woke with a shock of heat running through her, and she wondered if her pelt had defied her wishes and wrapped itself around her of its own volition, but her eyes focused on the flames of a small fire, then on the old hag woman who was stoking the embers and adding more driftwood.

"Stay under that blanket, child." Her voice was gruff. "What were you thinking? Your death was moments away, I'm sure." She stirred a cookpot slowly, balanced precariously above the flames. "You're no seal anymore. The cold will kill you and kill you swift."

The selkie reached beneath her to make sure her pelt was still in place, and indeed it was.

"I wouldn't take it. I've no use for it." The hag sniffed.

"How do you know —" the selkie started to inquire, but something in the old one's face stopped her.

They sat in silence for a time. The fire was a long-tongued god, and the selkie-woman was in love.

"I've never been so warm in all my life," the selkie said. "Never."

"Oh, that's not true, is it? You only didn't know what cold was," corrected the hag. "That's not the same as never having been warm. Humans need their opposites, you see. It's their language that robs them of possibility. It has to be this or that, never both, never neither."

This woman was a Witch indeed, thought the selkie.

"So, you'll be telling me my future, then?"

The hag grinned, handing her a cup of something salty and steaming. "I can, yes."

The selkie swallowed.

"Are you sure you want to know? You might go mad. Didn't the elder seals warn you about knowing too much?"

Something about the fire made the selkie bold, and she straightened her spine. "Well, what about you? Do you know your future?"

"I do," the hag answered.

"And are you mad?"

The hag looked stunned, genuinely shocked, then broke into an eruption of belly-born guffaws that echoed between the rock walls and shook the place.

"I honestly couldn't tell you," the hag answered when she'd calmed herself. "Very well. Are you ready?"

The selkie stood, letting her blanket drop and holding her palms upright as if she were about to receive some great rite.

The hag rolled her eyes. "There's really no need for all that fuss. I'm not about to tell you you're going to be some great queen, you know."

The selkie sighed, opening her eyes and dropping her arms. "You'll leave this cave in a few moments, after you've gotten what you've come here for. You'll only be outside the cave for minutes before you meet a pirate who's wicked in the best possible way, and you gift your pelt to him along with your heart. The two of you have a child together and spend many happy winters in love, dwelling high on the cliff's edge. In time, though, you begin to dry out. Every time you think of your time beneath the sea, your skin grows a little tauter, and your senses fade a little more.

"One morning, you wake, your boy grown and your pirate near death, and you cannot recall why you wear your jewels around your neck. Stricken by grief, you snatch your pelt from its hiding place and walk to the cliff's edge. In a fit, you toss the pelt and the jewels into the sea, but as they fall, you remember. You remember the blissful kiss of the currents and the rush of diving deep. You remember the sense of belonging you had only while nested atop a rock miles out to sea, laughing and singing with your sisters. You remember it all, panic, and jump off the cliff after your precious things, catching them midair and slipping into your pelt just in time, just before the sea was about to break open your fragile human flesh. Out to sea you swim, rejoining the other-world and having many, many stories to tell. Your stubbornness never fades, however, and as one of the elders, you break many rules, even venturing onto shore from time to time and coming here, to this cave, greeting wayward selkies who have lost their way and telling them their future."

She puffed right out of existence then, the ghostly grannies who tell this story say, and the selkie-woman woke wild-eyed and near frozen in the cave's shadows, wondering what Witchcraft had befallen her. There was no fire, and she could barely feel her legs. Crawling from the cave now using only her elbows, balancing her pelt on her back and scraping her belly on stones, the selkie resigned herself to a return to the sea. The air outside the cave was warmer, though the sun was sinking low into the western fog, and she took one last breath as a human woman on land before unfolding her pelt and stretching it thin over her feet.

Oh, and the warmth was glorious.

She pulled the skin higher on her legs and feeling came back into her lower parts. She couldn't get it back on fast enough now, and she lay back on the beach, arching her back. Her eyes fell on a man then, looming behind her with much curiosity and lust painted on his face.

She gasped. "Back away!"

She could see now that this man was clearly a miscreant, a bearded pirate with lawlessness in his soul. He raised his hands high, surrendering, and took a single step backward.

Now, the way this story ends depends on what medicine the ghostly grannies who tell it think you need, so I'll ask you. Do you need a bit of adventure or a risk-taker muse? If so, then the story ends like this:

The selkie saw the whole of her life, every bit of the story the old hag had shared in her dream, come true in this pirate's eyes. She saw their nights spent wild, her body pushing a babe forth with him at her side, the love songs he would sing her, and his face at the moment of his death. In that moment, she was up for all of it. Every flash was a yet-to-be-lived memory, and she would exchange none of them, not one, for the undersea life.

"The sea can wait," she said aloud, tossing her pelt into the pirate's arms and reaching for him, and they lived happily ever after until that fateful day when his mortality took him from her.

If, on the other hand, the ghostly grannies think you need the medicine of kinship and belonging, they'll end this tale just so:

The selkie looked to the pirate, then to the sea. Amid the waves she could see the elder seals swimming, their black-mirror eyes beckoning her to come forth, to come home, and she vowed to never again shun who she was, to never again lose her ancestral inheritance, and she slipped the pelt over her skin, melting into her lithe seal body before the pirate's eyes.

She returned to the sea then, now with a deep knowing of the wealth kept hidden beneath the waves, and the pirate had a very good story to tell that kept him warm for the rest of his days.

-->)(<--

The Sea Hag laughs then, an eerie and tinkling sound echoing from her chest more than her mouth; your feet touch the cool surface of the water, and you are left with a deep and wordless knowing that you are home.

Opening Practice: Your Autumn Initiation

Materials: Three candles and a secret location

There is a natural progression from our gratitude magick in summer to our grief ceremonies of autumn, and the bridge between the two are those tender and aching places that we attempt to shun or hide for fear of seeming too weak to exist in our hard-hearted society. Feel into the spirit of autumn now in a secret place where you can be alone. Depending on your location, you might sense the leaves dropping or the frost weighing down the most stubborn flower petals. You can be inside or outside, but do be in a place where you are not fearing the judgments of others. This is your time. Here, you are wild. Here, you are Witch.

When ready, you might cast a circle or simply give a nod to the four directions, to above and below. Let yourself be held by this place, wherever you may be. Ponder three tender edges now as you are here. In *Anam Čara*, John O'Donohue writes: "Transience is the force of time that makes a ghost of every experience. There was never a dawn, regardless how beautiful or promising, that did not grow into noontime."

Grief is the ever-present force that allows simple poetry to spark tears, a poignant word from a dear friend to crack our hearts wide open, and keeps us just on the edge of a beauteous and fertile mourning. We grieve not only for what we have lost in our personal lives but also for what our ancestors have lost, for what nature has lost at the hands of humanity, and the many, many myths that have failed to bear fruit.

Name them, these three griefs of yours. Is there a dream that is, as yet, unmet? Is there a long-held myth you are realizing holds no truth? Is there a wounded land you cannot save or a creature who will not love you the way you want to be loved?

Shed your armor now, and free-speak these three griefs, lighting a candle for the first and beginning with these words: *I am a child of the earth, and here, I feel tender.*

This is not defeat or retreat. This is looking life in the eye. Let this be a ritual of space making, of untethering binds. Do the same for the other two griefs, lighting a candle for each and then free-speaking a eulogy of sorts. Permit some ice to melt around your heart here. Let something move. Bid your body respond if it feels right, curling into grief shapes, then moving in ways that feel expansive and liberatory. Become a potent mourning. Wail if you like, and stay with this for as long as you can. Move into and through the rawness. Do not try to control or overcome.

Be kind to yourself then. Leave the candles burning, open the circle, and sip something hot and spicy while you nestle into this new way of being, this new way of sitting with the raw and the ache. We feel grief to better know joy. Trust that there is much power to be found here, and it is not solely the power of letting go. There is a sacredness to holding our grief like a beloved partner for a time, to admitting we feel tender and soft.

We are children of the earth, and here we feel tender.

Waxing Moon Practice: A More Sacred Gaze

As this Harvest Moon waxes, consider your tender places, and find three objects that feel tender in the way you feel tender, one for each of the three griefs. These might have been objects you used or will use for your equinox ritual, but they need not be. Set aside at least three sacred times while the moon is waxing, before the full Harvest Moon, to simply sit and gaze at these objects, one at a time for at least twenty minutes, pondering its death and its life, feeling into its spirit, and beginning to trust that you are more connected to this thing than you may have thought. Hold your eyes on this thing. Feel its weight. Speak to it: "I am tender, and you are tender, too." Before the full moon, work with all three objects in this way, and ponder whether your griefs have shifted, been nourished, swelled, or thinned.

These Broken Branches Are Bones
Rituals for Hard Times

———◄•————◄•-)(•-►————◄•—

Weighed down by layers of tear-wet wool, I was. Pricking at the frayed edges of death shrouds worn by nameless women now wrapped 'round my shoulders and slowing my pace, I barely made it to the place where my beloved blackthorn tree once stood. I come here when I hurt, you see. I come here to touch the ephemeral moments, to be reminded that all is temporary, that my flesh will indeed feed this ground, that these broken branches are bones left behind by a tree I once loved, and that this life is meant to be lived and lived well. A kinship with death makes one a better lover, an old hag once told me, and this Witch is the wildest vixen there is.

⟶⟩✕⟨⟵

Season of Orphaned Dreams: Full Moon

Grandmother Speaks: Where the Dead Swim

You are swallowed whole by the sea now, but the saltwater does not sting your eyes. There is much Witchcraft afoot here, you know, and the Sea Hag is holding you close so you might breathe beneath these raging waves. Still, you sink, the hag and you entwined and motionless, drifting lower and lower. The last of the sunlight goes, but you can still see somehow. You see the ghostly white fabric of the hag's gown wisping all around you, the shadows between her finger bones curled around your forearm, and the slow dance of the kelp trees — this swaying undersea forest — beckoning you into the depths.

"Another world, this is," says the hag into your ear. "The sea is the cauldron of birth. These are the waters of origin, of birth and death, the primordial ethers where the dead swim."

The seafloor holds you now, and the hag rests with you in this hallowed place. Ruins of shipwrecks surround you, and you see now that there are countless spirits swimming about, weaving around and through the kelp trees, some riding atop seals. All manner of dead are here, the somber stone-faced ones who still wish to live, the joyous angel-winged children who have found much happiness and belonging here in the deep below.

"You see," the hag begins, "this is sanctuary, and you will find much medicine here."

Full Moon Practice: A Eulogy Lived Out Loud

Materials: Journal, writing utensil, objects and candles from waxing moon practice

Ponder the crossroads now. Ponder the many decisions you have made that have brought you right here, to this moment, beneath the full Harvest Moon. Ponder the relationship between you and your three griefs, and write a eulogy for the wild one you used to be.

Our lives are full of small deaths. Every long-term relationship is full of deaths and births. Every time we make a weighted choice — to move to this place or to leave that partner or to become someone new or to take this job or to terminate that pregnancy or to attend that gathering or to tell that secret — we become someone new, while the person who might have made a different choice lies down, dead and gone.

You might consider a decision you made that has brought you to stand closer to those tender places, to hold those three griefs, or you might work with a present decision, a current crossroads. Whether you are marking a current or a past choice, do so with conviction. Compost the Witch you used to be and all their shame, all their guilt, right along with them. Write them a loving eulogy. Thank them for who they were and all they taught you. Let your grief candles burn. Invite your loving ancestors to join you. Wear black, and read your words aloud while juniper and cedar smoke rises.

Here lies the wild one who used to be. May they rest in peace. And so it is.

Season of Orphaned Dreams: Waning Moon

Grandmother Speaks:
Let the Current Lick the Shivers from You

Your heartbeat is quickening now, and the Sea Hag can sense your panic. She pulls you closer, and you feel her ribs pressing against you. You are so close to death here, closer than you have ever been, and if you're honest, it is the comfort of this place that frightens you.

"Do not fear the ease of this place, my love," the hag whispers. "You've been taught only to fear the depths. Let the current lick the shivers from you, and now your visit begins."

In that moment, from out of the dancing leaves stepped a spirit you knew and knew well in this life, one of your beloved dead. They come close, and you can see serenity in their eyes. You can feel their grace in this place, their belonging, their infinite compassion for all that is, and you smile, the salt of your tears becoming one with the waters.

Waning Moon Practice: A Letter to a Loved One Gone

As the Harvest Moon wanes and Samhain approaches, understand the cyclical nature of grief. We honor our dead now. We speak prayers to no transcendent god but to those holy ones who held us for a time, then left us alive to mourn them. Who would you speak to now if you could? Choose a loved one who has passed who truly would hold your best interest at heart, who would have no ill will toward you or those with whom you live, who would come and sit for a spell and then happily go on their way. Write them a letter now, as the moon thins toward darkness. You might speak of love or forgiveness, make an apology or confession. You might speak of none of these things and write only a gift of poetry or story. Keep the letter upon your altar, perhaps near a photograph of them, and continue to light your grief candles for your own raw and aching places.

Tonight, I Am Full
Words for the Healing Time

———◆◦◦————◦◦◆◦◦————◦◦◆———

"Yes," I hissed to my dead lover's ghost. "A persistent specter, you are. Yes, I remember you well — and, yes, you did indeed leave a star-shaped hole in my heart when you left me and this world behind. I mourned for you — for too long, some said — but, little by little,

*that aching place filled in with flowering vines and thorns, with ash
and beams sent straight from a silver celestial orb, with thin bones
and scar tissue. Tonight, I am full and whole again, made so by
memory and moonlight."*

━━━➤❖◀━━━

Season of Orphaned Dreams: Dark Moon

Grandmother Speaks: Your Soul Is Home Here

You speak all you want to share with this spirit, this member of your
soul family. You say all you wished you had said while they were alive,
and more. And, in turn, they tell you a secret. They gift you with some
small piece of medicine that serves as salve for your aching heart,
and — though no mysteries have been solved on this night — you feel
ready to sleep the heaviest sleep, to wake anew when the sun rises, to
ascend from these depths.

"Your soul is home here. Can you feel it?" the hag asks.

Yes, surely you can feel it, for a saltwater heart you have.

Dark Moon Practice: A Sweet Release

When the Harvest Moon turns dark, reflect on the weighted work you
have done. Revisit the three griefs, the objects with which you worked, the
death ritual for who you once were, and the letter to a loved one who has
passed. Ask yourself what connections exist between these experiences.
What common threads run through this work, this autumn? Light your
three candles for the last time. Breathe deeply, and again, as you did on
the new moon, free-speak about your raw places. Notice if the words you
speak have changed, if the feeling in your body has shifted. Conclude with
this incantation, if you feel called:

I am a child of this earth, and here I am tender. These orphaned dreams belong to me, to my beloved dead, and to the

yet-to-be-born. I will hold them well, cradling them like babes wrapped in pale blankets, and I will set candles to burn in the name of infinite hope and holy grief.

And so it is.

To the Season of Orphaned Dreams, Farewell for Now

You met me well, ye Harvest Moon, and I was swallowed whole by the deepest sea where my foremothers swim. I met the wayward wandering ghosts of pirates and the hungry undersea monsters there, too — but, all the while, my inherited wound kept me warm. All the while, I was falling in love with the great letting go, and here, I find myself anew. Here, I am a peace treaty struck between longing and loss, between gratitude and grief, and so I say to the Season of Orphaned Dreams, farewell for now. Until we meet again, in this life or the next.

CHAPTER 8

Season of the Haunted Heart

❖

Shadowing

The journey of the heathen soul is full of rough places. The road is red with the blood of the bodies we used to inhabit, with beliefs left for dead and smaller dream visions slaughtered by their wilder, wider offspring. Beneath this second autumn moon, often called the Blood Moon, we are led to such rough places, tasked with looking our shadows square in their unfeeling eyes and swallowing them whole. We consider that we might be the very monster we fear, that the only work left before the longest night comes is to face those deep knowings we have kept buried for so long.

Hag Lesson #18

Autumn magick is shadow work.

The Season of the Haunted Heart is thick with ghosts, not only of those ancestors who are here to help, here to hold a lantern for us at the crossroads, but also of who we once were before life stripped us of our vulnerability, of our ability to admit when we are lost or hurt.

Beneath this moon, permit the Sea Hag to teach you that the greatest medicine is in the wound itself, that your brokenness, your fractured spirit, is the holy entryway where stronger parts of your magick might enter and where others might meet you and say, "Yes, I ache there, too."

I Ache There, Too

Communion under the Bridge

———◆———

Beneath a painted bridge at the riverside I met a woman who looked much like me, though her house was made of paper. She invited me to sit and sip her whiskey, and I obliged, wanting to hear her stories of love and loss. But the drink drenched my mind and shook loose my voice, and it was I who began bewailing my dreams unmet and a planet gone too hot, my longing for well children and the death of xenophobes, my heartaches that would never heal and my angsty art that would never be born. She let me blubber on, that queen. She let me bemoan my beautiful life until my words went slurred and I had nothing left to mourn. Her black-mirror eyes held my gaze like no one ever has, entrancing me in an otherworldly glamour; then she said, "I know. I ache there, too," and we watched the river go about its business.

———◆———

Dusk Reflection: The Shadow Family

Shadow work is an infinite task, with no clear ending, no great reward once some well-defined goal has been reached. No hooded and bejeweled authority grants us a certificate or blesses us with an exquisite initiation once we have finished, and yet shadow integration is some of our most weighted soul work. Our power lies there, in the deep, murky pool, but so do the most gruesome monsters we will ever meet. To be sure, it is easier to not look, to turn our backs on that terrible place and live in the light, but should we wish to be Witches, mystics, healers, artists, storytellers, or dream weavers, we must — we absolutely must — learn to hold hands with the dark.

To begin, you first must look into that great, dark pool. Curl your fingers around its jagged edges, and see your own reflection in the water, only like you have never seen it before. In your Book of Moon and Flame, reflect on your shadow. Where are those too-bright places that blind, and where are those corners of total darkness? Ask yourself: Who are you absolutely not? Who do you refuse to be with all that you are? The answer can be seemingly positive qualities or be traits and titles you might deem wretched, even struggling to write them on the page. In either case, the binding thread, the telltale sign that yes, this is your shadow work, is that you would swear in this moment on a stack of the holiest books you know that you are *not* those things.

Who are you not, right now, in this moment?

Now, with your list of shadow qualities, ask yourself if you have had any loved ones, be they blood family or found family, who embodied — or whom you perceived to embody — those traits.

Very often, our caregivers during childhood as well as our partners later in life reflect our shadows back to us; part of this is projection, and part of this is a refusal of shadow integration. If, for example, we see our partners embodying the qualities of entitlement or laziness, then we do not have to own those parts of ourselves.

Afford particular attention to any loved ones who have passed into the spirit realm who may have embodied one or more of your shadow qualities. Who were your shadow teachers? What is your shadow lineage? What did you learn from them, and, most importantly, what qualities may lie beneath the seemingly sinister or overbright traits you have named?

During childhood, we decide that certain qualities of being, certain emotions, certain behaviors will not serve us well in life. We may decide being too loud or wild is not safe, or we might decide that being vulnerable equates to laziness or weakness. Neither wildness nor vulnerability are inherently negative qualities; in fact, they serve our wholeness well. By extension, we must look to what lies even deeper in that pool of shadow, to the source of that fecund wellspring we might so easily dismiss as grotesque.

Samhain Celebration: The Silent Supper

The Samhain cross-quarter day is a holy night indeed, a night when the ghosts surround us, when our stories of loved ones gone keep us warm.[*]

---

[*]   *Samhain* means "summer's end" in Irish Gaelic.

On this night, often celebrated on October 31 or November 1 in the Northern Hemisphere, hold a silent supper for your beloved dead.* Invite into your home only the loved ones in spirit you would truly wish to dine with, but consider including one or more of those shadow teachers. If you would not invite them to your home if they were alive, do not invite them now when they are dead. Cook their favorite foods; set places for them at the table; and build an altar of skulls, photographs, and dripping candles at the tableside. Play their favorite music, but otherwise spend the meal in silence if you are able. When finished, speak words of gratitude and grace, sealing the ritual with a meaningful walk in the wild, where you might leave a bit of food beneath an ancestral tree.

Adaptation for Families, Coven Groups, and Other Wild Circles: Gathering Beyond the Veil

The silent supper is quite conducive to small groups. Ask all living attendees to bring a loved one in spirit, cook their favorite meal, and bring an object or photograph for the ancestral altar. Set places for the living and the dead. Play the latter's favorite songs, and invite the group to eat in silence. There are, of course, some groups who do not sit well in silence, and making intentional space for storytelling, sharing memories of the dead guests, is always strong medicine as well. Once the meal is over, walk together into the night if you are able, offering just a small bit of food up to the spirits who walk heavier on this night.

Season of the Haunted Heart: New Moon

Grandmother Speaks: Dead Things Don't Spark

Shoreside now, you feel how the midautumn wind has frozen the fabric of your clothes to your skin. Somehow you are not cold despite the blueing shade of your skin, and you wonder if you met your death in

---

*   In Pagan traditions, this ritual is often referred to as the "dumb supper"; in my work, I have opted for "silent supper."

the depths of that ancestral sea, if you left your soul in the gray depths to join the others. An eerie light fills this land, as if the ground itself glows with a ghostly aura, and your hand emanates a similar soft halo.

"That's how you know you're still alive, little one. Dead things don't spark like that."

Jutting her elbow toward you like a formal, mannerly escort might, the hag bids you join her on a walk.

"Come. To the shadow pools we'll go. I've a story to share along the way."

Goldie's Shadow: A Ceremonial Ghost Story

To participate in this story ceremony, light a lone candle, wear black, and prepare yourself to become the hag in mourning.

Perhaps the wisest grandmother among them all, a true keeper of the elder medicine, is the grieving hag. She is not sad, mind you. Her grief is a beloved demon she has long since befriended, for she has lived a life full of both love and loss. She is skilled at the lost art of the keening, of whole-body mourning, and she bewails not death it-self but the absence of holy and rightful death ritual. We hear her before we meet her on these nights when the veil is thin. If we walk into the wild alone, her banshee's cry is a shrill and primal sound that says our dead are worthy of honor, that says the ghosts want to be mourned and mourned well.

Their stories are not ones of regret, nor are they the stuff of shallow inspiration that urges you to live only joyously. No, these hags speak of passion and pain in balance, of ecstasy and agony in wild waves of life and death. These hags have the long-vision, and their deepest hope for you is not goodness but wholeness. Should you resist the urge to run from their monstrous and creaturely sounds, they just might share such a tale as this with you. Their stories are brief but poignant, and they may pause at times to resume their funereal cries, to give you time to ponder their words, before continuing the telling.

Take a low-belly breath and howl here, sending your wildest sound moonward and feeling the heat of the candle on your palms.

The hags would begin with a howl, with a sound of pure and distilled grief that would set you shivering, then their voices would settle into an eerily soft and sweet intonation, introducing you to a bright and bubbly princess, a woman who had not yet met her shadow, not yet begun to sink her hands deep into the well of who she truly was. The grieving grannies would stop short of calling her, this woman whom we shall refer to as Goldie, superficial or trite, for it was only her circumstances that made her seem so one-dimensional, so lost in the light.

Goldie loathed all things that spoke to the darker side of this world, and if you were to ask her, she would tell you that she never once had a nightmare, never once was cursed by an errant fearful thought or caught in that sticky web of sadness. She shunned the time of year when skulls hung in windows and ghouls walked alive in the streets seeking tricks and treats. She did not believe in ghosts, you see, and she had never known death. Goldie was the sort of person who preferred to not think of the dead, you see, and would dance around the word itself if she were caught in a conversation about it.

The grieving hags would stop here, an opportune moment for a lesson, and they would say, "We can only feel joy as strongly as we feel grief, you see." Then they would begin a low keening while you pondered that truth.

Repeat these words three times, just whispering to yourself or to some unnamed soul who needs to hear such wisdom: "We can only feel joy as strongly as we feel grief."

When the hags were satisfied you either strongly agreed or wholeheartedly disagreed with that sentiment, they would continue the story.

Though Goldie did her best to surround herself with friends who thought like her — who would prefer to see romantic comedies to horror movies and had never once attended a funeral, who turned their faces away from cemeteries and boasted a fantastical belief that, while no other living creature in the world had managed to outsmart death, they would be the first immortals — every so often, a more realistic friend would begin a conversation about loss. Now, Goldie considered herself quite an expert on the law of attraction and would instruct her more interesting friends, those who wished to discuss the fecund indigo depths that color our lives as much as the sweet and brilliant shallows, to steer clear of such macabre language, lest her own delicate sensibilities be offended.

"Surely," Goldie would say, shaking her finger, "death will not visit those who refuse to say its name. Surely, if we turn our thoughts to love and light, only good will find us."

The grieving hags would pause just here, just for a moment, to see if you seemed to agree with Goldie. If you did, if you were nodding fiercely, they might just leave you right there in the woods, but if your expression was twisted in such a way that the storytellers believed you might be a shadow walker, a death Priestess, or, at the very least, a Witch who understands the merit of death and letting go, then they would continue.

Needless to say, Goldie did not have many friends — for, sooner or later, even the most sheltered life is met with grief, and the truest friends walk with you through the rough places. Goldie was a fair-weather friend in the truest sense of the term; she would be with you in the sun but never in the dark. Quite fearful of the night, she was, after all.

One evening — a hallowed evening, in fact, when children dressed as caped heroes and painted zombies, when the beech trees were lean and bare and looking much like skeletons — Goldie had locked herself away and turned on all the lights. She sat eating over-icinged cake and listening to sugary pop music, refusing to think of the potency of this evening, refusing to listen when the ghosts of her ancestors whispered in her ear to be vigilant, and wishing for warmer days when the sun was more stubborn.

Perhaps there was too much sweetness in her blood, or perhaps, as the grieving hags might say, it was simply time for Goldie to grow a little more whole. In any case, she could not sleep that night. Nearing midnight, a low rumble echoed from outside her tightly drawn shades. A storm was coming, and Goldie loathed such ominous and reckless weather. Before she could rush to find her many flashlights, the power was gone, and poor bubbly Goldie was terrified, shrouded in darkness, a lone candle glowing in the corner of her bedroom.

The hags would pause here to shriek just once, just to make sure you were still paying attention, and they would continue.

Shriek, cackle, and make the most fearsome noises you can muster.

Heavy raindrops pounded at the windows, and Goldie pulled the blankets over her head. A single knock came at her bedroom door, and she crushed her eyes closed. For all her brilliant manifestation know-how, she could not escape this living nightmare. She tried imagining the lights turning on, but it was no use.

The knock came again.

"Who's there?" Goldie summoned some courage but stayed beneath the blankets.

"Open the door and see," a high-pitched, childlike voice with a double reverberation answered her. Never before had she heard a sound more terrifying.

"I will not," Goldie refused. "Go away."

"Oh, come on." The voice was inside the room now. "How bad could we be? What's the worst, most terrible creature you can imagine?"

Goldie dismissed the question at first, shaking her head beneath the covers.

"Surely, even you can conjure an atrocious monster in your thoughts," the voice urged.

A fleeting thought came to Goldie then, a face of twisted bone and row upon row of sharp, pointed teeth. She gasped at her own imagination.

"That's it," the voice encouraged. "But you can do better than that. We're so much more horrible, so much more grotesque, the stuff of the true macabre. Think again."

Goldie could not help her thoughts now, and she was awash in nightmarish visions of decayed flesh and worm-riddled dead things. Where were these horrors coming from? She had tried so hard to distance herself from such terribleness, spent her entire life as far from death as she could be, and in this moment all her efforts were for naught.

The hags who tell this story tend to pause here as well, checking in with you to be sure you are not lost in your own nightmare vision, then they'll tell you of Goldie's great awakening.

Shrieking just once and shocked by the terror in her own voice, our heroine crushed her eyes shut again and ran from her room. She stumbled and fumbled, unlocking her door and crashing into the night, where costumed babes were giggling and howling, carrying totes full of goodies and ringing doorbells. No one seemed to notice

Goldie's distress, and she breathlessly bumbled down the street, slowly calming herself and wiping the tears from her eyes. By the time her heartbeat slowed, she was nearing the end of the street she normally avoided, and a certain panic squeezed at her gut again.

Goldie was on the edge of the old cemetery, a haunted place on any ordinary day, let alone All Hallows' Eve, but there was a moonlit softness to these grounds tonight. Goldie let a certain sadness come alive in her heart then, and she let it astonish her. For once in her life, she did not shun grief; instead, she allowed that wild knowing of nature's wholeness to bring her even more alive, and she opened herself to the night.

The hags who tell this story say that Goldie was found the next morning, asleep on a grave as if she were listening to the dead speak from underground all night long, and that awakening wildling was made all the better for a night spent in a haunted place. Feeling the presence of the dark made the light all the more sweet, and Goldie never shunned the merit of grief ever again.

Snuff out your candle now, wrap your arms around your shoulders, rock slow from side to side, and hum a comforting tune.

The hags would leave you then, of course, walking into the night and wailing, and you'd most certainly be more blessed for having met them, for having heard their ghost stories of life and death, beauty and monster.

●━❯❰━●

The Sea Hag falls silent then, pointing a bony finger into the distance toward what you know are surely the shadow pools, hallowed ground where the dead most certainly await you.

Opening Practice: Communing with the Shadow Creatures

Materials: Mirror of any size and candles

As this new, midautumn moon dawns, there is much work to be done. Set aside just a short time for this ritual, and create a small altar for shadow gazing. Then set candles to burn all around you as protective fire. Face west, sitting or standing, and gaze into the mirror. Feel yourself held by the directions, by the elements themselves. Look into your own eyes, and ask yourself this lone question: *Who am I not?* Answer aloud then, while you look at your own face, into those small black-mirror centers of your eyes. Who are you not? If no answers come, flip this question and ask yourself who you are, permitting your mind to rattle off all your roles, all your beliefs.

Eventually, you will come to a place of mystery, to a place where the words slip off into the ethereal and then stop coming altogether. Find that place of mystery, of not knowing. Still gazing into your eyes, see yourself as you have never seen yourself before, lit by candlelight, surrounded by memory, perfectly positioned in the spiral dance of time, a living and breathing fractal of the greater intergalactic whole.

Waxing Moon Practice: The Shadow Doll

Materials: A doll of your choosing

While the moon waxes toward fullness, find yourself a shadow doll. Whatever qualities are surfacing for you during the shadow work, find a doll that represents them to you. In *Women Who Run with the Wolves*, Dr. Clarissa Pinkola Estés writes: "Dolls are one of the symbolic treasures of the instinctual nature....No matter what mess we are in, it lives out a life hidden within us." This might be a stuffed creature, a figure you create out of clay, or a store-bought doll. Name it. Have conversations with it. Howl at it. Love it. Sleep with it at your side, or create a bed for it to nest in near your bed. If you are tattooed or have any birthmarks, let it have these marks, too.

As the moon waxes, slowly fall in love with this holy poppet. Come to a place where there is empathy for the shadow, where there is an interconnectivity that speaks of union and wholeness. Hold your doll close when you need to embrace those sacred qualities that lie beneath the shadows, under the water, in the psychic depths where it is difficult to venture.

Season of the Haunted Heart: Full Moon

Grandmother Speaks: Welcome the Monster to Your Table

The black-water pool is hidden, nested between two craggy boulders at the sea's edge. If the tide were higher, surely this place where you stand with the hag would be well beneath the waves, and you can feel the waters edging closer as sunset nears. Leaning close, you can see your reflection in the slow-rippling water.

"We must be quick about this," warns the hag. "Many a shadow worker becomes stuck here, staying too long while the tide turns high, getting stranded on the crags and praying to the seals to rescue them, only to be swept out into the depths. You must be vigilant. This work cannot be done casually, and should it feel too easy, well, you'll have to hold your breath and go under."

A serpentine tail whips itself up from the water, disrupting your reflection and making you gasp. You pull back and eye the hag. *What is this?* you wonder. In your fright, you notice how bony your hands are becoming, how tender your joints.

"Well, go on," the hag urges. "Reach in. Cup the water in your hands and drink. Are you ready to become a more whole version of you? Tonight, you welcome the monster to your table."

Full Moon Practice: The Darkest Medicine

Materials: Shadow doll

Beneath this full moon, we welcome the medicine of shadow. We integrate more fully those parts of ourselves we have shunned, and we ready ourselves to waken a more whole version of ourselves. Cast a circle, and in the west, prepare a place for your shadow doll. Begin to chant slowly, though the rhythm will naturally ebb and flow: "I am whole, and I am here. I am whole, and I am here." Stay with this chant as you gaze at your doll, recalling all the work you have done these last long nights.

I am whole, and I am here.

See in this poppet not only the parts of yourself that yearn to wrap themselves around your bones but also the lost fragments of ancestral medicine that have been ripped up from their roots, tossed about on the raging waves.

I am whole, and I am here.

The shadow holds some piece of the secret now, some small and humble ingredient that is precisely what you need right now, in this moment.

I am whole, and I am here.

Stay with this until you feel the energy shift, until there is a sense of swelling toward fruition, just as the Blood Moon has become the brightest version of itself. When you feel ready, let the chant slow into silence. Breathe low into the belly. Move into a softer shape, then a stronger shape, and back again. Weave this work around the spiral edges of your bones. Feel into your becoming. There is no shadow and light, no monster and heroine, no duality. There is only you here, whole and complete.

And so it is.

Season of the Haunted Heart: Waning Moon

Grandmother Speaks: That Magick Has Been Yours

With shaking, skeletal hands, you reach into the water, envisioning all manner of fanged creatures leaping from the depths, snaking around your neck, and pulling you under. As soon as you touch the chilled pool, though, as soon as your hands break the surface, you are overwhelmed with ease. You see your face, more skull than flesh, reflected back to you, and the water is clear as it wells into your palms. The thinnest ghostlike snake, as if it were only a stream of ink, slips into your hands and curls into a soft shape, its spectral diamond head resting atop your wrist.

"You see, that magick has been yours," the hag assures you. "Take it all in now. Swallow it whole."

The snake seems to puff in and out of existence — a dark shadow in the clear water, then fading to nothing, then returning again.

Obeying, wanting this sense of ease to stay with you forever, you pour the water, and the shadow with it, straight down your throat, tasting thick salt and the most ancient power of belonging to a place.

Waning Moon Practice: The Shadow as Gift

Reflect now, as the Blood Moon wanes, both on the ways in which your shadow's lack of integration has hindered you as well as on the many ways the medicine of the shadow can now become a renewed and restored source of power.

For instance, if the shadow qualities you are working with this autumn are weakness and dependence, and a more positive root quality might be vulnerability, then ask yourself now how your resistance to being vulnerable has been a hindrance, has blocked your clarity in relationships and sacred work. Perhaps it has kept you from asking for what you need, from voicing your desire for pleasure, or from forging meaningful connections at work or in other groups. Now that you have done this work, now that your shadow has been swaddled by the autumn moonlight, now you want to know how vulnerability is a power source. How can you become your own gift?

Write in your Book of Moon and Flame now, reflecting on these pertinent questions. You may use the prompts I offer here or create your own.

This autumn, I've given myself the gift of shadow and wrapped it well in...
I've named it...
At my best, I am...

You might read these words aloud to your shadow doll now, consecrating it in the elements and letting it rest in a sacred place.

Season of the Haunted Heart: Dark Moon

Grandmother Speaks: The Annual Witching Hour

The small fire built by the Sea Hag has warmed your flesh in just the right places, and you can see your fat returning slowly while you sip a warm drink. The waves are calmer now, and the wind barely blows. Though the two of you are alone on this stony shore, every so often some shadow catches your eye. When you look, it is gone.

"These are the most haunted nights," the hag affirms. "The annual Witching Hour. Tonight, we'll sleep well under these stars. Tomorrow, we'll find where our greatest treasures lie."

Dark Moon Practice: The Story of the Many Children

On the dark moon, perhaps write a myth of ancestral healing. Let the characters be you: a primal ancestor from at least ten generations ago and a member of a future generation at least three generations ahead. You can choose to work with blood relations or others. In this story, you are all living and breathing at the same time, with all your shared hopes and dreams and divergent experiences. You are all somehow healing one another by resurrecting dead pieces of yourselves, by integrating your own shadows and living and loving the way only you all can. You may use the prompts I offer here or create your own.

It was the Blood Moon when they met, these three wild...
The oldest among them was...
The youngest among them was...
The middle wildling believed themselves to be...
Despite their differences, the one gift they all shared was...
The demon they all faced was called...
On that fateful night, the battle began with...
In the end, these three told each other that all was...

Read your story before your ancestral altar. Let the forebears hear you, and reward yourself with something sweet.

To the Season of the Haunted Heart, Farewell for Now

Oh, blessed be, you wild season! I shall surely miss this, the bloodiest moon that knows me best. Until next year, until the ghosts walk heavy again through my haunted home, I will long for you like I long for no other time. To the Season of the Haunted Heart, farewell for now and begone. May you rest in the deepest peace.

CHAPTER 9

Season of Spice and Hearth

---◆---

Dying

As we edge closer to that primordial void that is the thirteenth moon, we begin to turn our intentions inward. The kinship we have strengthened with our own small deaths, with our many griefs and shadows, provides a much-needed resource now as the nights stretch longer. We have not only faced the monster but said to them, *I am you*. We have not only lit candles for our griefs but known those potent forces as gratitude. Now, beneath the late-autumn moon, we take on the long-vision. We decidedly befriend not only our own wholeness but that of the cosmic infinite, and we resist naming what cannot yet be named.

This, the Season of Spice and Hearth, is a time of truly slow living, of nesting and resting, of surrender. We ask questions that befuddle and defy any answer now. We are confronted with the discrepancy between all that nature is showing us, to gather and to rest and restore, and what society tells us, to attend all celebrations and to consume until we burst. Now, we seek to resolve nothing, to arrive at no hard-line conclusions, for there are some myths that offer no resolutions, only more questions, only more of that blessed gift called confusion.

Hag Lesson #19

Growth demands discomfort.

We live out these wilder myths in autumn, when we find ourselves at the hearthside remembering childhood — be it fondly or with much mourning, or both — and we sit at the holy intersection between past, present, and future. The lines cross here, and we live as our spectral souls will live, slowly and simply, carrying on and carrying through.

What If These Circles Can Hold It All?

A Nighttime Query Gone Awry

━──◆──━━◆❳❲◆━━──◆──━

Stargazing I was and pondering the merit of my witchery when I was struck by the sight of a meteorite spit toward ground, a sudden streak of silver fire that came and went so swiftly that I wondered if I'd imagined it. Another came then, and another still, and I watched those wildly ethereal things spark spirals to life in my mind's eye. I saw it all in those quiet moments, the symbols of infinity and the orbits and the fusion and those ever-expanding, always-shrinking circles upon circles that make up what we know of this beautiful and wicked world. I wondered then whether humans might not be good after all, if we would never be eligible for reward, if we were a blunder, a blight, an intergalactic misstep.

Another aborted star fell then, and I decided that, no, we were absolutely some great saviors of some great thing, that we would rescue the whole of the universe and humility was a lie. Still another silver streak sent my mental pendulum a-swinging once more, and I fell into a sudden certainty that we were a virus this planet must cure; then another fell, and I again believed myself and the human community to be gods, infallible and sovereign. But the new moon cooled the crucible of these hot and heavy thoughts.

"What if these circles can hold it all?" I wondered. "What if these circles can hold our certainty and our stubbornness, our heartache and our brokenness? What if the human animal can come back from the brink of extinction not because of the ferocity of its will and its technological know-how but because of its sudden willingness to sit back, to surrender, to be a soft-bodied creature, and to belong to this wild place? What if these circles can hold it all, and we need

not act to solve our problems so much as allow ourselves to be held, to rest, to know ourselves as star stuff?"

———✦———

Dusk Reflection: Inquiry into the Dud Myths

We wonder now what we have been told about Witches, heathens, or magick that presented the world to us in a certain way, with hard-edged definitions of good and evil, of success and loss. Take an inventory of these stories now and the lessons you might have learned if you took them at face value, if you believed that the morals of tales were always true or if you never questioned the happily-ever-afters.

What mythic promises have failed to bear fruit, and is there a sense of betrayal that comes from those aching places where lived experiences do not match the indoctrination? Perhaps you were taught to believe that a person was either good or bad, and that they would always stay such. Perhaps you were taught that certain milestones or material acquisitions equated to happiness, but you found more joy in places where you were less burdened by things. Lend attention to the stories you now know as being far more complex, far less this-or-that, than you believed them to be at another point in your life; in this way, such stories are not lies but rather it is the absolute that is a fabrication.

Find a certain freedom in this practice, if you are able. What if the fairy tales ended without any absolute resolution? What if the wildest stories had no objective interpretation? What if goals were an illusion and the sensual journey, the circle, held it all for us?

Season of Spice and Hearth: New Moon

Grandmother Speaks: You're Still Warm

You dream heavy that night, living a lifetime in the space of a single sleep. You are visited by spirits of tree and sea, gifted with old stories you pray you can remember when you wake, and celebrated by long-faced mothers made of moss and thorns.

"Wake, girl." The impatient voice of the Sea Hag stirs you, penetrating your ethereal visions. "You mustn't stay too long in that liminal place. You're still warm, still in a body, after all, and I've a morning story for you." She settles into her storytelling tone and begins.

The Soul Cages: A Ceremonial Autumn Tale

To participate in this ceremonial storytelling, gather four jars, remove the lids, and place one candle inside each.

If luck finds us on those late-autumn mornings, we just might meet one of those trickster grannies. They tell the greatest stories, these old ones, but you can only find them when you are lost near a crossroads at dawn, when you are bemoaning the state of the world, and when your mind has sunk into that dangerous place of complete certainty. Only then will the trickster grannies find you and send you spinning into oblivion with their bizarre fantasies, with riddles so thick you might chew on them forever.

These brilliant hags love a good show, though, and they wouldn't want you to just sit there and listen to them spin their yarns. No, they would want you to move through their stories, to let your flesh be moved more than your thoughts, to puff your belly when you inhale and welcome the story to sit low in your body, to take up residence in your blood.

"The Soul Cages" is a story loved well by those jokers, for it is a story that defies resolution but has a heartstopping title; those are the best tales, after all. Before the grandmothers would begin, they would ask you to ponder these questions: What are four gifts you might want to give the world now, in this moment? What four gifts might you bring to your more broken, your more recent dead? Four deep currencies, perhaps, that you believe are trapped somewhere, locked in your bloodlines, kept hidden until this very moment?

Name these four gifts now, but feel no need to define them too rigidly. Perhaps they are named wildness, empathy, earth love, and presence. Perhaps they are elderhood, song, plant medicine, and compassion. Stand facing the west while we begin.

The trickster grannies begin this story by spitting on your face to mimic the spray of the sea and, of course, to get your attention. "In a land of haggard gulls, near-dead birch trees, gray waters, and storm," they always begin, "there lived an ordinary Witch who knew too much."

The Witch was not cast out from her village but rather had developed quite a disdain for people over her few short years. Liked well enough, she was, but her heart was a hard one. People complain, and she had no time for such whining. People dithered when trying to make decisions, and she could not bear the thought of wasting even one more breath of advice on such indecisiveness.

She was a tough one, you see. She had learned to fend for herself as an orphaned babe and, having no fondness for friends, had moved to this place of storm and sea without so much as a mournful thought for the people or place she was leaving behind.

She was called crazy, as all the best people are, for this place where she built her home — with her own two hands, mind you — was quite difficult to reach. One had to scurry down a dodgy rope on the cliffside, being ever so careful to not look down, then balance quite precariously on a wind-rocked bridge. Even the best of her friends thought it best to let her be.

Some of the trickster grannies say the Witch built her house right here on purpose, trusting she'd never be in danger of houseguests, while others say the Witch's great-grandmother's ghost told her to build there in that rough place, promising her that great reward would come her way if she made a wild home of her own.

In any case, a wild home she did make, and no one came to visit her here. She was an outcast by choice, after all, and she liked it just that way. Weeks went by after the humble house was built. It was sturdy enough — shielded from the wind between the rocks — but, alas, even the lonest wolves grow weary of solitude; even the hardest heart wants a friend from time to time.

A storm raged that first evening when the Witch began to question her choices, as we all do. The full moon disappeared behind the thick of rain-full clouds. Thunder roared so loud that the rocks around the house shook, and the waves were coming so close to the house that the bridge had flipped upside down.

For the first time in her life, the Witch was afraid, and she wondered if she had let her stubbornness get the better of her. She lit a small and humble fire then, whispering prayers to Manannán mac Lir to protect her, to not ferry her off to the otherworld too soon.

Light the four candles inside the lidless jars now, setting one in each of the four directions, choosing which direction suits each jar best. Keep the lids nearby, and invite your beloved dead to join you here. Name each candle for one of your gifts, your deep values, the trapped medicine that might serve to heal your ancestral lines.

The Witch finally slept that night to the sounds of storm, dreaming of the face of her great-grandmother, who told her to relax, that all would be well, that even the bravest women must confront their own vulnerability. The Witch woke to find the sea calm and her house still standing. Relieved the bridge had also righted itself, she ventured outside her home and down to the stony shore to assess the damage.

She had scarcely made it onto the beach than she

saw them; dozens of immense crates and just as many barrels had washed onto the shore, along with a good bit of broken wood, and the Witch realized that a great ship must have wrecked in the storm. She shrugged off the disaster of it all, having no love for ships or sailors, and began to collect her bounty. It was no small feat, but she rolled the barrels to a safe and hidden place, breaking them open one by one and carrying casks of fine drink and spices back up to her house. The boxes were full of beautiful furs, leather shoes, and even small chests of gold. The Witch spent the day packing her home with these treasures, and with her body good and sore from a hard day's work, she rested at the hearthside then, draped in the finest clothes she had ever seen, smoking a pipe, and sipping some heady whiskey that made her quite pleased with herself.

"A queen, I am," she said aloud, and all her trepidations from the night before were washed away. That night she dreamed of her great-grandmother again, though this time she was less reassuring. Sitting atop a rock peppered with seals, she was. Sitting and singing alongside a red-haired merrow — a fishlike faerie with a human face and much, much old magick — her great-grandmother crooned a hymn of peril and tears, while the merrow played a harp with the kind of skill creatures have only in dreams.

The days started to drag on again then. Soon, after only a month, the food and drink were gone, and the Witch's clothes, though still very fine, had begun to bore her. At dusk on a particularly lonely day, the sky darkened and another storm began to roll in from the west. She prayed to the full moon to protect her, and she burrowed herself under her bearskins. Worse even than last moon's storm, this one rocked her house to and fro, and she scarcely slept at all, sure she would wake swallowed by the sea.

The sun did rise, however, and again the Witch found a bounty waiting for her on the shore. Even posher food and drink, robes and fabrics, and smoke and spice awaited her, and she spent the day hauling her gifts to her home. Like before, these beautiful things fed her for a time, kept her warm and satiated for a little while, and then, just when she grew bored, another storm would come and send her more bounty. With each full moon would come a fearsome evening of thunder and lightning, and with the torrent would come the treasures. For many years, this continued, and all the while the Witch would dream of her great-grandmother and the merrow.

The Witch thought she was truly living the best life she could, though loneliness would still come for her, and her aching heart was always soothed by her haul on the mornings after the full moon. She began to wonder, though, if this was all there was — the consuming, the storm, the gathering, and the taking. There had to be more to this precious life, she thought, and that errant thought — that small wonder if there could be something deeper, something even more rewarding than all her gold and silks — opened up the slightest crevice in her wholeness.

A tiny crack, it was. A slight fissure in this altogether and otherwise perfect existence she had built for herself.

The trickster grannies who tell this story — and you'll do well to remember that they are tricksters — often say that it was through that crack in her own perfection that the Witch began to see more clearly. She was gifted with the second sight, they say, and before the next full moon swelled to fruition, the Witch swam out to the seal-covered rock where she often dreamed of her great-grandmother sitting with the merrow, and sure enough, there atop the rock was the red-haired fish-woman, playing her harp and looking quite devilish.

"Ah, it's taken you quite a long time." The merrow shook her head. "What kind of Witch are you, anyway?"

The Witch was aghast.

"Your great-grandmother found me right away, she did, but you've been awfully gold hungry, haven't you?"

"You — you knew my great-grandmother?" The Witch began calculating the merrow's age, and her furrowed brows gave her away.

"Best not try to think your way into a faerie's mind, love. It never works. And, anyway, we are immortal. I might have known your great-great-great-grandmother, for all you know." She rested her harp down and tapped a seal lovingly on its nose. "Now, off we go."

She held out her hand and moved toward the edge of the rock.

"Where are we going? I can't breathe under the sea," the Witch protested.

The merrow smirked. "You can, and you will. I've been waiting a long time to meet my dear friend's great-granddaughter. You wouldn't refuse my hospitality, would you?"

The Witch thought for a moment, gazed at her house, no more than a dot on the cliffside from here, knew she would only spend the night drinking and lost in loneliness if she were to go home, and assented with a single nod.

Down deep they dove, and it seemed that so long as the Witch held tight to the merrow's arm, she would be able to breathe. It seemed hours went by, though perhaps it was only moments, before the two of them went so deep that they fell from the water onto dry land. Deep under the sea, they were, but in a liminal place that was not quite liquid and not quite air. Heavy with salt was her breath, but the Witch could move about on her own here.

The merrow led her to her house, a brilliant place full of garish shell work and treasures scavenged from shipwrecks, no doubt. What undersea luxury this place was! The Witch considered for a moment how lush her own humble house had become after just a few years of collecting her bounty, and she could only imagine what a majestic hoard an immortal life spent gathering would bring.

Late into the night, the Witch and the merrow drank and ate, telling jokes and stories, and the Witch had never known such camaraderie, such kinship. Alas, her lungs started to ache after a few hours, struggling to breathe well in this deep place.

"Before you go, I want to show you something, dear Witch." The merrow led her into a shadowy room, and the Witch shivered.

"What is this place?" she asked, taking notice of dozens of upside-down bone baskets strewn about the floor. "What might those be?"

"That's what I wanted to show you," the merrow answered. "Those are the soul cages."

The Witch clicked her tongue. "What a terrible name! What do you mean?"

"Each full moon when a ship crashes, I swim off into the deep and catch the souls of the sailors, keeping them here. I'm a bit of a soul collector, you might say."

Place the lids on the jars now, watching each flame snuff out.

The Witch started to question her new friend's goodness now. "Why would you do that? Do they not deserve peace?"

The merrow shrugged, ignoring the Witch's question. "Come, you'll need to get topside before you drown."

The Witch obliged, suddenly aware that she could barely breathe, and they swam up, up, and up, until they reached the seals' rock.

"There will be no storm tonight." The merrow looked to the half-moon. "You can make it to the shore from here on your own, I think."

The Witch nodded, still sick from seeing the soul cages but managing some words of thanks for the food and drink.

"Shall we do this again next month, perhaps on the half-moon?" the merrow asked with much hope. "There will have been another storm by then, and we'll be rolling in the drink!"

The Witch took a breath, then nodded, recalling the warmth of company, already plotting how she might set all those poor souls free.

"Lovely." The merrow bowed. "Until then."

The Witch sat atop the rock until dusk started to fall, pondering whether she would make it to the merrow's house on her own and be able to open the traps. In the end, she thought the journey would be the death of her, and she swam slowly to shore.

That night, the Witch spent nearly every second thinking about the soul cages, plagued by guilt that those were the very souls whose deaths had paid for her fine living, and she could scarcely look upon anything in her house without seeing a soul cage, without considering the names and faces of those who had died. Her father had been a sailor long ago. Was his soul trapped in the merrow's shadowy room? She started to see the hands of those who had packed the crates, the faces of those who had hoisted them high onto the ship, who had screamed for their mothers when the storm came.

The morning of every full moon, the Witch would normally wake full of excitement, full of small prayers for what she hoped might wash ashore, but this time she was full of dread. She prayed to the old gods to keep the storm away, and for the first time since she had left her village, she considered venturing back to the town.

She did not, of course, stubborn creature that she still was, and the storm did come. A beast it was, too. The Witch watched the lightning strike the waters over and over again, and she spoke words of blessing for the ships that might be caught in the fury. She had nightmares that evening of the merrow venturing out and collecting the souls, and she wept for her part in this sadness.

In the morning, she climbed down to the beach, dragged the barrels and the crates to her safe place, but opened none of them.

"These things are not mine," she muttered, making a sacred symbol of blessing above the lot.

When the half-moon approached, she began to plot. Down to the merrow's house she would go, as invited, but she would sneak away from the table at some point and release all the souls from their cages. It wouldn't be too hard, she thought, for the merrow liked whiskey more than she did.

On the fateful afternoon when the half-moon rose in the sky, the Witch waited on the seal rock for the merrow, who startled her, erupting from the water with a laugh.

"Well, let's go. I've prepared quite the feast!"

The Witch reached out, taking the merrow's arm, and down they went.

At some point during the fourth course of what seemed to be an endless meal, the merrow asked the Witch a poignant question. "So, tell me. I see that you've yet to enjoy any of last month's bounty. What's keeping you from the haul?"

The Witch swallowed, not wanting to give away her plans.

"I — I just haven't had the time," she lied. "And, anyway, my house is quite full. I'm not sure what I'm to keep doing with all of this."

The merrow looked perplexed. "Ah, well, you can always build another house."

The Witch grunted, shooing away the thought that, yes, she could build another house. She could forget the soul cages, forget the merrow, even, and go back to living in finery. She could, only she could not unsee what she had seen or unknow what she had come to know.

There was no turning back now. Her world was bigger.

After the seventh course, the merrow was leaning heavy on the table and telling the same story for the third time. The Witch wondered if she would die here, if the merrow would pass out and be unable to carry her to the surface before her breath became too heavy, but she shunned the thought of giving up now.

"I — I need to stretch my legs a bit," the Witch lied again, but the merrow's eyes were half-closed and she was droning on and on about some poor pirate she once knew.

Now was the Witch's chance, of course, and she quite easily slipped into the shadowy room. Still hearing the merrow's babbling, she was sure she was safe, and the Witch lifted up the bone baskets, one by one. There appeared to be nothing inside, but with every cage she lifted, there was the softest whistling sound and, often, a cool breeze on her face.

Lift the lid off each jar now, perhaps seeing a small puff of smoke, perhaps divining a shape within the smoke or even just a feeling arising within you. As you open the jars, envision that particular medicine being freed, being released from its binds and feeding you, your family lines, and your community.

Confident she'd freed them all, the Witch returned to the table, where the merrow was still slurring and blubbering.

"Ah, merrow, I hate to interrupt, but I'm starting to struggle a bit with the breath," the Witch lied yet again. "Would you mind taking me up?"

The merrow's eyes got a little wider now. "Oh yes, sorry. I've had a bit too much to drink, I suppose. Let's be off, then."

The journey was swift, and the whiskey hadn't seemed to slow the merrow's pace in the water at all. Once safely atop the rock, the Witch wondered if she should tell the merrow what she'd done, tell the creature to get another hobby, but she thought better of it.

"Until next month, my friend." The merrow waved before going under, and the Witch felt very light as she swam home — proud of herself, even.

That night, she slept better than she had in years, but as the full moon approached, she started spending her days dreading the storm again. How many times would she need to have dinner with the merrow only to release the souls? she wondered.

The night of the full moon she watched the sky like a raptor would the sea, but there were no gray clouds to speak of. There was not so much as a rumble of thunder, and the storm never came. She could scarcely believe it, but the moon stayed full and bright all night long. There was no bounty to be scavenged the next morning, of course, and the Witch wept with joy.

The trickster grannies who tell this story tend to leave it to you to decide: Was the merrow an ill-minded creature who caused the storms in order to catch the souls and who, knowing the Witch would keep her from claiming them now, moved on to another part of the sea where her affairs would not be meddled in? Or was the merrow testing the Witch all along to see if she loved her bounty more than she loved her fellow human creatures? Or did the Witch do what her great-grandmother could not, finding more bravery than her foremother had? Or perhaps it was all of these things. Or none of them.

The grannies agree that the Witch did, in the end, gather what finery and gold she had and return to her village, gifting her wealth to those who needed it more than she did and finding a certain peace and sense of belonging within this world she had sought so fervently to leave.

--)(--

The Sea Hag ends her tale and helps you to rise, offering you some brew and gauging your state of health, trusting you are ready and able to continue the work.

Opening Practice: The Living Ghost Story

Our magick is made stronger when we acknowledge our own interconnectivity with all that is — with our own flesh and blood, yes, but also with our ancestors, the land we hail from and the land we live on, the matrix of our local communities, the cultural and societal webs we both spin and are spun from, the human animal generally, the elements, the many creatures of this world, the stars, and the cosmic infinite. In a way, we are living ghosts. We are a consistent cocreation being done and undone, and there is no defeat in acknowledging the illusion of our separateness and isolation.

Imagine yourself now as a living ghost. You are omniscient. You have the long-vision. You are able to see across the expanse of time's fabric. You are able to fold it over on itself, to weave and reweave moments, to re-member experiences. As this living ghost, you hold the intention to nourish your wandering soul with precisely the medicine you need right now, in this moment, at this intersection of time and space while you read these words. Where would you go if you could visit any point in time and space to uncover this particular remedy, to glean this particular message?

Note that the question is not who you would be if you could be anyone, only where and when you would go to heal through the old magick. Choose three of these intersections between time and space now. Give these moments a soul. Give them breath. Grant them a life. Let it be part fantasy; it must be, after all. Rid yourself of the pressure of dates and even, perhaps, geography. Your bones and blood know where they must go, the soul of the moments you must encounter. You may use the prompts I offer here or create your own, but permit this to be a liberatory practice of becoming less bound by the confines of individuality. Know that such connection does not force you to relinquish all control or disrupt your sovereignty but rather plugs you into an immense, intense force of which you are already a part.

As a living ghost, I went on a quest to heal my...
Thirsty for integration, I first arrived at a moment of _____ and encountered
    the soul of this place and time; it was named...
Nourished but still seeking, I now met the soul at the holy crossroads between
    _____ [time] and _____ [place], and I sensed it was all...
Weary now but nearly whole, I sought out the last soul of a time and place,
    and I found it right where...
Returned home, returned to flesh, I now know...

Waxing Moon Practice:
Deep Listening and the Medicine's Resurrection

As this wild moon waxes toward fullness, sink into a practice of deep listening as often as possible. Begin in those liminal moments as you are falling asleep. Whisper a prayer of protection. Set the intention to encounter an ancient ancestor, one who is compassionate and holds potent medicine for you at this time in your life, one who lived connected to land, one who knew what it meant to belong to time and place, one who lived slowly and loved well. You may see an image or face more than you hear any specific words; even so, listen to what you see. Attend to all messages with your whole being, those that come in dreams, those that come from signs in nature, from pathworking dream visions, and from the unseen. Bring these messages out of the ethereal and into manifest reality by writing them down. Make note, and give thanks. Engage your ancient ancestor as much as possible while the moon waxes. Let them find you. Let them share what they know.

Before the full moon ritual, ponder the messages about this medicine, these gifts you are being tasked with resurrecting; then ponder what beliefs or ready-to-be-shed patterns are blocking this medicine from fully integrating, from being fully realized and lived out loud.

Season of Spice and Hearth: Full Moon

Grandmother Speaks: Pray into the Sunset

You are learning to love life here at the water's edge. Living close to the sea means having nature's greatest lessons constantly whispered to you. Each wave reminds you of the cyclical nature of all things, swelling to birth, cresting, dissolving, and receding, only to rise again. The landless horizon reminds you of the Mystery, of the mighty infinite, and the smell of brine reminds you that these depths are the womb waters out of which we were all born, and there is no separation, not here, not now.

"With dusk comes great blessings," the Sea Hag promises, handing you a bowl of fish stew. "Eat now. Pray into the sunset and wait right here."

Full Moon Practice: The Great Purge and the Great Switch

Materials: Paper, fire source, burn bowl, clearing herbs

After dark and as close to the full moon as possible, the Ancestors' Moon, set up a ritual space with a fire bowl at the center. This can be in the wilds or indoors, but take all precautions of the compassionate and careful fire tender. When ready, create sacred space by inviting the loved ones in spirit to sit with you here; then invite your ancient ancestor, the one with whom you have been working beneath this autumn moon. Ask your ancestor to bless your loved ones, to gift them with the same medicine you are seeking to integrate now. The intention of this ceremony is to make space for this medicine, be it wildness, a greater love of the land, stories or old magick, or whatever potent gifts and aged wisdom you know runs in your blood.

Having done the work while the moon waxed, write the blocking beliefs now, ones you are ready to banish, on separate pieces of paper. The blocking beliefs might be that wildness is not safe, or that the land is ours to be used as we will, or that old magick is evil. You need not have one blocking belief only for each bit of medicine; you will burn as many beliefs as you like.

When ready, raise energy by free-speaking a prayer to your ancient ancestor. You might include words from the mother tongue, if you like. You might move or dance, sing or drum. Whatever feels right as a means of invigoration, do it, and permit your ancestor to guide you. As you move, choose a phrase or a single word that will replace the outmoded beliefs when the time comes. How can your language give service to the medicine now? This replacement phrase can be taken from the prayer, derived from the name of your ancient ancestor, or born of simplicity. When the space feels full, feels ripe for magick work, begin the burn.

You will read the outmoded belief silently to yourself, not speaking it aloud, then set it alight. While you watch it burn, speak the replacement phrase aloud and with much ferocity. Mean what you say in this moment, and do this for all outmoded beliefs. Though you have only one word or phrase that is replacing all your beliefs, you may let the intonation change depending on the belief you are burning.

Once all beliefs have been burned, begin to repeat your replacement phrase now, over and over again. You might paint some of the ash on your face while you chant and imagine painting the faces of your heathen forebears. Imagine them chanting with you, invoking the same medicine you now have begun the work of remembering, resurrecting the old ways, your old ways. Offer gratitude to your ancient ancestor and the grandmothers when finished, then open the circle and place your hands on the ground with intention.

To integrate this work, while the moon wanes, keep your bowl of ashes atop your ancestral altar. When one of your old beliefs starts to surface — if you have an errant thought that feels restrictive, as if it might block the medicine — speak your replacement phrase aloud immediately or, if you are unable to do so, think it as loudly as possible.

And so it is.

Season of Spice and Hearth: Waning Moon

Grandmother Speaks: Let Them Come

The sky is a dusty-rose shade, the gray clouds veiling the sunset in such a way that the sea has taken on an eerie pink-gold glow. All is calm, but change is imminent. You can feel it.

"Such serenity cannot last." The Sea Hag confirms your precise thoughts. "Are you ready?"

Before you can answer, small shapes start to bubble from the surface of the ocean. You think them seals, but there are far too many, all bobbing to the surface, then sinking again, moving slowly shoreward.

"Let them come." The Sea Hag is grinning, nodding with approval. "Invite them."

You see now that these are your healed ancestors, those who have been the medicine keepers, those whom you have healed through your own work. They are winged Witches, scarred daughters, beloved land workers, healers, and midwives. These are the souls to whom you belong.

They lay gifts of herbs at your feet, speaking words of blessing. They show you the faces of babes in their arms, and they tell you they are well. They are without torment. These are not lost ghosts but warm and whole beings come to greet you, come to dream you into being.

Waning Moon Practice: Grieving Autumn

Our greatest task at autumn's end is to understand the blessings of the void, the gifts of the *prima materia* that has no name, and the merit of that hallowed ground between death and birth. Visit your dead now. Leave offerings that reflect the medicine of your ancient ancestors on their graves, if you are able; then welcome the short season of nondoing, of rest, of befriending the wild unseen and falling in love with unmanifest possibility. While the moon wanes, feel into the energy of the thirteenth moon as much as possible. Light your candles and write a eulogy for autumn that speaks well of its spice and hearth fire.

Autumn's Eulogy

———◆———

Farewell, my dying god. I will mourn for you as no soul has ever mourned. My body will shake with the keening, and I shall become banshee. Only for you, this Witch will bewail the darkness, and only for you shall I shed tears. These last three moons with you have taught me who I am becoming, have told me sea-soaked stories and shown me the still-beating spectral hearts of my wounded dead. Until next year, my lover, my friend. Until that first chill wind blows again and reminds me of your breath on my neck. You smell of rotting leaves and smoking pinewood, beloved, and no other has ever brought me such joy.

———◆———

Season of Spice and Hearth: Dark Moon

Grandmother Speaks: No One Can Tell You Not to Cry

Night has fallen, and your ancestral hosts have returned to the sea, returned to the salty mother that bore you all. The moon is near dark above you, only a single silver arch hanging between brighter stars, and you know you must leave this place. Consumed by sadness, you are, mourning for the sea before you leave it.

"Weep if you want to, child. No one can tell you not to cry." The Sea Hag places a humble necklace of shell and rope around your neck. "Into the dark you go." She motions north, and you see that the beach, the sea, the cliffs on the eastern edge, have all fallen into shadow in the distance. "Walk into that nothingness now; it holds it all for you."

Dark Moon Practice: Rest, Ritual, and Reflection

As this moon wanes toward darkness, begin to honor your right to rest and reflect, to spontaneously work simple rituals of root nourishment and deep breathing. Tend to your body. Watch the small creatures scurry about and make their preparations as you make your own, readying yourself for the longest nights.

To the Season of Spice and Hearth, Farewell for Now

—◆◆◆◆◆◆—

Just now, just when those prophetic first flakes began falling ceremoniously and pinpricking my lips and eyelids like icy nudges from a coldhearted granny, I remembered who I was, a winter-hungry Witch willingly housed in a place of eternal becoming. To the Season of Spice and Hearth, I must leave you now, but I leave you well. All blessings be.

—◆◆◆◆—

CHAPTER 10

Season of the Thirteenth Moon

---✦---

Becoming

There is a holy void that spans the space between autumn's end and winter's birth. This, the thirteenth moon, is a time of nondoing, of rest, of tending to those deeper states of being that remind us of this one wild truth: We are constantly being cocreated, molded and shaped by cultural, societal, and ancestral hands; by our own memories as we choose to harvest them and reexperience time; by our longing; and by our art.

This is the time of sinking back to source, of dropping down into mud. Though there are years when our calendar year contains thirteen moon cycles, most years do not have an entire thirteenth moon cycle. In the Celtic tradition, the thirteenth moon is a brief season that surrounds Samhain, and we are called to wield our intuition and feel this cosmic void when it is upon us rather than rely on a linear calendar. This moon wants us still and quiet. This moon wants us attuned to the ancient pulse, to our most untamed state.

Hag Lesson #20

Darkness holds it all.

In lieu of magick work, I offer you only a prayer, only a spoken dream and a nonstory of falling into fecund and hallowed nothingness for this, the thirteenth moon of the year, the annual dark moon. All blessings be during this season of grace.

So may it be for you, and so may it be for all your creaturely kin.

On This, the Darkest Hour
A Thirteenth Moon Prayer

On this, the darkest hour, I pray to the trees. Someday, may my bones become bark marked with those holy knots and forgotten sigils that stripe and spot the thin-limbed birches. May my blood feed loam and bewitch the graveyard yews shading those crumbling stones. May they, those elder trees of eternal shadow and infinite grace, sip slowly and become intoxicated by the rebel poetry that stayed locked in my veins until death set the verses free to water the ground. Until then, I shall pray to those wild and loving gods of berry, leaf, nut, and fruit. I shall sing them songs on these dormant days, and I shall ask nothing of them but to be my muse of wonder, my most beloved and treasured companions on this, the thirteenth moon.

Teach me to lay bare my branches and sink them low, grandmother oak. Show me the merit of my pricklier ways, ye blackthorn. Haunt me well, burned and severed cedar, for it is your ghost I love most on these cusp-of-winter midnights.

On this, the wildest night, I pray to the trees. Someday, I shall lie prostrate on their moss-laden roots and become their still, soft dedicant. Until then, may my breath feed them well.

And so it is.

The Unburnable Beloved: A Thirteenth Moon Tale

The thirteenth moon of the year illuminates nothing if not all our contradictions. We are at once raging activists spitting bitter vitriol on those we deem enemies of whatever particular justice we are backing at present *and* softhearted lovers grieving for a world we fear has never and will never exist. We are rebels and conformists, fighters and pacifists, destroyers and creatrixes. We will cast disdainful eyes down on those who profit from polluting our precious air but excitedly board airplanes to venture into the exotic. We love our vast oceans but also love the convenience of plastic. None of this is judgment; contradictions *are* until they are not.

Our collective journey of becoming is, in part, a navigation of these many contradictions, a slow and uncomfortable process of seeing and sitting on the edge of the unknowable. Resolving our contradictions too quickly is precisely the strategy that birthed many of the ills we seek to remedy, and there is the finest thread of a line between apathetic complacency and not rushing to define, act, and fix. Language encourages finite categories and a concrete naming of this or that — and, we might wonder, what would happen if there were words that meant everything *and* nothing, or action *and* stillness, or this *and* that. What if the words we spoke allowed for contradictions to exist, simultaneous opposites to sit and be? What if we invited our many discomforts, our innumerable shadows, to come home and rest?

Sometimes nonsense is the best medicine, but not just any kind of nonsense. So easily will we pack the nonsensical into our mental boxes labeled pointless, futile, and unimportant; that is, unless those preposterous ideas are flavored with a certain potency. The irrational is not particularly productive and therefore not socially valuable or economically viable; we might then ask ourselves if nonsense is a true currency of the outlaw.

Can a story be absurd and still make us feel deeply? Beneath the thirteenth moon, may we let the bizarre rule. May we hold hands with our deep confusion and, like the Witch in this brief nonstory, rest in that holy discomfort that always blankets us at this time of year.

While you read, imagine the tale being told by a loving and hateful creature with the face of a child and the voice of a hag.

> Once upon a time and then every day thereafter, there lived and died an enchantingly beautiful wretch. They had the bold and golden eyes of a sun sprite and skin made of dark moonlight. To look upon them was to fall into a certain trance, under a particular spell that had you knowing nothing and everything all at once. They, this Witch of many names, were both beloved and feared,

as all the best people are, and everyone said they could never be caught, never be caged, for to catch this Witch would mean the world would lose all its mysteries. Were this exquisite and elegant creature trapped, every shadow would be brought into the light. There would be no more illusion, no more theories. Everyone would have a name and a place, and every quest would end.

Naturally, because the human animal is a repulsive, fractured, beguiling, wholesome, selfless, selfish thing, there were those who wanted to capture that uncapturable Witch.

"Oh, won't it be just a blissful utopia once we can rest?" the peace-loving war makers would say. "No more will we tire. No more will we squabble over matters that don't matter."

Just as naturally, because that soft-bodied and hard-minded creature called human is an argumentative monster, there were also those who believed the Witch should remain free.

"Well, what will we do?" the war-loving peace makers would ask. "Surely, there will be no more adventure, no more motivation to move and climb or converse or weep. How will we know we've won when there is nothing to lose?"

Of course, the peace-loving war makers took it upon themselves to hunt that unhuntable Witch; it is far easier to take an action you believe in, of course, than it is to simply resist, far easier to attack than protect.

In a grove of unburnable elder trees, that Witch lived, hiding in the plainest sight, spending their nights sunbathing and their days howling at the moon, but those peace-loving war-making hunters came upon them at dusk, during that liminal 'twixt and 'tween when they were at their weakest and most powerful, their bravest and most cowardly.

"Come now, Witch," the confidently humble captors

half-ordered, half-requested. "Our minds are tired of so much pondering, and our bodies are exhausted from all this business. You are the ugly and beauteous heart of mystery, and we must — we simply must — take hold of you."

The Witch cocked their head to the side like a bird and said nothing with their tongue but everything with their eloquent eyes. Just then, the war-loving peace makers arrived, and the grove was encircled with those bizarre human angel-devils spaced like yellow-bellied brave-hearted soldier-babes between the elder trees, the Witch standing at the center point and the whole of the scene cast in the dusty-pink glow of twilight.

It was at once night and day, defense and attack. Everyone was victim and perpetrator, and everyone but that holy demon of a Witch was so sure of their position, of their rightness, of their morality. Every single human creature in that moment would have called themselves good, had anyone asked, and each of them would have gladly died, so sure they were that they served some grand purpose, so sure their lives had been lived with honor.

What none of them had considered was that, while they were all quite accustomed to quick-and-dirty resolutions, the Witch was quite at home in the precarious and on the edge. Long had they lived on the fringes, and they were fueled by that wild energy of infinite and unformed potentiality.

They lived for this, you see. Precisely here, with nothing and all things possible, was their domain, and those human animals began to sense their folly. It was as if some forgiving and vengeful god with sullen cheeks and a fat belly posed an unsolvable riddle that stopped time, that alerted all those so-reasonable, so-rational creatures to their eternal conundrum.

They were logical fallacy. They were actors in an infinite play, protagonists and antagonists in a never-ending story of becoming. The plot may have been written by a mad alchemist of sound mind and body who despised both lead and gold, and who was only interested in the brewing.

Those unburnable elders ignited then, for those haunted trees had lived long and learned to love those rare moments when human beings united in their common drama, when these humorous animals were stunned into silence by their own actions, genuinely surprised by their own behavior, and somewhere and everywhere, this grove still exists, eternally frozen and ever burning in time and space, and we human animals can all sense the necessity of both mystery and the quest to solve, of shadow and flame. We are at once the Witch, the hunter, and the hunted. We are the burning unburnable, and our fractured wholeness itself is radical.

Under the thirteenth moon, leave a little room in your witchery for nonsense. Feel into those moments when there is a blessed uncertainty, when some errant thought or external quandary sends you rushing to find resolution, and envision all those wild parts of your psyche coming together and simply being with one another among those firelit immortal trees. Confusion is participation in the grand conversation. Here, we rest, till life and death do us part.

WILD AUTUMN PRACTICES AND SACRED REMEMBRANCES

- Remember that grief, like gratitude, shows us what we love, and that our shadows are the most potent medicine.
- Check in with the groups to which you belong in autumn — collectives, covens, families, councils, work organizations, and others — and assess what needs to go, what is consuming time, energy, or money that could be better spent elsewhere. Banish and adjust accordingly.
- Honor the dead often and well.
- Grieve for orphaned dreams, for the childhood visions, the fairy tales that have failed to bear fruit.

- Nourish the body with warmth, with rocking, with small practices that bring about an ease to these drier times of release and letting go.
- Befriend the open spaces you are creating; don't rush to fill them too quickly.
- Check on your living beloveds who seem too strong to grieve.
- Name your tender aches, the soft and sad places, often; mourn for them and, perhaps, meet others there.
- Learn to love the mystery as much as the certain and sure.

House of the
MOUNTAIN HAG

Opening Winter's Portal

Invocation to the

Crone of the North

━━━━━◆)◆(◆━━━━━

Only hooded witches know

What lay buried 'neath the snow

Meet them in their mountain dens

Find them just as autumn ends.

Dawning on those grayest days of the elusive sun, winter whispers us dark rhymes by candlelight. The northern wind sets our house creaking and our bones cracking, and we look in that sacred direction of hard truths and cold ground. Those endless nights before winter solstice send us searching for her, that cunning hag who lives alone in the mountains, who seems to hold the deepest and most ancient wisdom this world has ever known. These moons are her moons. On the longest night, she serves us the sparse nourishment we need before challenging us to look inward, to reflect on our many battles, and to mark with ritual these holy Witching Hours that, like that wild and wily crone, will gift us with the precise faith we need in order to embody the wilds as our ancestors did, by infinite hope and firelight.

Overview of the Winter Journey

Season of Salted Bones

Nourishment: Resting
Story Medicine: The Storyteller Crone's Jewels

Season of the Wild Wolf

Challenge: Divining
Story Medicine: The Bone-Woman's Brew

Season of the Cauldron Keeper

Wisdom: Quickening
Story Medicine: The Moon Child and the Holy Wild Hag

The Winter Altar, Wildcrafted with Infinite Trust

The lunar seasons of winter welcome divination and darkness, ritual and reflection. Reverence for the sanctity and preciousness of light runs in our blood on these overchilled days, and we tend our many altars with great care and love. The wintertide altar is simple, bearing green branches and symbols of enduring trust in self, in others, and in the world at large.

Choose a luscious and dripping taper candle to stand at the northern edge of the altar; name this candle "Prophecy." Place a burn bowl in the east holding dried cedar or an earthy incense. At the southern edge, place an object that represents "hope" to you; this might be a statue of a deity, an oracle card, a crystal, or a photograph of some beloved one in spirit. Last, in the west, place a small dish or chalice holding water. The directional representations are the altar's bare bones, with potential additions including juniper or cedar branches; pentagrams made from sticks and twine; ethically harvested bones or antlers; or objects sacred to you that represent prosperity, the dark moon, or the wild-crone aspect of the divine feminine. The winter altar should evoke feelings of somber ease, holy solitude, hearth fire, and infinite trust in the ultimate perfection of all things.

CHAPTER 11

Season of Salted Bones

Resting

These last witching moons have wrapped you in a swelling darkness that was at once the warm water of the womb and the thick death shroud of the grave. Now, on the cusp of winter, your body craves sustenance and rest. Your soul hungers for stillness. You are meeting the coldest season with the weight of the last thirteen moons strapped to your back. You crave answers to questions you never dared to ask until this moment, and in time, you will leave winter behind bearing only the bones of who you used to be, wrapped in twine and woven into a humble crown.

This first moon of winter, this first lunar season of necessary nourishment, is a time of resting in the fertile dark, of discerning where to set your roots and how to best tend to your deep self. The short days are rituals of rejuvenation, and the long nights are warm, candlelit nests for coming home to the soul.

Hag Lesson #21

There is much magick in the mundane.

This moon is one that bids us nourish ourselves with those seemingly small and unplanned ceremonies of the senses, the hot drink sipped just before dawn or the smell of some steaming spice rising from a black iron pot. We must let such simple magick become a vital container for pensive reflection and pure, embodied presence.

Let these longest nights be a wide-mouthed cauldron slow-warming that unknown and potent brew that will be the next year of your life. May the hearth-tending Mountain Hag offer you up precisely what you need, and may winter wrap you in a blanket of perpetual hope, radical patience, and sensual nourishment.

Knelt before the Altar at Wintertide

A Solstice Prayer

To that floating, crumb-size spark of dawn nested in an ocean of darkness, to that pinprick of spirit light promising to ripen and swell to fullness after this long midnight ends, I pray to you on this solstice night. The eyes of the ancients are on me, and the brilliance of every quiet-glowing Yule tree ever graced by a babe's wild joy is warming these frigid bones of mine. Knelt before the altar at wintertide I am, stripped of the weight of last year's wounds and wants if only for this moment. Give me enduring peace and a long night's rest haunted by stone-faced ghosts who know of this season's solemn magick, who can teach me the ways of the flame tender before I wake, and who speak the language of the sacred trees so eloquently that those bark-skinned and bare-branched friends also bless this ceremonial nap of mine. May I wake a wilder version of this crone-hearted creature I am in this moment, and may I keep a candle burning on my ivory rib-cage altar for the wild heathen I once was.

Midnight Reflection: A Witch's Year in Review

Strike a match, Witch. Set some wild cedar to burn. Wrap a tattered heirloom quilt around your shoulders, and ready yourself for some raw-hearted reflection. Before the first new moon of winter dawns, before you hold your breath and knock on the door of that feisty Mountain Hag, tell a brief and poignant tale of the previous year's epic journey. Permit your deep soul to speak, and envision the words you write as truthful spells of their own, ancient incantations channeled through your voice but sourced from a collective lineage far older than you, far more resonant than any one voice could ever be.

> *Last Yule, I was aching for…*
> *Beneath a winter moon, I asked myself…*
> *By the time the gardens bloomed, I had already…*
> *Lit by the spring dawn, I wondered…*
> *In the summer heat, I followed the song of…*
> *On those long and sweltering afternoons, I busied my hands with…*
> *Those bewitching days of autumn renewed my sense of…*
> *Chilled by a colder wind, I banished all that was…*
> *Now, as winter finds me weary again, I long for…*
> *If there's one lesson I've learned from my year of _____, it's this: _____*

Solstice Celebration:
Prophecy 'neath the Pine on the Longest Night

When dusk falls on the longest night, our inner children all curl up beneath a strong-branched tree, their faces pressed to cold ground and their small fingers tracing spirals on the bark. Winter solstice celebrations are those that beckon the light to come home, and that first moon of winter is a snow-bright, celestial poem revering the dark as fertile gestation space warming the yet-to-come. In *The Winter Solstice*, John Matthews writes: "There is a moment of silence that occurs every year…a moment we have all experienced at least once in our lives, maybe more than once. It can silence a great city like London or New York, and it can bring stillness to our hearts, whoever and wherever we may be." This is a time of prophecy and divination, and the Witch's celebrations are those that do not overwhelm but instead quietly inspire, that do not deplete any emotional or material resources but instead nourish and replenish those precious stores.

There is a particular and ancient holiness to solstice night, but a Witch might celebrate on any evening during this first Season of Salted

Bones. If you're able, bathe with sea salt and imagine any unwanted dust from the previous year being washed away, gifted to the elements, and returned to the wild waters. Once you've been cleansed, surround yourself with firelight, quiet beauty, and silence. Near your altar, find yourself in a state of embodied presence, and become a living prayer to the night, lighting the northern candle and setting the herbs at the eastern edge to burn. Here in this ceremonial space, you will give yourself the potent gift of prophecy and nourishment.

Hold just one question at your heart center. Your query might be: *What do I need to know most right now?* or *What does this next year hold for me?* As with any form of divination, the tool you use is only a means of harvesting what you already know to be true. Gaze into the candle's flame, letting your eyes soften and lose focus without turning your attention away from the fire. Let your consciousness deepen, keep the gaze on the candle, then return to your question. Stay with this practice for ten minutes or longer if you are able, keeping a fixed gaze and returning to your question intermittently until you feel the answer has come.

The fire element has much to teach us of hope and desire, and this form of simple pyromancy is one our ancestors most certainly engaged in long ago, on those days when fire represented the very spark of life. The blessed flames were cook fire and light source. Fire was warmth, joy, and necessity.

On this solstice night, let this fire draw out your visions from their depths. When it feels finished, when you've received your answer, keep the candle burning and prepare yourself a blood-warming drink. Sip the liquid as a ritual of embodying the information you have received, of integrating this ceremony meaningfully and accepting the coming transformations with all the ease of swallowing a bit of honeyed tea or spiced juice.

Adaptation for Families, Coven Groups, and Other Wild Circles: Gifts of Divination

While sacred solitude is integral to the winter season, there is a particular and heart-lifting magick that comes from community on solstice night. Envision those hooded ancients dancing inside a stone circle around a high-burning fire, bidding the sun rise as a symbol of the end to the coldest days. Imagine them telling stories to one another, looking to their elders for vision and prophecy.

Consider guiding your group to gift one another with a blessing or prophecy for abundance, using either fire or another oracle of their choosing. You might have each group member secretly choose another member, so no one is certain from whom their prophecy is being gifted. Exchange the gifts as handwritten, decorated notes, and celebrate with a sweet and savory feast, hot brews, hearth fire, drums, and much, much laughter and storytelling.

Season of Salted Bones: New Moon

Grandmother Speaks: Warm Yourself, Child

Your pulse drums so hard that your frozen bones rattle, and your shaking hand knocks hesitantly on the hag's door. The smoke of her cook fire smells of blissful heat and spice; you long for your iced-over joints to thaw beside her hearth, and yet, part of you hopes this door stays locked, fears that you will not leave this house unchanged.

Even so, the door creaks open, and you finally see that knowing woman of the north you've traveled so long to find. Her wild graying hair is wrapped with bone and twine. She's dressed in sacred fur and adorned with jewels of teeth and antlers. Hers is the medicine of the midnight sorceress, of the wakeful grandmother.

She motions for you to sit at her well-worn, bloodstained table, and she dishes you out some steaming and strong-seasoned broth, some hot and holy elixir for whatever wounds this winter finds you nursing. Spooning through her brew, hesitant to taste her Witchcraft, you find little more than leaves and bones. The smell of salt and clove burns your nose, and you know that this sparse meal is precisely the nourishment you need beneath this first moon of winter.

"Warm yourself, child," the hag orders, and you raise the spoon to your still-thawing lips. "Here's a story for you while your guts thaw."

The Storyteller Crone's Jewels: A Yuletide Tale

In winter, if we are so blessed, we just may encounter that certain sort of elder who has the most bitter medicine, who has no time for small talk or niceties — for, after all, she knows she is not long for this world. "Why should I waste what precious few days I have left chatting about the weather?" these old ones often say after their "quit your blubberings" and "buck ups." Your pity party is not one they shall attend. We might call them too gruff, too prickly to be part of our worlds, but I wonder if these sharp-tongued grandmothers are not showing us the merit of the rough places when they speak, if there is a holy lesson in their meanness. And maybe, just maybe, if we can sit in the discomfort of their harsh words, we just might learn a thing or two about the darkness.

This Yuletide tale is the sort of story they might tell, these bitter hags, if they thought you could stay quiet enough to listen. They won't sit long for interruption, but they will give you something hot to sip and direct you to rest, to close your eyes, to breathe deep, while they gift you with their most pointed lessons. Though our elders are most certainly not beyond accountability, they might offer you a not-so-kindly reminder that the aged are not treated well in our world, and so, perhaps, they do not owe you their warmth.

The furrow-browed grannies begin: Once upon a darkening moon, there lived two curious and magick-hungry babes. Theirs was a weary and overmined land where the head was given priority over the heart, where the wisdom of the flame tenders was forgotten and the elders were locked away in sterile and unreachable towers. The town had lost its memory of the wilds, you see. The soul had gone out of the place. In the absence of those old and slow-moving crones and creaky-boned sages who could remind the young ones to pause, enjoy, and feel, time moved quite quickly in this place — so quickly, in fact, that parents would wake with fast-pounding hearts and rush their littles through the day without so much as a nod to the sunrise. Even the rowan trees had forgotten their majesty. Even the caves had lost their stories. Time moved at such a pace that the children aged to maturity in only a few short years, or so it seemed, and their in-born longing for the whimsical was snuffed out like a lone candle flame by a rushing winter wind.

Mind you, there were some children who were born with a certain resilience to the hyper rhythm of this place. One would know these outlaw innocents by the way they lumbered long behind their near-running caregivers, who would no doubt turn to urge them to run faster, screeching over their shoulders like harsh-voiced robots programmed with tunnel vision and narrow-mindedness. These resilient babes were diagnosed, their thirst for the wild pathologized as a sickness, as neuroses. You'd see those rebels often carrying flowers or stones in their small hands, and you'd know their long-staring expression sky-ward by its unmistakable sense of wonder, a wonder that would, so sadly, eventually be sucked away by vampiric to-do lists and the pressures of progress.

It seemed year by year, however, that fewer of these wild-eyed creatures were born to the town. More and more, even the infants erupted from the womb with anxious hearts and hypervigilant eyes that darted about their nurseries. In a time-impoverished land, stillness was monster, and the hag storytellers who once nourished the minds of the young, grounded the babes in a certain place where the old gods still ruled and roamed, were becoming extinct.

Even in this wonder-starved place, rumors always rode the late-autumn winds. There was something about those bare-branched trees, you see, that filtered the chill breeze in such a way that the breath of the north formed words, gracing the ears of those remaining outlaw innocents with tales of a bejeweled madwoman who lived deep in the pine forest bordering the northern edge of the gray-toned town. Each autumn, just before the Season of Salted Bones dawned, you could find the babes who'd heard the rumors searching the forest for the crone-witch who housed a million and one stories in her heart. Though there were fewer and fewer each year, it became a quite predictable event that the most untamed children would go missing under the dark moon, only to be found nestled and sleeping on a bed of browning pine needles or, more often, still wandering north in the hopes the hag would find them.

On this particular autumn, only two of these wild-lings remained, and their shared outcast nature had sparked one of those childhood friendships that molds the bones in two bodies to match and shapes a unique language only the two could understand. Indeed, theirs was a bond of the wild, a bond that could not be broken by discipline or authority. Their terrified parents locked their doors at night beneath this dark moon, knowing of their offspring's affinity for rule breaking. They covered their ears with woolen muffs to drown out the rumors of the hag, and they warned them over and over again about the dangers of the dark and the madness of the old ones.

Of course, none of this worked as intended, and the old Witches who share this tale at the fireside agree that the two wild ones heard the whispers at precisely the same moment, just as the clouds parted to reveal that haunted sliver of a dark Ancestors' Moon.

"Find the hag," the whispers hissed. "She's waiting for you."

No sneaking was required, as the wildlings' parents were blinded by their blue screens and did not even see their little ones walk right past them, out the door, and into the night. They found each other at the old oak tree that loomed large in front of those thin-boned pines just at the forest's edge.

"Did you hear it?" asked the dark-haired wildling.

"I did." The fair-locked babe nodded, and into the woods they went just as the first snow began falling.

They spoke to one another in that language only they could understand, sharing half-finished fairy tales and hopes that the hag might have answers to their questions about moons and mysteries. Long they wandered, nearly turning back just after midnight, but a dark-eyed snow owl swooped low over their heads and began leading the way north. They followed, their normally calm pace hastened by cold, and it was near to that thick time of night when the spirits walk heavier than the humans that the two babes reached the mad hag's house, full of trepidation and hope in equal parts.

"What if she won't see us?" wondered one of the children aloud, hair coated in a thin layer of ice.

"What if she eats us?" The other wildling upped the ante, shaking snow from frozen boots.

The owl sat atop the roof just above the door, blinking in rhythm with the babes' hearts and beckoning them to go inside. The house was stone, with much of it covered in a thin layer of sweet-smelling moss. Smoke waves of cedar and wet pine spiraled moonward from the chimney, and the children longed for a warmth they had never known. Yes, the amber glow emanating from the windows promised dry clothes and hot drink, but it was the sustenance of story they were after.

Thus, the young ones entered the house hoping for the solace of the wild, aching to hear tales of trolls and trees that walked. As the wide door groaned open, the little rebels saw themselves swaddled in tattered blankets and kneeling at the feet of a softly crooning granny as she rocked slow and easy in an antique chair, knitting and gift-ing them with songs of spells that last generations before finally coming to fruition, creatures who walk straight out of the otherworld and into the dreams of lonely-hearted mothers, and secret recipes for sweet cakes that contain all the truth-telling and lie-sniffing ways of the cunning elders; they had hoped for all of this, but what they found was something far more mysterious.

Much of what the children had heard about the hag was true, of course. Her graying hair hung in thin wires that were bedraggled and curled at the ends like ribbons chewed by mischievous kittens. She was indeed dripping in an odd sort of jewelry with a particular aesthetic; made of bone, stone, and dried flowers these bizarre baubles were, and the crone was so laden with these pieces that she could barely move, seated in the far and shadowy corner like a neglected queen figurehead whom no one cared to consult any longer. Her pale eyes twitched as the children entered, but she lifted her arms from her lap, garish bracelets clanging together, in such a way that the children knew she had lost her sight.

The wildlings shared an uncertain glance, then one of them swallowed and spoke: "Grandmother, we've come for your stories."

Now, the old cronely Witches who share this tale with their grandbabes as they drift off to sleep always say that right then, right at that moment, the old snow owl flew down the chimney, erupted from the hearth, and landed right on the hag's shoulder. The fire blazed even brighter then, and the old woman began to laugh.

"Did you?" she managed to say. The owl sidestepped and began nibbling on the elder woman's hair. "Are you not afraid of the madwoman who lives in the woods? Did they not tell you of my hysteria or warn you of my wildness?"

The wildlings opened their mouths to protest, to

say they weren't afraid in the least, but the crone kept speaking.

"In any case," she continued, shrugging softly and clicking her tongue, "I've no stories to share. Stories dry up when no one hears them, you know, and an old woman can only share so much with an owl."

The children's hearts ached in that way that feels as if a loss has occurred but there's no name for it yet.

"But, Grandmother," one of the babes begged, "we live in a place where the magick has been lost. There are days when we believe we're the only two people in the world who know it exists...and, well, soon even we will walk as the soulless walk, having forgotten what it means to be of the world, to be rooted, instead of whirling above it like some busybodied invisible wave."

"You're the only hope we've got," the other wildling summarized, grasping the friend's hand and awaiting an answer that wouldn't come. The hag cocked her head curiously, sending her many necklaces sliding and rustling. The owl moved in a way that mirrored its keeper, nearly turning its whole silver-feathered head on its side as if to say "Well?"

The children stepped forward, hand in hand. "That necklace with the long fangs and green stones; I very much like it," one of the wildlings offered cleverly. "Where did you find it?"

The owl righted its head, and the hag's face softened just a bit.

"Ah, well, I made it. I made all of my jewelry." She rubbed the ivory pendant of the precise necklace the wildling was speaking of. "It's a wolf's tooth, and I pulled it from the beast myself when my body was stronger. My husband was a great hunter, you see, but this creature nearly got the best of him."

The children shared a knowing smile and stepped closer while the hag continued.

"It was a winter evening, one of those nights when all the fire in the world couldn't warm this stone-walled house. Our bellies were empty, and our wills were waning. Still, I had begged that old stubborn goat to stay put. He had a mind to go after Mac Tíre, you see, the wily wolf-mother who's even older than my creaking bones. I don't know what it was that got into him, but he was obsessed with her that year, hungering for her blood with all the reckless ambition of a younger man who thinks himself a hero.

"'Don't you dare,' I told him. 'She knows these woods better than both of us put together, and she's got the spell of the ancients protecting her.' That wolf was an otherling, you see, and we mustn't ever kill what little magick we have left in this world.

"He listened to me for a while, but that frigid night the snow was falling and the only thought that could warm him, I think, was the satisfaction of putting an arrow straight through Mac Tíre's heart. I remember watching him leave, the snow blowing in through the door as he left, and I thought, *That's it. That's the last I'll see of the man who loved me well.*"

The children knelt at her feet now, holding one another.

"The night dragged on. I put the last of the wood on the fire, and a funny thing happened then. Now, you're most certainly too young to know this, but something happens as you get older and you have moments when you believe with your whole heart and soul that you are going to die; your thoughts begin to do this demon dance between fear and memories. I started seeing my love bloodied and buried under snow, then I'd see his face when he got down on his knee and asked me to be his bride, then I'd see my own frozen body right here on the floor, then I'd see my hands young and lithely working away at digging up roots, only to be pulled into my depths again and see my same hands with the flesh half-gone and riddled with worms.

"This demon dance is exhausting, mind you, and you can only do it for so long before you either slip into a terror-filled slumber or you make yourself get up and do something." The hag grinned, and the owl spread its wings just a bit. "Well, I chose the latter. I prayed to the Cailleach to grant me the magick of the winter wanderer, and I set out into the snow wrapped in all the furs I could find and carrying no weapons but a long willow staff. I don't know how long I was walking before I heard her howl, that great white wolf, and I walked straight into the sound, begging my grandmothers' ghosts to fight with me if need be.

"It happened quite quickly then; an arrow pierced straight through the flesh between my ribs, and I fell in shock. Somewhere in my mind the words my husband said as he wept and hovered over me are buried, but I can't recall them now. What I do remember is her eyes. The Mac Tíre had these silver-flecked eyes that only immortals have, and she walked straight out of the shadows and over to us both. My husband was so consumed with grief, thinking he'd delivered a kill shot straight into the breasts he used to love so dearly, that he didn't dare strike at her."

The hag half-snorted with humor. "Hell, I think the old fool fell over when he saw her, walking toward us not as huntress but as healer. She looked long into my husband's terrified eyes, and he bowed his head in submission, then that great beast took hold of the arrow with her mouth and pulled the thing free, spitting it into the snow, blood and all; it wasn't without effort, and she broke her tooth." The storytelling hag kissed the tooth pendant of her necklace and went on, "I don't remember much else except the feeling of a warm creaturely tongue on my wound and waking warm and safe in my bed. My husband never went after Mac Tíre again, of course, and

I made this necklace for him so that he might remember to leave the magick in this world be.

"There are men who think they can own it all, you see, but they end up stabbing through the very heart of what they love in an effort to claim and name mysteries that could never belong to anyone." She leaned forward, and the owl flew with grace to sit above the hearth. "Here," she said, lifting the long necklace and untangling it from her hair. "I think I'm ready to part with this story now." She coiled the thing in her palms and handed it to the wildlings. "It's made of stones that hold tales much older than that one. I pray you share them all."

The wildlings' cheeks were salt streaked now, never having heard a story from start to finish, and they egged the grandmother on, hungry for more now.

"What about that red bracelet?" asked the dark-haired innocent. "Did you make that, too?"

"Ah, yes," the hag answered, and went on to weave a potent ghost story about the lustful succubus who haunted these woods with a poetry-heavy tongue and a gaudy garnet-beaded shawl draped around her naked shoulders. She ended the story and gifted the wildlings with the bracelet.

One by one that night, the hag unloaded her tales of heathen revelry and feminine anguish, concluding each story by stripping herself of a single piece of jewelry. By sunrise, the wildlings were the ones covered in jewels, and the hag was breathing easier. The fire had nearly died, and the owl was pacing in front of the hearth, threatening to ascend and take to a tree for the day. The hag had only one piece left, a fragile ring made of spiderwebs and spit.

"And, Grandmother, what about that one?" the bleary-eyed babes asked in unison.

Now, the coldhearted grandmothers who share this story disagree on that final tale told by the hag. Some say it was a story about death and romance, as all the good ones are, and others say it was a story of a kind-hearted queen who saved the land from falling into the hands of pirates. Others say it was both. However the tale began, the grannies agree that it ended with the hag telling the children never to die with a good story stuck in their hearts.

"Stories are lifeblood," the hag said, "and I believe I've told my last. Be on your way, children, but remember the myths that warmed you tonight."

The wildlings left the hag there then, just as the owl flew up the chimney, and they rattled all the way home covered head to toe in the old one's words. Most of the grandmothers say the hag took her last breath that day, but all the grandmothers say that the wildlings shared those stories all over their sepia-toned town, and the color rushed right back into the place. The hag's stories flooded the town just in time for Yule; just in time for those still and quiet nights spent by firelight; just in time for handmade gifts to be woven from threads of grati-tude, grace, and once-upon-a-times; just in time to re-mind the world that its pulse beats in rhythm with the witch-storyteller's voice.

⊷⊱✳⊰⊶

The Mountain Hag stares you down then, lowering her head and looking up at you with only her wild eyes visible, an inquiring expres-sion that wordlessly wonders if you are ready, if you are worthy of what deep medicine she has for you here in her house.

Opening Practice: Your Winter Initiation

This new moon is a subtle awakening, a heavy-bodied stirring beneath a blanket during those haunted predawn hours. Mark this moon not with vision boards, resolutions, and hard-edged ambition but with divination and grace. Mark this moon with the soul-food of simplicity and be at home in the not knowing. This is a moon of necessary liminality, and your inner hag is telling you only to "warm yourself," to feel into the parts of your story left dry and aching from previous moons, and to rest.

By candlelight or hearth fire, open to your initiation by swelling your belly with breath, exhaling in a long, slow hiss, then reading these words aloud:

> This is my winter's initiation, and I can hear the voice of the holy hag welcoming me to this next, sacred turning of the wheel. I hereby surrender the armor I've outgrown and the masks that no longer fit. Breath by graceful breath, I am coming home to the wilds within me. In this moment, I am the truest and most whole version of myself I've ever been. I am the waking wisdom keeper, and I am minding these flames in honor of these coming seasons, in the name of those thirteen bewitching moons. All blessings will be.

Seal this ceremony in stillness, by feeling the heat of the fire element on your skin and thanking your ancestors for tending their altars, for telling their stories, and for being stewards of their heathen lands.

Waxing Moon Practice: Tending the Inner Altar

Spend the days leading up to the first full moon of winter opening to the shadows. On the nights when the moon is waxing, reserve just five minutes in the late evening to visualize your inner altar. Stand facing the north, soften your knees, and close your eyes. Imagine there is a single candle flame stretching from your midbelly to your heart center. As you inhale, see and feel this flame extending longer, reaching your throat center, and as you exhale, imagine the flame settling back to its original length but burning brighter. On your inhale, the flame dims and grows long. On your exhale, the flame settles and burns brighter. Stay with this visualization, adding these words on your out-breath: *I am whole. I am here.* When you are ready, end your practice in silence, trusting you carry your inner altar with you, no matter the weather.

As the moon swells toward fullness, begin to take notice of any subtle shifts you might experience, particularly in your sleep patterns or dreams.

Feel into any changes without judgment. Remember, this is a moon of nourishment, and your inner crone is directing you only to "warm yourself," only to hold yourself in the tenderest care, on these longest nights.

Season of Salted Bones: Full Moon

Grandmother Speaks: Tell Me, Child

The spice of the meal sends a current of heat running through your veins, invigorating your cells with desire and courage. The hag grins, knowing the power of her medicine, and she takes a seat across from you, sipping a brew of her own. You feel you've been bewitched, charmed by this old one already, then she asks you a question that beguiles all your senses at once.

"Tell me, child. When have you felt most alive?"

You swallow, opening your mouth to answer, but she stops you with a raised hand.

"I don't want to hear romantic drivel. Your loves and losses don't interest me; we all have those. I want to know when you've felt perfectly positioned in this joyous and wicked world of ours. I want to know when you've known in your gut that all of this was worth it, and I want to know what you were doing, where you were, and who you were with. Tell me it all right now, before your next bite, so I can picture it. When have you felt the most here you could be?"

Full Moon Practice: Cleansing the Altar

This first full moon of winter is the fruition of the Season of Salted Bones. It is the peak of our early-winter nourishment, the point at which we awaken to this new year, as we move slowly but with care away from the dark and toward the light. As close to the full moon as you can, set aside twenty minutes for this ritual of inner altar cleansing. Begin by creating sacred space, then stand facing north. Visualize your inner altar as you have during the waxing moon practices, breathing with your under-the-ribs flame and affirming your wholeness and your presence with the words *I am whole. I am here.*

Keep the same breath rhythm, but when you feel ready, shift the visualization in this way: On your in-breath, the candle flame swells, beginning to extend above and below, in front of and behind, its original position. It does not shrink or dim but grows brighter on the exhale. Inhale the flame bigger, exhale the flame brighter, until you are full of and surrounded by a brilliant glowing light. Shift the chant on the exhale to be *I am here. I am ready*, and imagine the golden light burning through any known or unconscious blockages to your presence, to your wholeness, and to the glory that awaits you under these winter moons.

Begin to notice, as you stand in the dark with inner altar blazing, if any visions come to you. Can you see yourself on warmer days? What second-sight images grace your psyche now, beneath this first full winter moon, while you affirm your preparedness aloud? You are here. You are ready. What do you see?

Let your chant soften to a whisper and imagine the Mountain Hag standing before you. Does she have any words of wisdom for you? Can you answer her question: "Tell me, child. When have you felt most alive?" Commune with her for just a few brief moments, honoring her as a keeper of these winter moons and permitting her to gift you with whatever she wants to share.

When you feel ready, seal the ceremony in silence, offering final words of gratitude to those ghostly gift givers who protect you from the ether; then open your circle. Your inner altar is clear. The dust has been swept away. You are whole, here, and ready. All blessings be.

Perfectly Positioned in This Joyous and Wicked World

Full Moon Incantation

———◄◆─ ◄►◆◄► ─◆►———

Perfectly positioned in this joyous and wicked world am I. Many, many moons ago, my hopeful soul sat atop a wild, crystalline comet and spiraled around a slow-dying star. Countless visions had I there, riding that blazing orb into oblivion, but the one I remember most clearly is this scene I found myself in right now. I saw it as if it were a soft-lined painting done by some dead and stone-faced master artist; it was I, just as I am on this wintry evening. It was I, standing in the cold with a heart overwelling with a senseless and infinite trust that all is as it must be, that all is an intricate weaving of pure, primordial chaos with silvery threads of purpose and poetry. It was I, perfectly positioned in this joyous and wicked world.

••➤)(◆••

Season of Salted Bones: Waning Moon

Grandmother Speaks: You've Come for Wisdom, Wild One

Your blood is warm, your belly is full, and your bowl is empty but for a few thin and meatless bones. The hag is still slurping on her own brew, and you lean back in your chair to let your eyes rest. In your haste to eat and to thaw your chilled body, you took little notice of how comforting to the senses this mountain haunt was. Now, in your stillness, you can hear soft-crackling fire and bubbling soup. You can smell the drying bundles of rosemary and lavender, and you can still taste the salt and spice of your meal on your tongue. The hag grunts sharply, and you open your eyes, noticing the care with which she has tended her home. This humble place is a sanctuary for the world-weary soul, a firelit altar built for the strange and wild wanderer.

"Why have you come here to me, hungry and with sullen cheeks?" she asks. "What nourishment have I, a fierce old woman who has chosen to live her life on the edges of the mapped world, to offer you, a loving and soft-bodied creature?"

Her words bite at you, and you resist your instinct to defend yourself, to demand she see you as a strong-hearted warrioress.

"Ah," she continues with a smirk, "I know why you've come, after all. You haven't come for food and warmth. You haven't come to gawk at the lonely Witch on the mountaintop. No, you've come seeking something far more dangerous, haven't you?"

She pauses, but you know she isn't looking for an answer.

"You've come for knowledge. I know your kind. Well, don't think I'm going to teach you a thing you don't already know. Don't think — not for one second — that I can show you how to live as a Witch in a single joyous weekend of song and dance; it doesn't work like that.

"You've come for wisdom, wild one, so here's some advice for you: I can't teach you what I happen to know. I can only craft the conditions for you to remember your own innate magick. I will feed you. I will tell you stories, and, yes, I will challenge you, but I cannot give you anything gift wrapped and tied neatly with a bow. If you're looking for a swift and easy end to this visit, your chance has already come and gone."

Waning Moon Practice: Something Far More Dangerous

As the first moon of winter wanes, as those gray days grow ever so slightly longer, the Witch feels the seeds begin to stir beneath the soil. They wonder what magick this year might bring. While all the world is telling them to consume, to pad their nest with glittery frivolities, the latest technologies, and unnecessary trinkets, their spirit craves something far more dangerous. The Witch wants answers, and they want direction; they must look within for both.

Beneath the waning moon, take just five minutes each evening to journal your answer to this one question in your Book of Moon and Flame: *Where do I go from here?* Begin your answer with these words, writing for the full five minutes and repeating this introductory prompt as many times as you need to:

From here, this wild one is moving toward...

At the end of each of these short rituals, circle just one word you have written that seems particularly potent, then write this word on the next page of your Book of Moon and Flame to inspire the following evening's writing. Notice how these words relate to or oppose one another, but try not to judge yourself. We harbor a bounty of contradictions beneath our skin, after all.

I've Come for Your Magick

A Winter Resolution Made over Salted Bones

Said this Witch to the leafless trees, "I've come for your magick. This is my winter resolution, and my offering to you is a humble one. Bear with me while I bury these salted bones at your roots, while I pray to myself as I will be in one year's time, thirteen moons older and many lifetimes wiser. A ripe vixen I will be, to be sure. A bejeweled queen, I will have become. This year, my gift to you is but a bowl of bones, but next year I'll come swinging baskets full of treasures. I'll prance about like a thankful sprite, pouring pitchers of milk on the browning grass just for the faeries and humming songs written for me by the fallen angels. This is my Year of the Wild, and I hereby vow to spend it well, waking with a subtle yearning in my ancient soul each morning and enchanting my soft-drumming heart with a grateful prayer each night. I'll remember the ways of the hags moon by precious moon, and I'll make offerings to you, the trees, by day. Bless these bones and bless those crones. So mote it be."

Season of Salted Bones: Dark Moon

Grandmother Speaks: Let's Not Be Too Hasty

The Mountain Hag is grinning, pleased by some small mystery as yet unknown to you. You move to stand, to clear your place, but the old one motions for you to stay in your chair.

"Let's not be too hasty," she warns. "Let's not move too quickly. Now's not the time for speed, after all. Let your food settle, open your third eye wide, and see what you can see now that you've had time to rest. It's nearly time to feed the wolf, and you'll need your senses sharpened."

Dark Moon Practice:

A Puzzle-Piece Hymn, Handwritten by the Witch's Apprentice

The day before the new moon dawns is never a time for spellwork or heavy ceremony. This is a time for reflection, when we are tasked with assessing the work we have done during the past lunar cycle. Spend just five minutes on the first dark moon of winter reviewing your writing, feeling into your soft body, and examining your relationship with your inner crone, that Mountain Hag whom you've come to know well these last few weeks. Look to your Book of Moon and Flame, reviewing all the words that stood out for you following your waning moon practices. Rewrite these words on a new page, and create a short incantation that includes all of them. Speak it aloud as if it were both a blessing for your inner crone as well as a sealing ceremony for the Season of Salted Bones.

And so it is.

To the Season of Salted Bones, Farewell for Now

Until we meet again, you cold gift giver's moon. Farewell for now to the Season of Salted Bones, to the longest night, and to those far-reaching arms of darkness that swaddled me and kept me from sinking too deeply into mourning. Good night and rest easy, you wild winter moon. You've taught me well, with all the grace of a knowing mountain dweller. All blessings be.

CHAPTER 12

Season of the Wild Wolf

❈

Divining

We find ourselves here again at midwinter, and this is surely a time of deep shadow and fertile nothingness, a time when our psychic beasts are as desperate as a lone mother-wolf after an epic snow has blanketed her wilds and threatened her babes' survival. This is a moon of challenge, a time of standing our ground and permitting what has been pure and unformed potentiality to begin to take shape, a time of unknotting the fraying, inherited fears of scarcity.

The lessons the Mountain Hag has for you now are not easily learned. To be the crone's student now is to admit you belong to some great and numinous nature you have no name for and permit such mysteries to keep you humble while your fiery will sparks to life yet again.

This moon wants our fortitude. Here, we are tested, tasked to not forsake our soulful grace for fear of not doing enough or being enough. This lunar season is a twenty-nine-day-long stare-down with a snarling beast; if we flee too quickly, we will be taken down. If we stay frozen too long, we may never move. How do we know when it is time to act? We listen for the hag's direction, and just for now, just maybe, we shun the weak-bellied second-guessing that would be the death of us.

Hag Lesson #22

Winter magick wants discernment.

The Bride's Brew

Salve for the Imbolc Ache

———◆———

I'm sorry you found me this way, my beloved, my betrothed. My lace is soiled with moon blood and grass stains like I'm the ghost of some vengeful Yuletide bride. My veil looks as if it's been shredded by mountain cats, and my eye paint's left pitiful inky streaks from lashes to lips. I know I must look a fright, but I promise there's still warmth to be found beneath this overchilled skin of mine.

Hold me close! This ache always finds me here at midwinter. I can feel it haunting me as soon as the bustle of Yule settles, when my floor is littered with pine needles and wax drippings, when the nagging orders of the human world ring louder in my ears than that sweet hum of the slow and lumbering wilds. Always, I try to run, my love — but, alas, that ache knows me better than I know myself.

Even so, I'll be damned if I haven't figured out the best remedy for those midwinter heavyhearted ills. I fear you'll leave me if I share with you, dearest, but there's no point in my hiding such secrets from the kindest lover I've ever known.

Here goes: When I'm certain the ache has me, when I can feel its long-nailed grip on my ribs and hear its voice hissing low in my bowels, I give in for just a bit. I don't try to paint over the black-mold winter muck with the pastels of spring, and I sink into a necessary solitude. I roam the loneliest forest roads, I press my forehead to pine bark, I weep, I rest beside near-frozen streams, and I bid the wilds swaddle my annual Imbolc darkness in blankets of moss and fur.

Nothing fixes it, of course, and I can't say I find any laughter out there. But, my brave-hearted mate, I am armed with infinite trust that this, too, shall pass. Smooth my hair while I sleep soundly now. Wrap your arms 'round these wide hips of mine, and sing me those rebel songs that stirred my heart so long ago and ensured I'd be forever yours, forever your cunning, cautious, sultry, sad, joyous, jaded, giggling, grieving, righteous, raging Imbolc bride. And so it is.

———◆———

Midnight Reflection: Dream Visions of the Near-to-Come

Midwinter magick is the magick of muted manifestation. Here, we creep forward, moving subtly toward what we can envision as our own. We need not know the name of the destination in order to begin the journey, and the Witch understands that the desire to know everything about what might manifest limits the cosmic infinite's ability to support us. As Imbolc approaches, that holy cross-quarter day between winter solstice and the spring equinox, the seeds begin stirring beneath the ground, the hag begins dreaming of warmer days, and if we listen, we can hear the hymns of our deepest desires whistling through the still-bare trees.

Take to your Book of Moon and Flame now. Light your altar candle called "Prophecy," and begin the work of dream-visioning. Beckon those unseen beloveds to surround you now, and ask the Mystery to grant you a dream vision of yourself beneath the first moon of spring. You may use the prompts I offer here or create your own. Feel free to scrawl and scribble images if words do not well serve to represent what you see, and resist the urge to assume, label, and know anything other than this singular vision.

> *The Mountain Hag has taught me well, and I am staring straight into...*
> *The brightest colors here remind me of...*
> *This place reeks of...*
> *I'm listening close, and I hear...*
> *I reached to touch...*
> *On my tongue, I taste...*
> *These are holy days indeed, and I feel...*

Imbolc Celebration: A Bridal Bed and a Flame Alight

Materials: Natural materials for doll making, box or basket for a doll bed, long-burning white candle, writing utensil, paper

The precise night of midwinter is the Celtic Goddess Brighid's day, the eve the flame-tending maiden does battle with the skull-faced crone for her right to nest, nurture, and birth even as the land lies barren and the sun stays feeble in the sky. This holy day is often celebrated on February 1 and February 2 in the Northern Hemisphere. Mark the halfway point between winter solstice and the vernal equinox — or Yule and Ostara, respectively — with an evening ritual of hope and fire.

Return to your Book of Moon and Flame, and read through the winter work you have done thus far. Tonight, you seek to give shape to your desires for the looming spring season. Ponder what you truly want as the days stretch longer. For what will you keep the fire burning now, and for what will you petition that flame-tending mother who guards your hearth and gifts your inner altar with the warmth of infinite trust and enduring faith that the seeds you plant now will bloom into your wildest and most flourishing garden yet?

Invoke that playful inner child who inhabits your psyche, and fashion a doll from natural materials; these might be wool roving, grasses, corn husks, stones, vines, or any other found and ethically sourced materials. You might also use a doll you already have but know you will not keep. Handcraft this humble poppet with great care, for she is the magickal embodiment of the forge keeper and altar mother. She is a sacred relic, an homage to that part of your deep soul that, for all its tribulations, still harbors hope that, just maybe, all things are indeed possible. The doll once finished will need a bed, so gather a basket, shoebox, or more majestic sort of vessel that can be filled with a small blanket or cushion. Unlike the doll, the bed can be repurposed, so it need not be something with which you are willing to permanently part.

On a small piece of paper, inscribe a very short description of what you are invoking for spring. Best not be too specific, as these are fragile days of medicine and mystery where there is still much to learn. You might consider your vision from the midnight reflection as if it were a painting, and then ask yourself what the title of that painting is, writing your answer on the piece of paper and nesting it beneath the blankets in what will be your doll's bed.

To begin this short ritual, affirm that you are in sacred space; then light the candle. Permit the candle to symbolize both your desire for this vision to come to fruition as well as an ode to who you have always been; a sovereign prophet and sensuous mystery keeper. In this moment, you are the flame tender. You are the Imbolc bride, and you are guarding your dream like the wolf-mother guards her pups, with great care, vigilance, and ferocity. Hold your doll close to your heart now, and begin to envision that dream with all that you are. You want to feel it, yes, but also see, smell, hear, and taste it. In this moment, you are there at that single instant in the future, sensing the yet-to-come so powerfully that it feels like a memory.

Begin chanting the title of your vision now, the words written and nested beneath what will be the doll's bedding, and allow them to wave through you in quiet whispers, then loud howls. Stay with this until you feel a subtle shift occur, a soft sort of pressure in the air, perhaps, or a sensation that maybe you are not alone here; then let your chanting quiet to a still point. Tuck your doll under the covers like a granny would a babe, then open the circle, ground the energy by placing your hands on the floor or earth in front of you, and, importantly, keep that fire burning.

Do not snuff the candle out but let it burn out naturally or, if you are blessed to be using a long-burning candle, keep it safely alight for at least a full day, staying close to warm and nourish your seed dreams. Beyond the ritual night, you will move the doll's bed near you while you sleep, placing it under or next to your own bed and giving her a nod every so often. On the spring equinox, she shall be released in a wild place, an in-nature ornament honoring the merit of your desire.

Adaptation for Families, Coven Groups, and Other Wild Circles: So It Is for the World

The Imbolc ritual can be adapted easily for families, groups, and other wild circles by providing a space for all to create their own dolls and beds, to share their dream visions, and to raise energy together in unison, for the good of each other and for the good of the world. The sanctity of a circle or group provides a range of immense resources, including significant energetic potential as well as the opportunity to have your magick seen and validated by like-minded seekers. At midwinter, at a time when immense loneliness threatens to overtake many souls in our rapidly paced society, to be engaged in spiritual work with others is to begin the annual business of returning to the light.

Gather all the wildlings you can, and cocreate a larger doll and bed that represent an enduring vision for an equitable world. Within this nest have each individual place a brief description of their hope for future generations, for planet Earth and her beloved creatures, and, perhaps, for current forces that might govern these blessed and urgently necessary transformations. Co-cast the circle then, if it is in your group's practice to do so, then raise energy by permitting everyone to free-speak their dream vision for a sustainable world. Depending on how many wild ones are present, this can be an intense event of simultaneous Pagan prayers riding waves of tears and laughter.

One by one, each participant might move to the center of the circle and touch the doll then, supported by the holy words being offered up from the others. When the space holder feels a shift happen, similar to that described in the individual ritual, they will cue the free-speak to wane to whispers and conclude the ritual by having all individuals repeat these words: "So mote it be for us, so mote it be for me, so mote it be for the world. And so it is." Open the circle then, ground the energy, and keep a long-burning candle at the doll's bedside overnight, choosing a participant to be her guard until the spring equinox calls her to the wild.

Season of the Wild Wolf: New Moon

Grandmother Speaks: She Can Smell Your Fear

What solace the hag's house had brought your hungry heart has left you, and the warmth that wrapped your bones only moments ago is cooling and freezing over in familiar ripples, beginning in your joints and spiraling deeper toward your spine. You are an ice sculpture called *Fear*, and the wolf is staring you down with primal and hard-knowing eyes.

"If you listen to what I tell you, you'll not only live through this; you'll be a better Witch for it," the old crone warns, her gruff voice muted by the rush of the northern wind. "If you think you know better, if you try to be that beast's master, she'll sink those fangs into your neck like your flesh is butter, and the last thing you'll know in this life is the warmth of your own blood running down your body and the stench of iron and snow."

You swallow, shifting your weight from side to side in rhythm with your own pulse. Random thoughts rise, swell, and burst like bubbles, a feeble psychic attempt to distract you from the all-consuming terror of this moment — a moment the hag warned you was coming, yet nothing could have prepared you for that visceral, in-the-gut quake that comes only from an instinct, only from that singular root fear of death we all share, no matter the size of our bank accounts or length of our résumés. The patterns of the wolf's fur remind you of the burnt-ended needles from childhood sleepovers when piercing one another's ears was the most rebellious act, but then the sun hits her pearlescent canines just so, and you wonder if her teeth will feel as the needles felt. Something in that creature's readied stance seems akin to a once-beloved and now-gone dog, and you wonder if this beast has ever nuzzled against the hag's skin the way your sorely missed pet used to crawl onto your lap at the fireside.

A snarl rumbles from low in the wolf's throat, and you are brought back to the present, to the looming danger.

"Don't dare move. She can smell your fear, and you've yet to learn to differentiate between instinct and intuition." Out of the corner of your eye, you can see the hag moving with a smooth and feline grace, but you and the wolf are locked in an unbreakable gaze. You are both bound by this primitive battle of wits, and you sense that this creature knows things about you that even you yourself have forgotten.

"Don't look away from her now." The hag moves close to you. "Reach your arm toward me very slowly. Take this bucket of meat, and ready yourself for winter's greatest lesson. I've got a story for you to get you out of your head." She begins, spitting her words.

The Bone-Woman's Brew: A Midwinter Tale

Should we be so lucky in winter, should we soften our hard edges enough to visit them in their isolation and lay a hand-knitted blanket on their laps, we just might meet the tree-loving grandmother. I'd say she was nothing like me, but nothing pains her or me more than the indoor life. So, if you wish to hear her stories — and they are hearty stories indeed — you must bundle her and take her to sit beneath the branches if you are able. She adores alder trees but prefers the willows, most likely, but any long-limbed beauty will do — for, while her words to you may fail, she speaks the language of those heathen trees quite well indeed.

The stories these tree-loving hags tell are short, but they take their time with the telling. They told their first tales to oaks and yews, after all, and tree time is longer than ours. This is a story they might share with you, to a weeping willow left bare at midwinter, and do not be surprised if their poetry incites a swift snowfall, for there is something otherworldly about them, as if they are eternally surrounded by the faeries.

"Do you know the bone-woman?" the tree lover begins.

"No," you'll likely say.

"Ah, well, the bone-woman lives in the Between," she'll clarify. "She is neither alive nor dead, neither a ghost nor flesh and blood. So easily can she stretch her arms long to the sky and root down into the dirt with her feet that she seems a bare-branched birch in winter; only the most curious of Witches can see her for what she truly is."

"What is she?" you might ask the tree-loving crone then, and delighted she will be by that question. For what seems an unnaturally long time for a normal conversation, she will fall silent and stare into your soul. If you have brought her to a willow, she will place her palm on the bark to feel it breathe, and you might think her lost until she gasps, as if the tree has told her to answer you.

"The bone-woman is an ancient," she will answer. "The first woman, some say, the mother of us all. She is part creature, part tree, and all wild, a god before there were gods."

The tree-loving granny will stop then, distracted by the beauty of the dried willow branches swaying in the winter wind.

"Well," you'll break the silence, "what of her? What of this bone-woman?"

The grandmother will sigh, and you'll wonder if she had forgotten the story.

"Oh, the bone-woman!" she'll squeal. "How do you know the bone-woman? So few do."

You'll get frustrated and wonder if your time might be better spent. But, I assure you, there is no other place you should be than right there beneath that willow.

"You just told me about her," you'll say. "She is part creature, part tree, and all wild. She was a god before there were gods."

The grandmother will smile then. "Yes, good. I was just making sure you were paying attention."

The snow will begin falling, and she'll say that many people have sought out the bone-woman. "Many have wandered long to find her, to hear her stories and sip her brew. Some seek her out of pity, some out of intrigue; so few understand that they look for her because they are her. They seek her, that primal and green-blooded part of themselves, in order to become whole, at long last."

You'll wonder precisely what she means, but you won't ask, and the flakes will start to gather in her gray curls.

"The bone-woman's brew," she'll continue, "is born of sheer mystery and deep belonging. She remembers what so many have forgotten, that kinship with nature is not the medicine but the truth. Her brew is simply words spoken at just the right time, in just the right way, and then she is gone, leaving the one who sought her out quite changed indeed, though that change is best left unnamed."

You'll be entranced by her, caught up in the rhythm of her voice, and you'll scarcely notice that her skin is toughening into bark, that her lips are pulling back ever so slightly from her teeth, and that her hair has taken on a greenish tone beneath the layer of ice and snow.

"That bone-woman will make you remember your most primal ancestors," she will say. "Not those prayerful grandmothers but the ones who came long before, who remembered what it meant to belong to a land, who had stolen nothing and had nothing stolen from them, whose bodies wanted the same ground that wanted them."

You'll sit near her now, transfixed, and she will stretch her arms long toward the slow-dancing willow branches. Her legs will begin to fuse together, and her feet will sink deeper into the earth.

"That bone-woman is muse, you see. She is not one soul but billions of souls come home to rest, to nest."

Her lips will stop moving then, and her eyes will turn to mere knots on bark. The fabric of her clothes will sink into the wood, and her arms will stretch longer and longer still.

Somehow you'll still hear her, and she'll say, "So, I ask you now, do you know the bone-woman?"

"Yes," you'll whisper, staring up at the tree-loving granny turned to willow. "Yes, I know her well."

Sitting then you'll be, beneath not one tree but two, with soft flakes falling all around you, perfectly positioned in this, our most beloved world.

❧

You can feel the heat of the wolf's breath now, and the Mountain Hag is humming a low song. The story has calmed your nerves, and there is nothing left to do but feed the wolf.

Opening Practice: Welcoming Sovereignty Home

At midwinter, the season of sovereignty begins. This is a time of early manifestation, of moving *toward* but not *at*. As this new moon dawns, we must begin to know the difference between our intuition, that inborn gift that attunes us to the intimate body-to-cosmos connection we all share, and instinct, a necessary but far more fear-based sensation that demands we save ourselves. The hag archetype governs intuition and early winter, while the maiden archetype rules instinct and late winter. Both serve us well, and those early stages of true manifestation magick are fed by intuition and instinct in equal parts.

Beneath the new moon, welcome sovereignty home by adding two objects to your altar; one will represent intuition, or, if you like, the Goddess of Prophecy; and one will represent instinct, or the Goddess of Sovereignty. Whatever sacred relics you choose, one will remind you of your omniscience, of your kinship with the Mystery, and of your ability to see in the dark; the other will remind you of your primal power, of your relationship to nature, and of your ability to move as the wolf moves, with power and purpose. One reminds you to listen, and the other reminds you to act.

As the Season of the Wild Wolf dawns, hold your object that represents the Goddess of Prophecy in your left hand and the Goddess of Sovereignty object in your right; then speak these words aloud with much righteous resignation:

I welcome my sovereignty home on this holy winter's night, for I am a wild creature, to be sure. I am still healing. I am sovereign. I am still healing. I am sovereign. My fear might well be a gift as I move into this new year, as I shatter old patterns and cast out the hungriest and most vampiric ghosts. May my hag ways serve me well, so that I might know the difference between deep knowledge and a fear of pain. Grant me the clearest sight I've ever had, for I see as the wolf sees, for I know what the wolf knows. I am both prophecy and sovereignty embodied in soft creaturely skin, and I am a cunning Witch, indeed.

Waxing Moon Practice: Choices Made, Choices Owned

As that bright moon waxes toward fullness, spend some mornings taking stock of your life's choices; mind you, these are not the turning points in your story that feel as though they were scripted by someone else's hand. These are moments when, in retrospect, a single choice could have set you on another path entirely. In your Book of Moon and Flame, you might structure this page accordingly:

Title: *Intuition and Instinct*
Relationships (briefly describe at least one "choice" but as many
    as you like relative to relationships, be they romantic, familial,
    platonic, or otherwise)
Sacred Work
Health/Body/Food
Sexuality
Movement/Location
Communication/Conversation
Art Making
Learning/Psychic Development
Beliefs/Spiritual Practice

Go back through the moments you listed, and reflect on them according to both intuition and instinct. For each moment, you might freely and
briefly respond to the following two prompts:

> *If I made this choice out of fear, then it was because...*
> *If this choice was born of intuition, then I had known...*

Remember that all reflection is simply a mirror of who you are in that
moment you are doing the reflecting, rather than a finite cage in which
to place all your experiences, and ponder the roles played by fear and
intuition in your personal story. Importantly, many of these choices were
likely made from a combination of forces far beyond simply intuition and
instinct, but do not let this understanding stop you from beginning the
weighted work of feeling the difference between the two under your skin.

Before the full moon dawns, go back through your inventory and
see if you can pinpoint any choices that were made around this time of
year — this pivotal inception of sovereignty season — and, if so, whether
there are any patterns in these midwinter decisions that seem to hold potent lessons for you now, as you begin your wildest year yet.

Season of the Wild Wolf: Full Moon

Grandmother Speaks: For the Gods' Sakes, Be Bold about It

The meat smells fresh, and the wolf's face softens infinitesimally. She moves her eyes from you to the bucket you are holding, then looks to the hag. You are suddenly sovereign in this moment, and the chill threaded through your joints thaws just a bit. You can see a way out now; if you had to, you could throw the bucket of meat down and make a run for it. You'd be well into the woods before the wolf had finished her meal, and her full belly would no doubt keep her from wanting your fatty flesh. If you ran, though, if you played the coward, could you go on without reliving this moment over and over again, wondering if you'd made the right choice?

"This is it, child." The hag's voice interrupts your mental battle. "Now, feed her. Breathe; move slow; and, for the gods' sakes, be bold about it."

Releasing a breath you didn't realize you were holding, you dig out some wet and bloody strips from the bucket. The wolf licks around her whiskers and sits heavy in the snow. In that moment, you and she are one. Her hunger is your hunger, and there is a mutually honored bond between you two. You will feed her, and she will let you live.

Full Moon Practice: The Bravest Gardener

Materials: Seeds, soil, a vessel, water

This winter moon of challenge often has a manic sort of energy to it, as we sense the seeds stirring beneath the ground and the quickening of nature as spring approaches. Art is medicine now, a means of channeling the high-fire creative energy into something tangible, a small way of proving to ourselves that our actions have an impact. For this ritual, we shall let our art be made of soil, seed, and water.

Choose any seeds and vessel you like, then create sacred space. From the waxing moon practice, select a single decision you made that, perhaps, feels as though there is some unease attached to it; this might stem from a lack of closure or another uncertainty as to why this choice was yours in the first place. Perhaps this was a choice made at midwinter, one you feel is somehow linked by a silver thread to this very moment in time, no matter how many linear years have passed.

Begin the work now of planting the seeds — but, as you do, recall the moment that pivotal choice was made. Feel it in your body and notice whether it seems to be gut based and therefore sourced straight from instinctual fear or, alternatively, rooted under the skin at the heart or higher, in which case the choice may have been born of calculations, love, or intuition. As you plant these seeds, you are acknowledging this choice that was made, owning it fully not just as yours but as critical nourishment for the present. You, right now, are working this magick as the sovereign Witch you are because this decision was made, because you are able to reorder, to *re-member* the past, to accurately reflect on and own the choices you have made. When ready, repeat these words while watering your newly buried seed babes in a clockwise, spiral motion:

> *Fullest moon of sprouting seed*
> *Illuminate my choice and deed*
> *I've laid it down, the worst, the best*
> *Now, I'm ready for the rest*

Opening the circle if you cast such a boundary, ground the energy by placing your hands on the floor in front of you, then set your potted seeds on your altar until the dark moon comes. And so it is.

Season of the Wild Wolf: Waning Moon

Grandmother Speaks: You Did Good, Witch

The snow between you and the wolf has been stained with much blood, but thankfully you remain whole. The wolf finishes the final scraps, and the hag steps close to your side, so close you can smell the scent of pine smoke wafting from her hair. The wind has calmed, and your heart is swollen with a sense of accomplishment and pride.

"You did good, Witch," the old crone grumbles. "Let's leave her be now. She'll be wanting a nap, and we've got our own supper to think about."

The wolf licks the last bit of flesh from the frozen ground and grants you a soft-eyed glance, blinking once and turning her back to you. Strangely, as much as that beast rattled you, you are sad to see her go; such is the way of winter.

Waning Moon Practice: Such Is the Way of Winter

Winter's middle moon wanes quickly, and we're left with subtly longer days and a quiet longing in our hearts. After the full moon, begin a daily practice of seeing your actions having an impact on your world; these can, importantly, be small and mundane results of a direct act, such as washing a dish until it's clean, feeding a pet, or scribbling a drawing on a piece of paper. In these days of screen validation, when many of us rely on "likes" or "followers" to assess the impact we are having on our worlds, we must strategically simplify our understanding of action and impact, lest our will and our agency be too constrained by the realities of our technology.

Late winter can indeed dampen our will, and we must continue to tend that inner altar well. On those days when a sense of apathy or weakness threatens to overcome your senses, these words are yours:

> *I have the fire of the ancients surging through my veins,*
> *and I am a living ode to my ancestors' strength.*

Season of the Wild Wolf: Dark Moon

Grandmother Speaks: It's a Wonder

Indeed, she is pleased with you, that Mountain Hag, and she brings you a strong-smelling brew as you sit hunched beneath heavy blankets at her fireside. You nod in gratitude, sipping the bitter cedar tea sweetened by a flavor unknown to you, and a serenity overcomes your weary spirit. You are so much at peace, so abuzz with an ancestral understanding of all that is, you scarcely notice when the hag opens her door.

A cold nose on your cheek shocks you back into your body, and you are eye to eye with the wolf. A dull squeezing low in your belly threatens fear, but you tame it quickly. She, that great beast, seems more sloth than wolf now, rocking her body onto the floor next to you, laying her immense head on your lap, and drifting off to sleep. The wolf's snores and the crackle of the fire are the most welcome winter hymn you've ever heard, and the hag busies herself in the kitchen behind you.

"It's a wonder, isn't it?" The hag speaks after a long moment. "How there's victory in every action? Small challenges overcome every day, tiny battles fought on the road and in mere conversation. We throw our own glorious marches then, our own coming-home galas, our own heroine's holiday balls. It's not the fight we're after, you see. It's that after-battle joy that comes only from making it through some great thing that might have broken you. Therein lies some good medicine, the sweetest reward, the proof that we are alive and breathing in this great collective."

Dark Moon Practice: Naming the Fears

As winter's moon of challenge wanes to darkness, ask yourself to recall the dream vision from the Imbolc ritual. What lies beneath the doll? Go out under the dark moon and name any fears that emerge when you consider that vision, gifting them to the darkness, to the cold, letting the late winter hold these trepidations for you so you might move forward with greater ease. Whisper them in the softest voice so as not to give them more power than they deserve — and, when finished, simply grant a nod to the moon for listening. And so it is.

To the Season of the Wild Wolf, Farewell for Now

Until we meet again, you beast. I'll not say it's been grand, but I will say you are my wisest teacher. When you first set your hungry eyes on me, I was deep winter. I was icicle blades and spiderwebbed frost on windowpanes. Now, into the light I go, with chin lifted and blood far warmer than when we first met on those days of the short-lived sun. Tell that Mountain Hag I'm ready, for surely I've recovered that long-lost crown of mine. Surely the final snows are upon us, and all shall be revealed in good time. All blessings be.

CHAPTER 13

Season of the Cauldron Keeper

---❦---

Quickening

Breathe it in, Witch. The integration begins now, beneath this last winter moon. It is that sacred moment known to all the kitchen-witching grandmothers when the long-simmering spices begin to meld in such a way, when the scent of the work, the promise of completion, first graces our senses. This is a moon of wisdom, when we make good use of the lessons learned at midwinter and bravely step out of the darkness and toward the next stage in our yearly becoming. We become the cauldron keeper now, having learned all the Mountain Hag had to teach us, and open ourselves fully to what spring may hold.

Whatever challenges we faced at Imbolc, whatever wolves waited for us outside our doors, we find ourselves here more fully alive, our bodies abuzz with possibility, our holy hands busy with the weighted work of art making and ancestral healing.

This is a cunning maiden's moon, kept well by those altar-tending wildlings who did not pretend to know it all during winter, who sat patiently listening to the hag's tales while the snow fell. These wily ones are ready to be unleashed now, to return to the world with discernment and wildfire packed in their bags.

Hag Lesson #23

Birth is inevitable.

If you listen, you can surely hear them coming, their drums a harbinger of rising, sun-hungry sprouts and yellow blooms.

One Poem at a Time
Prophecies of the Cunning Maiden

———•——— ——•◄•►•—— ———•———

She was a student of mysteries and wildcraft, that one, and I remember her prophecies well. Her manner was quiet, but she had this way about her, this way of saying the harshest things in the gentlest singsong voice. Perhaps an unseelie Fae haunted her blood, or perhaps she had simply learned at a young age what it takes most of us lifetimes to understand: that the elder's truth is better than the knight's ambition. It's her kind that will heal the world, I think, for these are not times for sugarcoated small talk and half-hearted performative activism.

That cunning maiden taught even me, cranky and embittered Witch that I am, that often the best and bravest act is to shrug and sit down, that I am healing my mother lines just by breathing, that my glorious babes must be taught the sins of their great-grandfathers and taught them well. In my dreams, I am just like her, a swift-moving truth teller who changes the world one poem at a time, but then I wake with the same arrogant ghosts hissing in my ears. Even so, I'm a better woman for having met her — and, in those moments when old patterns threaten to grip my shoulders and take me down, I remember what she said about this wounded world: that to be rich is to have a moment to make art for art's sake, and that all else is frivolity. I hope to meet her again someday, that cunning maiden, and we shall sip earthen nettle tea, smoke mugwort, and speak of simpler times.

———•◄•►•———

Midnight Reflection: The Muse of Our Own Becoming

To manifest is to remember the yet-to-come, to make real what we know in our bones is already coming but not yet arrived. We rise to be muse of our own becoming as this last winter moon dawns, spreading wider wings and being so beauteous now that we have no choice but to become the majestic creatures of our dream visions. We reflect now on the missing pieces, on the blank spots, and on the persistent unknowns. In *The Witch of Portobello* by Paulo Coelho, the main character, Athena, seeks to master calligraphy from an elder, who tells her, "although you have mastered the words, you haven't yet mastered the blank spaces." This is a moon for tending the darkness and the Mystery.

Consider the dream vision from Imbolc, from that midwinter season of quickening and wonder. Begin to flesh it out with a bit of word-witchery. Who is this wild-hearted one who stands beneath the first spring moon? How do they hold themselves, and what do they know that you do not? Write them real now, as the oil lamp burns low, as the final frosts struggle to form on those fragile young buds. You may use the prompts I offer here or, as always, create your own.

> *They are more alive than they've ever been, that one, and they are beginning to...*
> *If they trust anything, they trust...*
> *If they could teach me one secret, I'd ask them for...*
> *I am their muse, you know, and they'd be nothing without my...*
> *I can tell they remember me, and I want them to know...*

Be muse to your own becoming now, as that new moon rises and winter comes to a close, as the Cailleach hardens into a crag by the sea, and be full of faith that your garden is blooming just as it should.

Season of the Cauldron Keeper: New Moon

Grandmother Speaks: A Secret Good Enough

You wake to the rhythmic song of wolf snores and the intermittent scraping sound of wood on iron. The hag is stirring her cauldron, and you recall your vivid dreams of tall-stretching wildflowers, drums, and dancing. Even here, amid the comforts of a firelit mountain home where the darkness promises a security the light never could, the spring is bidding you leave your sanctuary.

"Those warmer days are calling you, aren't they, you heathen?" The hag speaks without looking up from her pot. "Feel no guilt. The wisest Witch among us cannot resist the lure of the long afternoon, the joy of shedding our furs like snakeskin and chanting sunward those songs of love and lust. A time comes when we've no choice but to snuff our fires and leave our proper altars, to show the world our winter-weary face and come down from the mountain a softer version of that lonely hunter we were when the snows fell."

Your throat makes a knowing sound, a grumble of agreement that was a sort of hag noise you might not have been able to muster before this moment.

"Well, stand up. Leave your dreams there on the floor for now, and come close." The hag stops her stirring and waits. "You'll leave this mountain soon, but first you must tell me what you've learned. I want to know what you know, as the Witching Hour approaches, and I want to hear a secret good enough that it will keep me warm once you've gone. Before you share your wisdom with me, I have one last story for you to hold in your heart. Call it up to warm your bones on your long journey east."

The Moon Child and the Holy Wild Hag:
A Ceremonial Late-Winter Tale

To move through this ceremonial tale, gather these materials: candle, burn bowl with dried juniper, bowl of ash, small container of water, and a small vessel filled with mud or dirt. Create an altar with the lit candle at circle center, the burn bowl with dried juniper in the east, ash in the south, water in the west, and dirt in the north. Read aloud then, your voice ringing loud and true in all directions.

On the coldest nights when even the ghosts fear the winds, should you be brave enough to venture outside the warmth of your firelit nest, you just might meet one of the most majestic, queenly hags, though she will certainly wear no crown. You will know her from her blue-tinged skin, from her red teeth, and from the long willow staff she carries. This hag is a loner, to be sure, and she tells the sorts of tales that leave parts of you dead and parts of you more alive for having heard her words. She is the Yaga and the Cailleach, the elder of the wild.

First, the Cailleach would certainly begin with an invocation:

Moon of Hawk, Moon of Crone
Strip my flesh down to the bone
Wake me wild, wake me true
Cast your spells like Witches do

And then she would tell you a deliciously wicked tale of prophecy fulfilled and sovereignty regained:

Once upon a bitter moon, 'neath swelling veils and late-winter storms, there lived the wildest of moon children. Deep in a forest she was, trapped in a house haunted by dreams unmet and magick lost. She, this wistful maiden, was much like we all used to be, knowing of herself only what others told her, so she believed she was too sour and too sweet, too thin and too fat, too loud and too quiet, too this and too that.

The ancient wood she lived in was one of those holy places that had its own heartbeat, where you walked on the land and could hear the bones of the earth rattle beneath your feet, where you could feel the underground rivers run like lifeblood through the veins of the earthen Mother-Witch. This was a land of prophecy, where the old grandmothers would speak of a hag even older than they were who lived deep in a forest haunted by both cold-gutted monsters and the healer-women they burned. This hag was no savior, no initiated High Priestess or revered royal of high birth. Even so, this hag was the wisest among us — an immortal, perhaps, or more likely, the flesh-covered unbeauteous spirit of the oldest of ways. She kept all her knowledge of the mysteries and the dark inside a flaming skull she carried with her all the time, the grandmothers would say, and she could never be found, because her house was always moving about by itself, standing on two chicken legs and, if the need arose, sprouting wings and taking to the sky.

The prophecy said that one day, an apparently ordinary creature would seek out that hag and demand her secrets. One day, those old grandmothers would hiss to their bleary-eyed grandbabes, an uncertain creature would walk straight out of the mundane and into the magick, the hag would swallow her whole, and the Dark Goddess would rise from her depths to crush those crumbling institutions of corruption once and for all, hissing hellfire and free-bleeding on the government steps.

Every child in this land had heard this story, most often told as a warning to not venture into those woods too far, lest the skull of the hag be the last thing you see. Every child had heard this story, but only that wild moon child chose to ignore it.

A good story wants a rebel.

Why, nearly every day that wild one would be in those woods, gathering rowanberries, acorns, and juniper branches. As we all do, she had set rules for herself that she thought might keep her safe. She would never venture too far from her home, you see, and she would never, ever stay in the woods past dark.

Though she wished very much for a sacred solitude she had never known, this wild moon child lived among three lonely hearts. We might call them a wicked stepmother and two wicked stepsisters, but we know better. Women of the modern world, these were. Women made of polished and pristine puzzle pieces placed together just so, raised to quash their lust for the primal wild 'neath rigid straps and etiquette.

Indeed, they were hungry. Nay, they were starving.
To see these three lonely hearts at midnight was to see
their true forms, teary-eyed embodiments of longing for
all things wild and mystical. They were told that to be
wild was to be sinful, and they believed it. They were
told that to be a Witch was to be burned at the stake,
and they believed it. Years of these lies had turned these
three, the thin-waisted matriarch and her two manipula-
tive and doe-eyed spawn, into something far worse than
"wicked."

They had become...boring.

But this story is not about them, though they play a
very important part in the beginning. Don't we all know
these lonely hearts, though? Don't we all know these
sullen creatures who long ago covered over their deep
wells of passion and purpose? Who put the lid on their
blessed cauldrons of bubbling ancestral inheritance and
soul-feeding ways?

Sometimes, we must remember to not speak the language of rebellious blooming to those afraid-to-sprout
seed people.

We know this — but, alas, that wild moon child did
not.

Day in and day out, the wild child spouted all she
knew about the way the stars moved and how the night
birds spoke to her in dreams. She'd go on and on about
green leafy medicines and the whispers of the beloved
dead. On the better days, the lonely hearts would pretend to listen, only waiting for their own turn to speak
about the waking nightmare that was their small-minded
beliefs. On the worst days, the lonely hearts would be
so fed up with the moon child that they would conspire
to send her away, insulting her over soup and wine, letting their dining table become a sad and feeble war room
where they planned their feckless battles by firelight.

"She doesn't belong here," one would begin.

"She certainly doesn't," another would follow.

"Ugh, her nonsense. I just can't take it anymore," the oldest of the lonely hearts would say.

"I don't know how we could ever send her away."

"Yes, she never listens to us."

The three lonely hearts bickered among themselves about the best way to be rid of the moon child once and for all, yawning and nearly boring themselves to death with their lack of imagination.

"We could dare her," the youngest lonely heart said just before nodding off into her soup.

Now, on all the many nights when the three sad ones had done precisely this, no one had ever said that before.

"That's a good idea," affirmed the other two. "Yes, she can't resist a dare."

Now, the next part of the story is unclear, and the grandmothers never agree on precisely how this next bit happened. Some say that the three lonely hearts did, in fact, dare the moon child to go into the woods at midnight and stay until dawn, but if you want to know what I think, it's this:

The wild moon child was onto them. She'd been listening the whole time, led to the dark corner of the room by the spirit of the hag herself, hearing what trite machinations her family was planning, muttering to herself, "Fuck this," packing only the bones of who she used to be in her bag, and heading for the woods all on her own, just before the Witching Hour.

Now, the grandmothers who tell this tale agree on one thing: As soon as the moon child left, what little bit of wildness had lived in that house left with her. That fainthearted pulse that had kept the place breathing, that had kept the lonely hearts half-fed by sucking some of the passion right out of the moon child while she slept, died. Without their source of wild nourishment, those three lonely hearts quickly dried out, turning to heaps of dust and leaving no ghosts behind.

The wild moon child wandered through that forest, tales of zombies and demons and ghouls — oh my! — echoing in her ears. Even so, she never considered going back, not even when a raven swooped down and landed in her path, not even when that black bird snorted and coughed with a smoker voice, not even when it said out loud in the gruffest of tones, "You best go home, child. This place changes people."

By 3 AM, the devil's hour, the wild moon child had gone farther than she'd ever gone by day, and by 6 AM, the maiden's hour, she had forgotten what names had been given to her.

Walking within the warmth of mystery and grace now, that wild one saw something: a fire, she thought. The sun had yet to rise, and the morning birds had yet to sing. The comfort in knowing that orange glow was imminent on the eastern horizon made the moon child bolder than she might have been otherwise, and she walked straight toward that crackling, humble fire.

As she got closer, she could see a shadow there. Closer still, and that shadow stood to be an immense and be-muscled horned hunter. Even closer, and the moon child could feel something stirring in her heart, in her belly, then below. Even closer, and the moon child wondered if she'd been searching for some undefinable thing, some particular source of nourishment she'd never known, not really.

"I want you," the moon child said.

"I want you," the hunter replied.

And that was the end of that.

There was something about the way the sun rose through the trees while the wild one rode that hunter straight into oblivion that felt like a sacred and holy rite, and the ghosts of burned women began clawing their way up from the ground, hearing that primal call of wild feminine climax that is unmistakable, covered in mud and licking every tree along the way, chanting to themselves as they made their way to surround the moon child and bless that great rite:

Blessed be these heathen trees
Branches birthing infant leaves
Roots wrap bones so no one sees
On winter mornings just like these

Chant these words while setting the dried juniper alight, bathing yourself in the smoke and awakening the sensual wildness within.

And surround the two they did, lighting pipes off the hunter's fire, dancing with their own madness, and singing, "I'm a wild, wild heathen child!"

When the rite was over, the moon child went to each and every one of those maidens to be blessed by their smoke, then left the sleeping and satiated hunter there by the still-smoldering coals.

The morning sun had risen; the heathen women had returned to the soil, or so the moon child thought; and she had reclaimed a certain autonomous lustfulness, a certain sexual power she didn't know could belong to her, and while she was nourished in one way, she was still empty in others.

Her belly snarled like a wolf in winter, and she couldn't recall the last time she'd eaten.

She hadn't thought of asking the hunter — what was his name again? — for meat.

She tried to let the sound of the autumn wind through the trees be sustenance enough, as it sometimes was, but she was past the point of spiritual nourishment being adequate.

She needed food.

There's a particular ache to that wilder hunger, is there not? That bone-deep desire to be fed by something more than what we're told is good.

She licked some dripping sap from a maple tree, drank from a clear-running stream beside an eight-pointed stag, and nibbled like a fluff bunny on some wilting cabbage. None of it fed her in the way she needed to be fed.

Just after the sun had started to visibly sink below the treetops, just when the moon child was sure she was going to have to return to the places where she knew she could forage, where she knew for sure the berries were safe and the mushrooms wouldn't send her mind to the rainbow realms — just then — she smelled it.

Oh, it was the way the summerlands smelled, she was sure. It was the scent of stringy, salty flesh, of hearty dripping juices and fat. Wafting through the air so pungent, so perfect, this beautiful and blessed reek of a sacred kill, she was sure, and the wild one let her nose lead the way.

Dusk had fallen, and her guts were grinding against themselves. The scent of the majestic forbidden pulled her forward, even so, and then she heard them.

First came cackles. Then came drunken song and dark poetry:

We've laid to rest, the worst, the best
Suck the milk from our breasts
Come to die upon our nests

Chant these words now while painting your face with ash and awakening your wild art, your cunning and worldly inner bard.

She saw them then, these wild mothers. Covered in ashes and blood, they were, sitting around a cook fire and tearing flesh from bone. Were these the ghosts of the burned women, the heathen maidens who blew smoke in her face and blessed her with their ecstatic dance? She couldn't be sure, for they had aged.

Had she not been so hungry, she might not have been so bold, but ravenous, she was.

She stepped right up to their circle and demanded, "Who are you?"

The wild mothers weren't bothered, scarcely looking up from their meal.

"Who are you?" the wild one asked again.

Only one of the mothers looked up from her plate of bones and met her eyes.

"That's the wrong question," the mother said, and the others made sounds of bemusement.

"Okay," said the wild child, drool dripping from her lips now. "What's the right question, then?"

Every one of the mothers stopped chewing and turned to look at her then, but it was the one with the bloodiest face who spoke: "Do not ask us who we are. Ask us who we are not."

"Yes," hissed the other mothers.

"Okay," she acceded. "Who are you not?"

The mothers smiled now, their teeth stained red, and they rose from where they sat, beginning to dance in pairs as if it were a dark, underworld ballroom. They giggled, twirling about like demon debutantes.

"Well, we're certainly not sweet," said one of the mothers.

"And we're not civilized," her dance partner added.

"We're not quiet and mannerly."

"We're not demure."

"We're not perfect.".

They started chanting in unison then, scarcely hearing the moon child when she demanded food.

"I need to eat!" she cried. "May I please have some of your precious meat?"

Some of the mothers kept chanting, while others mocked the moon child.

"May I pleeease?" they squeaked and laughed.

"You don't want what we're eating!" shouted one of the wild ones over the chaos. "Trust me."

"I do," the moon child countered. "I'll do anything for it, in fact."

"I don't think you understand. This is no fresh meat from a bear or a deer. This is the flesh of who we once were, little one."

"We're eating our old selves like a meal!" two of the mothers shouted.

The moon child paused, wavering but hungry enough that she was nearly unbothered by the gruesome words of the wild mothers.

"Do you still wish to eat?" two of the mothers spoke together, ceasing to dance and bringing a bowl of red and running meat to the moon child.

It smelled so luscious, like it would satisfy every craving she had ever had with just one bite, and the moon child snatched it from them.

While she ate, the mothers chanted around her, painting her face with ash and welcoming her home to her own magick and ferocious nature. The moon child not only emptied the bowl she was offered but devoured every piece of meat, licking every plate clean.

"We are mothers, like no others," they said.

Full and fed, the moon child fell into a deep sleep now. When she woke, she could tell from the sound of the raptors that it was a few hours from midnight.

The mothers had left, or so she thought, and the fire had gone dark and cold. The moon child shivered, standing and heading westward, moving in the direction of mystery, muse, and death. She had reclaimed her lustfulness and her ferocity. Now, covered in ash and blood, she longed only for the warmth that could come from a certainty she had never known.

Never before had she trusted her own intuition. Never before had she moved with that sure-footed grace that those grandmothers with low-hanging breasts used to speak of. And yet, now she found herself on the edge of midnight, deep in an unmapped and haunted woodland, all without fear.

Never before had she been so in touch with the truth of who she was and who she might become.

She heard them before she saw them then, the hooded crones. They were hissing like snakes and howling like wolves, moving in slow, smooth, and lithe movements like felines. Were these the wild mothers from before? She couldn't be sure, for they had indeed aged.

Their faces were more skull than flesh, and their lips had begun pulling back from the teeth as if death had taken them. Some of these slow-moving crones carried dolls with them, fearsome handmade things with wide eyes and a poppet's nature.

The wild child knew she should be afraid. She should be, yet she was not. These crones seemed to know something she didn't, you see, and she longed to be wise the way they were wise.

She swallowed, stepped toward them, and asked in the most robust voice she'd ever mustered: "Who are you not?"

The crones stopped dead and stared at her. The oldest among them, a mere skeleton, really, stepped forward, doll in hand. "Who taught you to ask that question?"

"The wild mothers," the moon child answered truthfully.

"Ahhh." The crones nodded. "Yes."

"That is the right question," a short and spectral shadow crone affirmed. "We're not religious zealots."

"We're not shortsighted."

"We're not small-minded."

The crones fell into a chant then, just as the mothers had, but the wild moon child interrupted them with some Pagan poetry of her own.

Crone of wolves, crone of crow
Tell me what those old gods know
I shall learn your wildest spell
And I will sing your chants so well

Pour or drip some water atop the crown of your head now, chanting these words and granting your wild flesh a new name.

The crones smiled then, cackling like banshees, and moving again, continuing their journey and bidding the moon child join them. It seemed only moments they walked together, arriving at a moss-covered well just before midnight. They chanted while the oldest among them raised the bucket filled with the holy water, and, one by one, they blessed the moon child, bidding her look in the well to receive her message:

A wild, heathen crone am I
Scry your future in my eye

In the well, she did not see a white picket fence or a prince. No, she saw her own face, aged to perfection, and she saw all of time spiral-dancing. She saw the cosmic whirl of alien worlds, and she saw her own self reborn as a humble elder. She drank her fill of the water then, suddenly awake in a way she had never been before, and one of the crones handed her a tattered doll.

The stitching was pulling apart at the seams, and one of the eyes had fallen off — and yet, this doll had a magick about it that could not be dismissed. Another crone stripped herself bare, wrapping her cloak around the moon child and raising the hood.

"Listen to the doll," the crones hissed together. "She knows the way."

With that, the crones sank back into the shadows, leaving the moon child wild-eyed with hood raised at midnight, covered in ash, blood, and well water, clutching her precious poppet. She recalled the raven's words then. Yes, this place changed people indeed.

Now, the grandmothers disagree on this part of the story as well: Did the doll tell the moon child how to get to the hag's house, or did the moon child simply know? We cannot be sure, and that's how intuition works, after all, is it not? Do we receive these messages from the ethers, or do we simply know, omniscient creatures that we are?

In any case, the moon child did walk, straight as the crow flies, from the crones' well to the hag's house. It did stand on chicken legs, as the prophecy had said, but it certainly seemed anchored in place. Perhaps only the most magickal creatures can see it, so not many do. It was long past midnight now but not yet dawn, that time of night when the ghosts walk heavier than people do, and the moon child could see smoke rising from the chimney quite ceremoniously. There were fat handmade candles glowing in the windows and blood on the door; it was as if the hag was expecting her.

The moon child knocked timidly with the ominous bone-and-metal knocker. No answer.

She knocked again. Still nothing.

Finally, the moon child beat her fist on the door and demanded, "Let me in!"

The door squeaked open by itself.

The hag's house smelled of burning cedar and some

unknown bitter brew, a certain warmth hitting the moon child in just the right places.

The hag wasn't hiding, either. She was right there, stirring her cauldron at the hearth. Cheeks tattooed with sacred symbols and black-mirror eyes wide as could be, she had an ancient and ancestral wisdom about her that nearly glowed, and the moon child was not afraid.

"Who are you not?" asked the moon child.

The hag made a low and knowing sound.

"Ah, that is the right question, you wise one." The hag kept stirring and motioned for her to come closer.

The moon child did just that, peering curiously into the cauldron and thinking that the mothers' meal had prepared her for whatever gruesome feast might be inside that black iron pot.

She was wrong.

Just as she leaned in, a flame-eyed skull bobbed to the surface of the brew, spitting hot stuff at her and startling the moon child so much she fell back onto the floor. The hag sniffed and sang softly:

The Yaga, the Witch, the wild hag
She'll feed you guts and make you gag
She'll tell you tales that make you old
And you'll forget all you've been told.

Repeat these words now while you bless your feet with dirt from hallowed ground, knowing yourself as the wise one, feeling into this moment as it is, perfectly positioned within your epic story of becoming.

Now, we're not sure how long it took for the moon child to muster the courage to stand and return to the pot. Some of the grandmothers say it was only moments; others say it was ten years or more that she lay there on the hag's floor fearing the skull, fearing the forbidden knowledge she might gain if she looked into those black-hole eyes again.

We cannot know, but the prophecy says that stand again she did. What moved inside her that sparked her will? Was there some mystical convergence of her stars that aligned in just the right way, or was it simpler than that? Maybe she was just ready. Maybe it was her time. Some say it happened only when the hag wished it to happen, and others say only the moon child could decide when her initiation should be complete.

All we know is that at some point beneath a late-winter sky, perhaps this very time of year when the vernal equinox looms like an old salty grandmother, the moon child did stand, march straight to the pot, snatch up the skull with both hands, hold it high, and nod just once. And then, this moon child, this wild one who had journeyed so far, found herself alone here in the house of the hag, alone with all the wisdom of the blood mysteries, at one with the cycle of death-birth-death, and, indeed, she had become the hag.

The grandmothers say she's still there, stirring her pot and beckoning the Dark Goddess to rise, praying to the weepiest willow trees, and chanting to the descended mistresses to wake the sleeping ones:

A Holy Wild hag am I
We die to live and live to die

Our story ends here, just as it began, on a darkened moon when all possibilities writhe and wriggle in the womb of the world, with the Cailleach hissing an incantation in your ear.

Moon of Hawk, Moon of Crone
Strip my flesh down to the bone

Wake me wild, wake me true
Cast your spells as Witches do

»)(«

The Mountain Hag spits out the last words, settling into her chair with eyes closed, drunk on her own words, and waiting for your wisdom.

Opening Practice: Becoming the Crone-Weaver

As the Season of the Cauldron Keeper dawns, that last moon of winter buzzes with infinite promise and possibility. If it feels right, remove the object that symbolized the Goddess of Prophecy from your altar, leaving your winter practice space marked by the Goddess of Sovereignty and those bony remnants of your wild wintry ways. The vernal equinox is a balance point of darkness and light, a holy cosmic vow straight from the stars to our flesh that we cannot have hope without fear, joy without grief, or life without death.

Become the crone-weaver now, the knowing one who deftly braids the light with the dark to reveal glorious stories of ecstasy and agony, love and loss. In *The Spell of the Sensuous*, David Abram describes his experience watching a spider weave a web: "I sat stunned and mesmerized before this ever-complexifying expanse of living patterns upon patterns, my gaze drawn like a breath into one converging group of lines, then breathed out into open space, then drawn down into another convergence....My senses were entranced. I had the distinct impression that I was watching the universe being born, galaxy upon galaxy...." Our magick is energetic web weaving, no more and no less.

Birth the universe into being now. Weave a web. Face northeast, that midpoint between the direction of winter and spring, and call up some spontaneous truth that wants to spill from between your lips. Speak story now. Let it be a tale from your lived experience that reeks with rust and rot as much as it emanates fresh spice. These are the stories we need, after all, those that honor the fallows and the fruition, the nadir and the apex. Gift your story to the northeast, encircled by your foremothers and not worrying about the linear order of events, eloquence, or having the proper storyteller's inflection.

Share the story that wants to be told in this moment, beneath this new moon, and release it to the wilds like the sovereign sorcerer you are. So mote it be.

Waxing Moon Practice: Beginning Again

If deep winter is a time of rest and reflection, when our magick turns toward the early stages of manifestation sourced from our prophecies, from our wolf-mother's intuition, and from our wild divination, those late-winter weeks before spring dawns call our magick closer to healing. We become the elder Witches we needed when we were younger, yes, but we also acknowledge that we are healing severed mother lines, brewing salve for the wounds of our forebears, simply by continuing to move forward on our healing journey. All our magick is stronger when we draw from our ancestral legacies, and there is much merit in acknowledging our familial wounds as well as the wounds of the collective as part of this incarnation's particular inheritance.

Drawing from the work you have done so far this season, spend some time under this waxing moon pondering what particular theme in your family's story you are being called to heal, honor, or transmute. If you are not familiar with your specific blood ancestry, ask yourself what wounds within the collective you are being called to work with now. Begin with your prophecies from Yule, your dream vision from Imbolc, your visceral and sensory understanding of what you are calling in for yourself, and your story spoken beneath the new moon, then reflect on any persistent aches that might be serving as blockages to moving forward.

Importantly, these aches, these wounds that still bleed, are obstacles only if we fail to compost them, to integrate them into lived-out-loud experience. And just as salient to our healing is the deep and continued knowing that we can frame the wound as ours, however temporarily so, without dismissing any wrongs done or condoning any abuses committed against us or our kin.

Bring your Imbolc doll out of her nest now, and let her be a poppet for your healing magick. Imagine that she represents the wounded ones, the hunted Witch, the great-grandmother who left her body with dreams unmet, the warrior who mourned for a land lost, the babe who was assigned a gender that was not their own, the accused healer, and the lonely crone. As this last winter moon waxes, be midwife to your becoming by holding the doll close to your heart and speaking these words if they feel true:

> I am the living answer to the prayers of my forebears, and I am breathing their dreams into being one precious dawn at a time. Blessed be the hag magick that runs in my blood, and holy is the healing of the Witch. On this day and every day, the spirit wakes wild.

Notice your dreams as you do this work, Witch, and make note of any realizations you might have as the moon swells toward fruition. Choose whether to leave your poppet in her bed by your altar on these days or to continue to sleep with her near your own bed. You are the cauldron keeper, after all, and only you know best.

And so it is.

Season of the Cauldron Keeper: Full Moon

Grandmother Speaks: All Ways Are True

This brew smells of the fondest childhood memories, and you stir the thick, herby soup in slow infinity symbols. The hag nods in approval, hands on her hips and hellfire in her eyes. She's about to gift you with something, it seems, some new direction or long-sought answer.

"So, tell me…where did you learn to stir a pot like that?" she asks, chin raised.

In that moment, you see the skin on your hands age and spot and remember your grandmother's patience.

"My grandmother showed me," you answer. "Once, she said this symbol blesses the food and shows the gods we'd like more of their bounty."

The hag makes that low and knowing sound only those with a crone's heart have mastered, and you continue spiraling the spoon through long leaves and oil bubbles.

"It weaves in the lessons of the day, she also told me, and once when I was getting older and no longer asking questions, she said this symbol keeps us curious."

The hag clicks her tongue. "Your grandmother was a wise medicine keeper."

You stop stirring for a moment and meet the old one's eyes. "Well? Which answer do you think is true?"

Her eyes narrow then, and you know you made a misstep with your words. "If you can't answer that question, you're not ready to leave this mountain."

You sigh, continuing to stir, and that fertile symbol of interconnection and unending grace offers you solace and solution.

"All of her answers were true," you realize aloud, and the old salty hag's face sparks with a certain joy.

"Yes," the hag hisses. "All ways are true."

Full Moon Practice: It Is Finished

Materials: Your Imbolc doll in her bed, clearing herbs such as juniper or pine, burn bowl, fire source

On this last full moon of winter, honor the immense work you have done on those coldest, longest nights. Take a moment to read through your Book of Moon and Flame, to touch your altar in fleeting reverence for your Craft, and to welcome the coming spring storms that shall surely cleanse the dust from your hermitlike ways. On this fateful night, you shall release your winter's work and trust it is finished. If your planted seeds are still on your altar, decide if they shall stay or go. Create sacred space and raise energy through this chant or another you feel is more suited to your witchery:

> *Moon of seed, moon of storm*
> *Take this spell, keep it warm*

Set the herbs to burn, waving your doll through the smoke and re-flecting on the initiation of your ancestral healing work you have done since this moon dawned. Also burn the piece of paper on which you la-beled your vision, setting it free to swell to fruition. Keep chanting and call to mind your Imbolc vision now, seeing it more clearly than you have before, and feel your body as the body of the person in that vision. Step into their flesh now. Become them and shed the skin of the person you were at midwinter. Stay with this sensation of becoming for as long as you have, eventually allowing the chant to quiet and sinking into stillness.

Feel into the energy around you. Have any of your beloved dead, those who hold your best interest at heart, those who dream your dreams with you, come to join you here? Seal this work in gratitude to those un-seen warrioresses who surround you, then open the circle. Take your doll to a tree that seems maternal to you now, nesting her in its branches or at its roots, then gift the ashes from your work to the soil.

And so it is.

Season of the Cauldron Keeper: Waning Moon

Grandmother Speaks: Lighten Your Heart

This night is somber around its edges, you think, and a sweet sort of grief is squeezing at your heart. The hag sits at the table with you, slurping the brew you stirred to perfection and grunting in satisfac-tion and out of uncharacteristic kindness. You shall be sad to leave her, this old woman who put you face-to-face with the wolf of winter, but you are surely braver for having traveled here to this mountain.

"Lighten your heart, and enjoy your soup," the hag orders, read-ing the ache in your eyes. "You'll be back next year, after all."

The wolf exhales sharply at the fireside, stretching her limbs long, and you wonder how such a gentle creature could have been so threatening. *Sometimes we must give our demons what they crave*, you think. *Sometimes our midwinter fears are best faced head-on and with the support of ancestral ghosts at our side.*

"Yes, I'll be back," you agree. "I'll leave the darker parts of my soul here for safekeeping, lest the wolf forget my scent."

The hag laughs then, a genuine belly-wobbling sound, and her face takes on the shape of youth for the first time since you came here to her mountain.

Waning Moon Practice: Grieving Winter

Permit yourself to grieve the loss of those darker days now, as this last winter moon wanes. Do the work of the death ritual, honoring what is falling into its annual shadow before rushing to welcome what comes. Spend as much time as possible walking in nature, if you are able, giving a nod to not only those fragile emerald sprouts but also what is decaying. Ponder what parts of yourself you are leaving in that house of the Mountain Hag, the ways in which winter both humbled and heartened you, and speak spontaneous eulogies for those moments of joy, of oneness with that holy void, that graced you these last long months.

Take a brief inventory of these fleeting memories now, these times of feeling a sense of peace or ease, and do not be awash with guilt if you can only find one or two. If this winter was a struggle and the hungry wolves were many, you may find that even a single moment of peace eludes you; but perhaps this moment right now as you claim time for yourself and read these words might be sufficient. Choose just one moment to honor now, and handcraft a small and sacred relic that can stand in honor of that one moment — it might be a feather painted in just the right way or a carved candle; let it be simple, and let it mark winter's end for you. Place it on your altar as the moon wanes, and welcome what comes.

Winter's Eulogy

━━◁▷─ ◁▷◖◗◁▷ ─────◁▷━━

This winter found me weak, creeping up on me from behind on one of those lonely evenings when wine stained my lips and tears tracked my cheeks; it was not my finest moment, but that old hag of winter wrapped her heavy cloak 'round my shoulders and spoke the rawest truths. She told me bitter stories of anguished birth and the ancient walking dead. Her medicine was unlike any I had ever tasted, for she made no promises of healing or redemption. She, that salty woman, only held me while I wept and sang songs in a language my soul remembered but my mind forgot. I fell asleep in her arms, dreamed of snow-blanketed wastelands and full moons, and woke to find her dead and gone. Winter's lips curled back from her teeth right before my eyes, and she left only her bones behind, draped over my still-warm skin like a skeletal shawl, and I carried her into my slow-blooming garden.

Here lie the bones of winter, a hag who taught me well.

Season of the Cauldron Keeper: Dark Moon

Grandmother Speaks: Admit It, Witch

You've bundled yourself as best you can, though this rising sun promises only pitiful warmth, and you've packed the bones of who you used to be in your bag. The hag stands behind you in her doorway, mighty wolf at her side, and you ready yourself for the long journey down the mountain to the gardens of the east.

"Aw, go on. Admit it, Witch," the hag urges. "You're excited to find a bit of warmth. Best leave now, and you just might make it before nightfall."

You nod in gratitude and turn toward the forest, saying a quiet prayer that the snows will soften as you descend this mountain, that you'll remember the way down, and that you'll not forget the lessons you learned here.

"Tell that sultry garden keeper I said hello!" the Mountain Hag shouts after you.

You lift your hand to acknowledge that wild grandmother, and you leave the winter behind.

Dark Moon Practice: Spring's Sacrifice

Beneath the dark moon, winter's last exhale, offer a sacrifice to spring. Take some small thing that was precious to you in winter but belonged to the Witch you once were and not the sovereign sorceress you have become. Gift it to nature, to the elements, or to a dear friend — a symbolic action of not only release but transaction. You are giving this thing over to the graces of spring as a symbol of your commitment to what comes. As you do, perhaps speak this blessing-prayer aloud:

> May we find ourselves hooded and hearthside this last dark moon of winter, sipping some sour pomegranate nectar and staring long into the dying embers, underworld queens that we are. May we hike our skirts up between our legs and lean close to better scry those soft-glowing dream visions of a spring well lived, to better hear the smoldering smoke prayers hissed from our foremothers through generations of ash, blood, and soot. Here, may we come to know the longing that haunts every flame tender, that deep and in-the-blood desire to melt our iced-over parts, to thaw the ancestral magick frozen with atrophy, to warm, at long last, the secrets of the dead altar keepers hidden away and masked with frost so the wicked ones wouldn't claim such precious mysteries and wild stories as their own. Here, by the feeble light of this late-winter moon, may we remember why we were born into these bodies of ours, why this slow-brewed medicine is worth saving, and why, for the love of all things true and holy, we still tend these quiet fires of joy and witchery, of bone-and-hair art and poetic rebellion.

And so it is.

To the Season of the Cauldron Keeper, Farewell for Now

━┥◀╟─────◀╟─╫──╢▶─────────╢▶┝━

I've stirred that mighty cauldron well, and I'm on to brighter days. I bid you good night, ye moons of shadow and ice, and I'm tucking you in tight to keep you from haunting me too soon. The faeries are calling, you see, and I can't ignore them any longer. Don't look for me, for I'll be sky clad and twirling in the spring rain, child of lightning that I am. This heathen has come out of her winter cave, and she's singing songs of thorn, petal, and mud. And so it is.

———•⊰❍⊱•———

WILD WINTER PRACTICES AND SACRED REMEMBRANCES

- Remember that rest, ritual, and reflection are radical and necessary.
- Know that there is much magick to be found in simple and solitary moments.
- Appreciate that great art, great work, is born of the still and the dark, from periods of nondoing and not knowing.
- Recognize that an oracle can be made from anything.
- Check in with your collectives, families, and work organizations. Reflect on the past year, on the many seasons you have lived together, on the dreams fulfilled and losses mourned.
- Be present in this wild body of yours. Turn off the screens while you eat. Do not rush away from the small sensations. Close your eyes; taste, touch, smell, listen.
- Understand that any act of creation or manifestation is also an act of banishing or release. Only balance is sustainable.
- Practice intentional awe by finding some small piece of nature to strike you, to inspire a sacred gaze that fills you with wonder and reminds you of the bountiful magick on this rock called Earth.
- Honor the human animal, who wants the cave, the secret cocoon, to house our annual becoming.

Return to the House of
INITIATION

At long last, we return to the House of Initiation. Here, we become the hag. We step into our own wisdom, and we are at once beloved elder and curious youth. In the cauldron of infinite possibility, we are. Within the primordial womb of the world, in touch with the *anima mundi*, the world soul, we find ourselves yet again poised and ready to welcome what may come.

Hag Lesson #24

Every ending is an initiation.

We return here, time and time again, if for no other reason than to question all certainties and feel into the wild ache that is our humanness. This is our house of flesh and bone, of timely solitude, whimsy, and wonder. From here, the best stories are born.

CONCLUSION

Seasons of Moon and Flame

———◆———

Each of our many seasons of moon and flame is a story, a breathing myth to be lived, sensed, shared, and remembered. Every spell we cast — from our high-magick enchantments made under full moons to our quiet and simple incantations spoken over the kitchen sink — is a story we are telling; a place of beingness we are shaping; a once-upon-a-time we are slow-crafting through language, longing, and much, much love. The elders of the Earth-based traditions tell us that all things have a spirit to be revered. In *Grandmothers Counsel the World*, Carol Schaefer writes: "There is an order and a structure to the universe, the Grandmothers say. All things are dependent upon each other. This is why reciprocity and remembering to hold the relations among all people and all things as sacred balances the universe. Any actions that destroy life lead to imbalance, which is what we are facing in today's world." All of nature, including but extending well beyond the human collective, is an integral part of the world soul, and we all seek to feel this belonging in our lived-out-loud stories.

The story of our communal becoming is a tale with no poetically named ending, no simple moral we can derive and use to justify or condemn our actions, to validate our attempts to heal what may just be a wound necessary to spur us forward, to keep us inspired, to serve as the raw and bleeding material for our art and our many sacred quests. Just maybe, our brokenness, our grief, is the beating heart of who we are, and our diverse attempts to flee from this tenderness, from this holy and wild ache, perpetuate the monstrous distance between our individual stories and the grander tale to which we belong.

The hag teaches us to slow down — to look to where we feel both joy and hurt and find, right there, the impenetrable wildness of who we are. We look to the most ancient medicine of our people, to their gods and fairy tales, and we cocreate our stories of becoming out of a bone-deep desire to belong the way those long-gone ancestors of ours belonged and a simultaneous knowing that ours is a more wounded, more watered, more fragilely interconnected world. We Witches live close to that knowing. We can feel the future pulsing in our veins as much as we feel the echoes of the past, and we sense both the past and the future being reordered, re-membered, through our everyday movements, by our morning prayers and our evening ceremonies.

Hag Lesson #25

Our bones want belonging.

We hear our grandmothers calling, yes, but we also feel their greatest dreams coming to fruition through us. We weep for the babes of the future, yes, but we also see their precious faces loving the way we love, lighting candles and looking to the moon with the same longing that rolls off our own fertile tongues every time we chant and sing. They are beguiled by this world, and we are beguiled, too. We are their forebears, after all — and, if nothing else, we aim to be worthy of their reverence.

May our magick be a conversation with the babes of the future as well as our ancestors, for we are all the beloved living and the beloved dead, if only on different cross-stitched seams on the cosmic fabric of space and time. May we look to those wild places of contradiction where we are at once overwelling with the sweet nectar of hope and cracked by the driest apathy and dusty hopelessness. May we be good hags. May we make good art. May we slow down and taste the marrow of the magick we are brewing. May we move the way we want our ghosts to move, and may we let our stories stretch and breathe, leaving room for those impossible miracles that are, as yet, unwritten.

These Fallen Trees

These fallen trees have taught me much
'Bout death and life, and grief and such
And now, as ghosts, they teach me still
They know things I never will.

Epilogue

---◆---

As I finish writing this book, I am sitting lakeside at my grand-parents' cabin, and two mallard ducks have waddled ashore and nestled unnaturally close to my feet, their beaks burrowed and twitching under their wings, their nap unbothered by my keyboard clicks. I want to snap a picture, but I am without my phone. I want someone else to witness the scene, to share this bizarre moment with me, to listen and believe me when I say I think these ducks are my grandmother and grandfather come to bless my morning, come to tell me I have not given away too many family secrets. But I am alone with the water, the mountain trees, and these two sleeping creatures.

I decide this unlikely visit will just have to be a good story. I decide a snapshot or a witness would diminish the magick of these hours, and I look to the looming hemlocks above for validation. A west wind rustles the long grasses and curls the petals of the forget-me-nots, gracing the feathers of my companions, and the words of Dr. Clarissa Pinkola Estés from *Women Who Run with the Wolves* start playing on repeat in my mind, as they often do: "Among the best teller-healers I know, and I have been blessed to know many, their stories grow out of their lives as roots grow a tree." Since I began writing this book, I've been pondering, sometimes painfully so, the stories I was told as a child, and what sort of tree I might be if these stories had grown me up from their roots.

There were those tales of fire and brimstone, of course, the vengeful-god and shamed-woman stories that were full of judgment and never open for interpretation. These particular myths, these parables and presumed prophecies, I've come to think, might well have been damn good stories had they been allowed to breathe; had they been permitted to grow over time and had the natural cocreation that affects all old, great stories been allowed to occur; had the hands of forest dwellers, hidden healers, and all who did not use story as a weapon to maintain social and religious power been able to take hold of them and mold the words in such a way that they could be met and met well by the many instead of the few. These were not my stories; had they alone grown me, I might be much like the charred stump that sits at home in my backyard, a certain fire survivor with no name and no softness left.

Then there were the magick stories, and the fairy tales I most often begged my grandmother to share were not conducive to Disney. I was in love with the rebellious hedonism of the "Twelve Dancing Princesses," and I used to covet their shoes. I had a strangely illustrated copy of *The Little Match Girl* — a book I scavenged my grandmother's boxes to find upon her death but to no avail — and she made me appreciate warmth, fire, and my elders' laps. Quite morbidly, my favorite fairy tale was "Hansel and Gretel," and I longed to be a hag in the woods who lived in a house made of candy; cannibal or not, that Witch surely must have kept some deep magick, and I wanted to know what she knew. Had these stories alone grown me, I think I might be a blackthorn with an even sharper tongue than I have now, fearless, a bit heartless, and full of mischief.

Then there were the tales of scarcity, the in-the-blood stories told by my grandfather about growing up in Detroit with a single mother during the Great Depression. He had one story, a story that was not really a story at all, that my sister and I would beg him to tell us, perhaps because it was the only childhood memory he ever shared. "Go on, tell us about the potato, Grandpop," we would beg as if it was an epic myth with the happiest of endings and the strongest of morals, and he would.

His eyes would get soft, and he'd tell us about being young and hungry, about how his mother — my great-grammy Ross, a heroine in her own right, who divorced her abuser in 1928 knowing she would have five small children to feed — would split a single potato into small pieces for their dinner, and we, my sister and I, would feel that elusive thing called gratitude. It was that rare and overwelling heart we were addicted to, I think, that deep knowing that something had been healed. For all our family's many faults, our table was full enough to feed us, and some great battle had been fought in our blood and won. This nonstory story about the potato had a breath to it. Sometimes it was used to ensure we ate all our dinner, and sometimes it was wielded as a weapon against our wanting more than we had. Always, it was mutable, malleable. We could make what we wanted out of it. Had the potato story alone grown me up from its roots, surely I would be a willow burdened by tragic memories, forever weeping, trembling in the wind for fear of future storms.

Then there were the stories that turned the villains into heroes. One of my favorite family stories, told at countless holiday dinners and then, last that I can recall, at my father's funeral in 2007 by my uncle Dwight, is one we unimaginatively call the "Duck Story" (and the title is legendary enough that it's unlikely to be replaced by this small lakeside story I am living now). The story goes that one year for Easter my father and my uncle, his eight-years-younger brother, both received ducklings as gifts. My uncle's hatchling died almost immediately, and their parents conspired with my father to lead little Dwight to believe that it had been my father's duck who had died, thinking that the other duck was not long for the world, either, and hoping, at the very least, to grant my uncle a few more days of innocence and happiness. Of course, the duck lived for years, and whoever was doing the telling would usually highlight some epic snowstorm when my uncle had to head to the shed to feed the duck, my father snickering at the window.

Uncle Dwight did not find out about the loving betrayal until many years later, and my father, devil trickster that he was, would continually gift my uncle with creative reminders of the experience, severed stuffed-toy duck heads most often; he did this to mask what was actually a story of great compassion on his part, I always thought. The perplexing notion of my hard-hearted biker-soldier father selflessly acting to protect his little brother from a certain sadness, from that first deep grief of losing some wide-eyed fluffy creature with which he instantly fell in love, always made this story breathe for me. Even so, had this been the only story that grew me, I would be a thin-limbed jokester pine, always giggling, taking nothing seriously.

I want to tell my two wild-eyed children stories that breathe, and I have sometimes succeeded in this endeavor, I think. I want to tell them stories that will grow with them in a wounded world; spark more questions than answers; gift them with the humility, curiosity, and land love required of today's children. I want to tell them stories I hope they still tell when their witch-mother is feeding the trees. I want to remind them that we all have stories that matter, that any memory is a story, and stories shape the world.

I worry for the loss of the breathing stories, for the stories that grow us, and I am tender in those places where I feel the wild stories dying, killed off in the name of progress and distance, never again to be resurrected. In the time since I began this book, the powers that be have begun developing the wild lands near my home, the hallowed ground where I have held countless rituals, wed my love, and spoke to many, many ghosts. Long-toothed machines are running roughshod over the ground, ripping even the most stubborn junipers up from their roots and leaving the land bleeding, severed wildflowers strewn across leveled dirt, condos to be raised on the boneyard. I'm holding my grief like I might hold a slow-dying hatchling, the way I like to think my father held his baby duckling that Easter in the late 1950s, with great care and a protective, loose, and loving grasp.

I am conjuring more fireside songs and word-witchery. I am setting my mind to the Great In-Between, that mystical place that lies just beyond the offered language of a story but before the hearing, that climactic and Tantric pop where the story gets met. The great Dr. Maya Angelou said words stick to walls, "they get in your wallpaper; they get in your rugs, in your upholstery, in your clothes, and finally, into you." And so, too, I think there are stories that stick to bones; if this is true, my bones are stuck through with fallen biblical women; Depression potatoes; frozen match girls; and the corpses of hatchlings, which is an image I call to mind when I fear I might be taking myself too seriously, when I forget I am a mere mortal, Irish-German-Scandi-American woman living in a wounded world.

If you, the reader, were here with me now by the lake, I might ask you, *What stories are stuck to your bones?* What stories have grown you, and for what do you grieve? What breathing tales have you to tell in this moment, and how is it with your heart?

My heart, in this moment, is full of faith, brimming with my quintessential Aquarian optimism that stubbornly believes all will be well, despite much evidence to the contrary; that believes art is still a world shaper; reparations will still be paid to those whose true histories remain egregiously excluded from textbooks; we will all acknowledge that the existence of one person's particular gender does not threaten our own and act accordingly; the Earth will forgive us; we will all cease dismissing our stories — the stories without an apparent, sword-raised victory, stories that do not end with an boom but with the ordinary, perhaps with two curious ducks hobbling into a lake — as too plain to be told; and every news headline that could be read as a warning that times are dire could also say *Times have been dire; now they are visible, now we begin the healing*, and our story of becoming shall continue its grand unfolding, with the wilds as the perfectly flawed heroine and the human animal as her devoted lover.

And they lived happily ever after, will say the omniscient Witch narrators. Long after death did them part, long after birth brought them together again. Once upon a time in a new world...

APPENDIX 1

Hag Stories of Moon and Flame

————— ✦ —————

Spring Seasons

The Chicken-Witch of the Grove: A Ceremonial Equinox Tale

Medicine: Ancestral Belonging
Season of Tender Roots

Born of my personal understanding and stubborn certainty that there are wild and unseen forces at work in our lives that hold us, that support us without our conscious knowing as we do our work in the world, this story is about mundane initiation, the simple acknowledgment that we are held by our ancestries whether we know the stories of our forebears or not. Those who seek to drink the ancestral medicine can get overly focused on the inherited wounds, on the ills of the past few centuries, which are, after all, but a fleeting breath within the scope of human history; they neglect the inherited joy, as a result. This does not mean excusing the sins of the colonizers or bypassing the need for real and lasting political shifts that require the living to admit wrongs were done by their dead. The line is a fine one, indeed. It means not letting the ills of the recently dead ancestors become blocks to finding what is rich and spiritually fertile inherited ground.

It was my hope that this story would acknowledge the pleasure-filled light and the rich shadows that run together in our blood, as we continue to be held up firmly by the ghosts of those we may never have met in this life, trusting that we love what they love, that we ache the way they ache, and that, for all our loneliness, we have always belonged.

When people move through this ritual, there is often a sense of childhood wonder, as many were raised hunting and collecting eggs on Easter morning. There is laughter and, of course, tears, but the movement and the breath are healing. The communal gathering is healing, and, in the end, there is a sense that the primal ancestors surround us, have witnessed our work, and are nodding in approval.

For Reflection:

1. Choose a time frame within your life that feels highly transformational, then consider what your grandparents might have been doing at that same age. Are there parallels? What has been healed through you?

2. In reading the story, how did you want it to end? With Juniper finding love or remaining in the grove?

3. If you moved through the ceremony, what unexpected memories came up for you while collecting the "eggs"? Are there any patterns to be traced here?

Temple of the Flame Tender: A Ceremonial Tale of Wild Redemption

Medicine: Long-Vision, Intergenerational Healing
Season of the Elders' Altar

As many of us come to realize that the work of leaving a better world behind for the children of the future is arduous, fraught with innumerable obstacles and, in the end, the only work worth doing, a certain sense of pity arises for our long-dead forebears, I think. We wonder how they could possibly have been fulfilled, how they coped with all the same heartaches we feel with fewer resources, what wild art they made or poetic prayers they spoke after the little ones were in bed, art and prayers they thought no one would ever see or hear. An old salty Witch once told me that the absolute worst energetic act — indeed, an unintentional hex in its own right — was to feel sorry for someone, that we do not want the heavy energy of pity hanging on us. And, while I have not personally found this to be true — not yet, anyway — I can sense the futility of pitying our ghosts.

This story was born of the idea that somewhere inside all of us we can feel that some prayers will only come true for those yet-to-be-born babes; even so, we do our work, we light the candles, in perfect love and perfect trust. Having witnessed groups moving through this ceremony, I have seen how that simple collective ritual of lighting fires together creates a common bond. Some long-gone memory wakes up, and there is a communal yes. *Yes, we are the altar keepers indeed.*

For Reflection:

1. If you were to light three candles each day from now until forever, what would they be named for?
2. Envision an ancestor whom you have never met, your great-great-grandsomeone, and ask yourself what they might have lit their candles for. For what and to whom did they pray?
3. If you moved through the ceremony, how did you feel once all nine candles were lit?

Bawdy Betty and the Lady in Beige: A Late-Spring Tale

Medicine: Humor, Shadow Work
Season of Mud-Caked Hands

In truth, I cannot think of any women like the "lady in the white house," though I know countless characters like the ones of whom she was terrified. I am thankfully surrounded by those wildlings who are the stuff of Betty's nightmares, and I am a better person for it. I like to look under the perfection, and I am quite certain that purity — particularly the unflawed and overbleached performances on social media — is always a lie. I'm always in love with the shadow psyches of heroes and heroines, always asking who this glorified person does not want to be or what names they might shun. To my mind, you aren't really in a relationship until you've asked yourself those questions about your loved one and, of course, yourself. We're all a little bit Bawdy Betty, and we're all a little bit of her shadow.

For Reflection:

1. How much Bawdy Betty do you have in you?
2. Have you ever dreamed of your shadow, that buried part of your psyche that terrifies you when you encounter it in other people?
3. If Bawdy Betty at the end of the story were to integrate more of her "lady in beige" shadow, what do you think she might do? If there is a part of her screaming to have more order, to be more in control of her circumstances, how might she invite more of this into her beautifully messy, rainbow world?

Summer Seasons

The Faerie Doctor's Daughter: A Ceremonial Solstice Tale

Medicine: Story Harvesting, Belonging to Nature
Season of Wild Delights

We've been conditioned to run away from our own stories, I think. Countless systems have benefited from our secret keeping, from Witches staying hidden and isolated; a partial consequence of this is our discounting of our own tales as unimportant, our ancestries as boring, or our grandmothers' experiences as too mundane to matter. If we are to heal the ills of this world, in particular that of colonization, we can no longer run from the stories we keep. We can no longer frame ourselves as completely separate from whatever lineages we hail from. We have to sit with our particular tenderness and breathe.

This story ceremony was born as part divination, part pathworking, and I love hearing the whispers of stories pour out of people as they move through this ritual together. We all become awash in our shared stories of becoming. Some sing, some dance, many weep. Some are silent, and this is perfect, too.

For Reflection:

1. If you moved through the ceremony, what stories emerged for you? Are there common themes within them? To which

direction — north, southeast, or southwest — did you feel most akin?

2. What does the Celtic trinity of land, sea, and sky mean to you? How do you feel about the absence of fire?

3. When have you felt storyless in your life? What shifted this feeling for you?

The Witch and the Lightning Tree: A Midsummer Tale

Medicine: Remembrance, Inner-Child Work
Season of Holy Thunder

Since I was a child, I have been fascinated by lightning storms; they're like suddenly opened portals where anything is possible, where you can be anyone or believe anything. I think every storm is an opportunity to change, a mini — or not-so-mini — spell cast upon you and your world. My grandparents had a tree I was in love with, a mulberry that truly had the deep stories (I recall that a horse was buried beneath it, but I cannot remember why, and maybe no one else could, either), and this was the tree I was envisioning when I wrote this little story. My grandparents' house and the tree along with it have long been torn out at the root to make room for a McMansion, but both still live on in my memory and always will, so long as I myself live. In a few ways, this story is a distillation of this entire book, as I continually come home to the realization that all the wisdom we need is here in our quietly aging and unassuming bones.

For Reflection:

1. Did you have any childhood trees that seemed more like friends?

2. How do you feel right now, at this point in your life, about the spiritual quest?

3. What does home mean to you?

Biddy's Retreat: A Late-Summer Love Story

Medicine: Hope, Nature Love
Season of Midday Grace

I wrote this story after revisiting the tale of Biddy Early, a faerie doctor who is rumored to have disappeared for several years, returning from the faerie lands with much knowledge of plant medicines and other wise-woman, *bean feasa*, ways. The first novel I ever wrote, a terrible young-adult romance that will never, that should never, be published but still holds a special place in my heart, was about a half-faerie woman named Cloda and her love Sage (a character I loved so much that I named my second child after him), but were I ever to rewrite it, it would be about Biddy Cloda and Dot, I'm sure. We need those hopeful stories in late summer, I think, those stories that hold the long-vision and tell us our hope has a place, that our faith has merit.

For Reflection:

1.   What messages did you receive about the earth, environmental consciousness, or the elements as a child?
2.   What is your greatest fear and your greatest hope about the future of our beloved planet?
3.   In what psychic places do you feel simultaneously full of hope and completely lost, devoid of all hope, with respect to our precious environment's future?

Autumn Seasons

The Selkie-Hag's Pelt: A Harvest Moon Tale

Medicine: Divination, Time Bending
Season of Orphaned Dreams

The old myth of the selkie-woman is one of my all-time favorites, and I don't know that a better myth of women's wild feminine redemption exists. We all fear that our pelt will be stolen and we'll lose ourselves. We all long for the deep medicine of the sea. This story is a reminder that it is never too late, that we can always become someone else, someone more whole. We can be a rebel one day and a conformist the next, and all the while those old salty foremothers are poking their heads surfaceward and checking on us, holding space for us, and waiting for us to return to that home that is wild beyond all definitions.

For Reflection:

1. If you could know your future, every little thing that would happen, would you want to?
2. If you would wish to be selective about how much you wanted to know, what things would you choose, and why?
3. Of the two ways the story could end, which would you prefer, and why?

Goldie's Shadow: A Ceremonial Ghost Story

Medicine: Shadow Work, Grief Validation
Season of the Haunted Heart

I know I have some old keener woman as an ancestor; I dream of her often. I love funerals. My wedding was a death-themed ceremony. Throughout my tumultuous private- and public-school career, the death-riddled stories and poems I wrote were always cited as evidence of my madness; all the while, I was talking only about an everyday experience, the destiny that awaits us all. I think the root of our unwillingness in the West to talk about death and dying is the same as that which grounds our resistance to the hag, the shadow, and the Witch. Goldie, to me, is the embodiment of all things twisted in the love-and-light New Age community, the very reason we shun the aging and neglect the richness of elderhood.

Now, some might feel protective of Goldie and wonder if she had gone through some great tragedy as a child and simply did not want to be reminded, but it has been my experience that among those who fear all things shadow, the opposite is true. They have not been around death enough. We have to be able to say the word *dead* if we are to appreciate living, and autumn is the perfect season for sharing stories of our beloved ones who have left this plane, who are dead. Long may they rest.

For Reflection:

1. What feelings does the word *dead* evoke? Move through a quick word association. Begin with *dead*, then say the next word that comes to mind, then the next, then the next. What does *dead* become in the space of only a few thoughts?

2. Who are the elders you surround yourself with? Do you visit places where the aging live? Why or why not?
3. Do you know people like Goldie? What have they taught you?

The Soul Cages: A Ceremonial Autumn Tale

Medicine: Deep Knowing
Season of Spice and Hearth

"The Soul Cages" is an old Irish folk tale, and one that speaks to my heart. The part I fell in love with in the W. B. Yeats version is that, for all the hero's good work, he is offered no grand reward for freeing the souls from their cages. He hears only a whistle, a faint sound that tells him he did well. That is such a powerful message for activists, for those who are continually doing the hardest work of social justice, community organizing, protesting, environmental cleanups, and other movements for which there is no great financial reward, no celebrated awards ceremony; there is only that faint whistle that says, *Yes. You did good.*

For Reflection:

1. What seemingly selfless acts do you do, or have you done, without reward? Why did you do them? What was in it for you?
2. What medicines do you keep that are your unique soulful gifts you offer to the world, that you give without reward?
3. How do you feel about the merrow's motivations? Why did she trap the souls?

The Unburnable Beloved: A Thirteenth Moon Tale

Medicine: Nonsense, Mystery
Season of the Thirteenth Moon

I love nonsense. When I was in fourth grade, I read what I thought at the time was the most obscene poem ever written, and the best part was that I read it in my born-again Christian school textbook. Of old but unknown origin, the poem begins: "One fine day, in the middle of the night, two dead boys got up to fight." The rest of the lines are full of contradictions, full of unsolvable riddles that exist only for the sake of our befuddlement. The thirteenth moon is nonsense season, and this story is a tale of loving the liminal, of shunning reason, of paradox, of posing questions with no answers. The enemy of my Witchcraft has always been the same poison that affects my art, and it is that insidious belief that *I know this for sure*, that *this is the way it must be*, without qualification. This story is a nonstory that, I hope, validates the questions that have no answers at all, the living riddles that are these confounding stories of ours.

For Reflection:

1. What beliefs have you, at some point in your life, known for sure, only to dismantle them later? What caused that dismantling?
2. Finish this sentence: "I know for sure that…" What could happen to make you rethink that statement? Would you have completed that statement in a different way last year?
3. What voids have you experienced in your life? For instance, one job has ended but another hasn't begun, or a relationship has ended without another to replace it. How did it feel to be in the void, and what pulled you from it? Was it an external or internal force?

Winter Seasons

The Storyteller Crone's Jewels: A Yuletide Tale

Medicine: Mythic Memory
Season of Salted Bones

When I was little, there were times in my life when all I wanted was to run off into the woods and meet the old hag from all the fairy tales. As I've gotten older, I still wish that, though now I more want to be her someday. This story was born of the idea that our stories keep our hearts beating, that we can't die as long as we have at least one good story left to tell, and that stories keep the land alive as well. If I had a language of my own, the word for "story keeper" would be the same as that for "healer" and for "jewel." Those who keep the stories are themselves jewels, precious ones who keep us living, who remind us what is important.

For Reflection:

1. Do you know an elder who seems to be a story keeper? Do you know any elder who isn't a story keeper?
2. Look around your house and choose three objects. If you wear jewelry, you might choose three pieces of jewelry. Now, ask yourself what stories these objects have to tell. If nothing comes to mind, tell the story of the object's origin, who crafted it, if it was crafted at all. What are the epic tales of these apparently nonepic material items?
3. What stories were you told as a child about the lived experience of your elders? What themes were apparent in those stories?

The Bone-Woman's Brew: A Midwinter Tale

Medicine: Clear Sight, Tree Love
Season of the Wild Wolf

My mother was a night nurse in an assisted-living facility when I was growing up, and I spent a lot of time as a young child around the old and the dying. I recall some of their faces even still. Some of their names are burned in my memory — but, of course, I did not realize what a beauteous gift it was to be so close to the dying during middle childhood. Many of my elder friends would give me candy and tell me tales. We would watch *Dynasty* together; then, the next night, they would be gone. I imagined returning to that place when I wrote this story, wheeling one of my old friends, Dorothy, out under the willow tree and letting her share her magick with me once more, taking nothing for granted.

For Reflection:

1. Did this tale remind you of any winter moments?
2. Who are your bone-women? Who have you known who seemed otherworldly, full of the hidden medicine?

3. What single conversations have changed you, made you rethink the way of the world?

The Moon Child and the Holy Wild Hag:
A Ceremonial Late-Winter Tale

Medicine: Integration
Season of the Cauldron Keeper

I wrote this story while a red-tailed hawk sat perched on the fence outside my window for hours, not moving, stalking the birds at my feeder but never attacking. I wanted to write a story ceremony of being blessed by the elements, of reclaiming those haggish parts of ourselves. It is a heroine's journey, of sorts, and I've been blessed to witness many wild hearts moving through this ritual, smearing dirt on their faces, getting hissed at by my beloved friend Shine Blackhawk, who sometimes plays the wild hag. It is a story of familiarity, I think. Those who move through it sense a subtle coming home — but, overall, there are no surprises, no shock or sudden revelation; there is just a resonance, a feeling of *Oh yes, I do know this*. And, in the end, we do. We know the directions, the elements, and the wild, for we are built from them.

For Reflection:

1. When have you felt like the moon child at the beginning of the story, when she was being cast out of her home?
2. What quests have you been on, either metaphorical or physical journeys? What prompted you to set out on this quest?
3. Who is the hag to you? How is she you?

APPENDIX 2

Hag Spells and Rituals of Moon and Flame

House of Initiation

The Circle as Story
The Pentagram of Being

Season of Tender Roots

Spring Equinox Celebration: Twin Eggs of Birth and Renewal
The Chicken-Witch of the Grove: A Ceremonial Equinox Tale
Opening Practice: Your Spring Initiation
Waxing Moon Practice: Writing It Real
Full Moon Practice: Cosmic Eggs of Creation and Will
Waning Moon Practice: The Great Galactic Fabric
Dark Moon Practice: Memories of Joy and Grace

Season of the Elders' Altar

Beltane Celebration: A Fire of Demand
Temple of the Flame Tender: A Ceremonial Tale of Wild Redemption

Opening Practice: Flame Tending for the Yet-to-Be-Born
Waxing Moon Practice: The Wildness of Our Longing
Full Moon Practice: The Truest Healing
Waning Moon Practice: The Feeling Body
Dark Moon Practice: A Wild Walk

Season of Mud-Caked Hands

Opening Practice: A Helper Tree Found
Waxing Moon Practice: Humble Offerings by Morning's Light
Full Moon Practice: Sweet Reward
Waning Moon Practice: Grieving Spring
Dark Moon Practice: The Purge before the Fruition

Season of Wild Delights

Summer Solstice Celebration: Rejoining the Band of Storytelling Heathens
The Faerie Doctor's Daughter: A Ceremonial Solstice Tale
Opening Practice: Your Summer Initiation
Waxing Moon Practice: A Practiced Thanks
Full Moon Practice: The Three Stories
Waning Moon Practice: A Moment of Pause
Dark Moon Practice: The Spirit of the Moment

Season of Holy Thunder

Lughnasadh Celebration: The Bread of Life and Death
Opening Practice: Our Web of Being
Waxing Moon Practice: To Make Peace with the Mystery
Full Moon Practice: Held by the Long Arms of Time
Waning Moon Practice: The Made and Maker
Dark Moon Practice: Calling On a Dream

Season of Midday Grace

Opening Practice: Pondering the Fractal
Waxing Moon Practice: The Witch's Retreat
Full Moon Practice: An Offering to the Broken
Waning Moon Practice: Grieving Summer
Dark Moon Practice: Welcoming the Great Letting Go

Season of Orphaned Dreams

Autumnal Equinox Celebration: The Best and Last of Their Names
Opening Practice: Your Autumn Initiation
Waxing Moon Practice: A More Sacred Gaze
Full Moon Practice: A Eulogy Lived Out Loud
Waning Moon Practice: A Letter to a Loved One Gone
Dark Moon Practice: A Sweet Release

Season of the Haunted Heart

Samhain Celebration: The Silent Supper
Goldie's Shadow: A Ceremonial Ghost Story
Opening Practice: Communing with the Shadow Creatures
Waxing Moon Practice: The Shadow Doll
Full Moon Practice: The Darkest Medicine
Waning Moon Practice: The Shadow as Gift
Dark Moon Practice: The Story of the Many Children

Season of Spice and Hearth

The Soul Cages: A Ceremonial Autumn Tale
Opening Practice: The Living Ghost Story
Waxing Moon Practice: Deep Listening and the Medicine's Resurrection
Full Moon Practice: The Great Purge and the Great Switch
Waning Moon Practice: Grieving Autumn
Dark Moon Practice: Rest, Ritual, and Reflection

Season of Salted Bones

Solstice Celebration: Prophecy 'neath the Pine on the Longest Night
Opening Practice: Your Winter Initiation
Waxing Moon Practice: Tending the Inner Altar
Full Moon Practice: Cleansing the Altar
Waning Moon Practice: Something Far More Dangerous
Dark Moon Practice: A Puzzle-Piece Hymn, Handwritten by the Witch's
    Apprentice

Season of the Wild Wolf

Imbolc Celebration: A Bridal Bed and a Flame Alight
Opening Practice: Welcoming Sovereignty Home
Waxing Moon Practice: Choices Made, Choices Owned
Full Moon Practice: The Bravest Gardener
Waning Moon Practice: Such Is the Way of Winter
Dark Moon Practice: Naming the Fears

Season of the Cauldron Keeper

The Moon Child and the Holy Wild Hag: A Ceremonial Late-Winter Tale
Opening Practice: Becoming the Crone-Weaver
Waxing Moon Practice: Beginning Again
Full Moon Practice: It Is Finished
Waning Moon Practice: Grieving Winter
Dark Moon Practice: Spring's Sacrifice

APPENDIX 3

Hag Lessons Unpacked

---

1. THE BEST STORIES ARE NOT HEARD BUT MET.

Not every story my grandmother told me was an epic myth that forever changed my worldview, but there were certainly some that fit that description, by my own definitions of *epic* and *myth* at least, and these were stories that I wanted to hold hands with. I did not just hear them; I took hold of them and they of me. I wanted to know them better, to have tea with them. I wanted to mine the dirt under the words to see if there was more. These are the stories we live for.

2. THE REVOLUTION WILL BE WILDCRAFTED.

"The revolution will not be televised," sang Gil Scott-Heron in 1970. All the many hidden rebellions — the kitchen-table movements and street-corner protests, the seemingly small acts of social courage done not to perform but to truly make a shift — these are what will save the earth. Human beings must name our of-the-earthness imperative. In her book *Emergent Strategy*, Adrienne Maree Brown writes: "My dream is a movement with such deep trust that we move as a murmuration, the way

326

groups of starlings billow, dive, spin, and dance collectively through the air.... There is a deep trust in this: to lift because the birds around you are lifting. Imagine our movements creating this type of trust and depth with each other, having strategic flocking in our playbooks." Why do we exhaust our resources time and time again to learn about our own nature from others who are similarly separate — similarly wounded in their severance from the natural world — when, in fact, nature holds every lesson we need?

3. JOY LIVES IN MYSTERY.

We must claim a felt, in-the-bones joy during those times of uncertainty. We have learned to find discomfort in the not knowing, been trained to run toward those who will tell us, *This! This is the way!* What if we found pleasure in the unknowns of life? My grandmother's life was an apparently simple one; she lived and died in the same small part of the world, was married to the same man for over five decades before he died. There were many knowns in her life, many for-sures; and yet, she was still able to not only sit in silence and stillness for long periods of time but love those between-the-knowns moments. When dementia clouded her world, she seemed at times to return to a state of childlike wonder. Every moment was new, in the absence of memories, and, even there, she found joy; you could see it on her face when she was served the cake she liked or the sunset was particularly stunning. Memories of the past do not alone make our joy.

4. NONLINEAR MOVEMENT IS REBELLION.

Countless systems profit from our fast-forward, never-look-back movements. One of my teachers, Bayo Akomolafe, says we have learned to equate distance with success. We have learned to run as far away from home, from our bodies, from our creaturely nature as possible — and, in so doing, we have turned away from cyclical time, away from the wild feminine. Having long-vision, caring about the babes that will not be born until long after we ourselves are in the ground, is radical in the short-sighted, individualistic West. We must rise above the straight lines and see that they are, in fact, our own tiny segments of an ever-widening spiral.

5. Our circles can grow wider and wider still.

As Witches, wild ones, or however we might identify ourselves today, we must continually examine the ways in which our work, our activism, our magick, and our art are a new conversation, a true disruptor of the patterns we have named outmoded or harmful, an authentic invitation to shift. So often, we find ourselves saying the same words that have been said, only using a different tone of voice, inadvertently repeating the most problematic — the least just — stories but titling them more palatably. Our circles, our communities, are wider than those of our grandmothers, but they can always get wider. We cannot dismiss anything as *good enough* these days. We can always do better.

6. Everything is participation.

All actions and nonactions, all stories and nonstories, all spells and non-spells are participation. Apathy loves to declare that it is simply not participating when, in fact, countless systems of institutionalized discrimination are fueled by apathy, by complacency, by that particularly powerful sort of participation that gets to mask itself as nonparticipation. We are removed from nothing. We are part of all.

7. What is wild must always change.

Only change is predictable, and nature shows us this truth over and over again. There is a birth, a swelling, a fruition, and a decay to all things, and the sooner we come to know change as fundamentally natural and an inevitable aspect of life, the sooner we can get down to the business of being present, of not running, of getting dirty and feeling it all — our many agonies and joys.

8. We must be gentle with ourselves.

Life is hard. We can be resilient, be challenged, and still be gentle with ourselves. We can let ourselves feel the discomfort of learning, of integrating old truths that seem new to us, and still feel the sun on our faces.

9. THIS CRAFT IS YOURS AND OURS.

The way you live your magick is your own. No one can tell you how to walk that spiraling road that is the spiritual quest, but also know that your Craft is participation. Your spells are conversations, and your own witchery does not exist in a vacuum. You may not be part of a coven, but you are part of a collective just the same.

10. THE ALTAR IS A TOUCHSTONE.

We need symbolic reminders that our Craft matters. We need touchstones that will ground us when the world shows us that our slow-living and cyclical ways are not socially valuable — not yet, anyway. My grandmother was a queen of plastic yard-sale-bought seasonal decor, and season by season, she would build her small altars anywhere she could. In particular, she had two stone room dividers topped by wooden lattice that stretched to the ceiling, an unimpressive feat in her small, one-level home; these separated the living and dining rooms, and — though she certainly would not have named them as such — these were her altars. In plain view and for all to see, they would be covered in red hearts and cherubs for Valentine's Day; bunnies, chicks, and eggs at Easter; American flags in July; then skulls, pumpkins, and black cats all the way until Christmas. There are altars everywhere, you see. They need not be grand. They need not be noticeable to anyone but you. Our altars only need remind us of our wildness from time to time, validating our changing nature and reflecting back to us an ancient part of ourselves.

11. SPRING MAGICK IS LINEAGE-MENDING WITCHERY.

Years ago, I began to notice patterns in my healing and my Witchcraft. In spring, I've been known to tell people that I become a gopher, furiously digging out ancestral wounds and deep secrets, particularly but not only among the women. I've uncovered countless painful stories and raised far more questions than I've answered, all the while nourishing my Witchcraft with that unique sense of belonging that comes only from such inquiry. Boundaries around this work are good, of course — and, yes, I have been the bleary-eyed insomniac awake at 3 AM sifting through genealogies and census records — but grant some room in your witchery for the ancient ancestors to come through and support you always, but particularly during those fertile days of spring.

12. WE CAN BE FULLY SOVEREIGN AND STILL BE HEALING.

It has never been a choice between sovereignty and healing. We are all broken, all wounded, never fully fixed. So, too, are we all integral aspects of the whole, sovereign fractals of a collective. Our magick is made better by our tenderness. Our aches show us what we care for, and there is much power in belonging.

13. IN THE END, WE ARE ALL OF THE EARTH.

That is all.

14. SUMMER MAGICK IS BORN OF ACTIVISM AND GRATITUDE.

In his book *Consolations*, David Whyte says our anger is born of love. We rage against injustices out of a great love for a more just world. We despise the mistreatment of animals because we love them. We protest, we rally, and we demand to be heard out of what looks like rage but is really an intense passion for the global community we know is possible. In summer, our magick is activism, yes, but it is also gratitude. It is heart-born compassion and deep, deep love.

15. THE INTEGRITY OF MAGICK DEPENDS UPON COCREATION.

Magick means, in part, holding hands with unseen energies in space and time. Such interconnectivity demands a certain sense of power, yes, but also a necessary humility. You are not and have never been doing it alone. Spells go by many names and are cast with many hands.

16. GRATITUDE BECOMES GRIEF.

The gratitude of our summer magick becomes good grief in autumn, as we mourn not for what we have lost but for what we have loved and loved well. We hold our grief like we hold our gratitude, as if it were a precious soft-bodied creature, and we let our why-mes naturally become thank-yous. When my grandfather died, my grandmother's character shifted like the weather. She had a season of tears, to be sure, but then there was an intense storm season when her rage was irrational, swirling in all directions like a chaotic torrent. But, after all of that, there was a long and enduring season of softness, of openheartedness and the purest gratitude for the life she had with him and the life she was still living in his absence.

17. OUR WHOLENESS DEMANDS WE MOURN.

The prevalence of the human ache is so immense and enduring that to shun our mourning, to run from our grief, would be to shun our wholeness, to willingly remain fractured creatures who deny their most fertile tenderness. We do not mourn to process loss, heal, or get over our grief; we mourn because we are feeling creatures and loss is as much a part of life as the gain, as the win. We mourn because we love.

18. AUTUMN MAGICK IS SHADOW WORK.

There is no greater personal power source than the shadow, in my humble opinion. Shadow work is a lifelong psychic task of becoming larger, more whole, more empathic versions of ourselves. If it feels easy, it is not shadow work.

19. GROWTH DEMANDS DISCOMFORT.

Healing is hard. Change is inevitable, and growth demands we get uncomfortable. It is not enough to wish for a better world. It is not enough to wield our manifestation magick without acknowledging the role of our privilege in obtaining the lives we long to live. We must get comfortable with discomfort, and often we must love the world more than we love ease.

20. DARKNESS HOLDS IT ALL.

Befriending those voids we have faced in our lives, and indeed will continue to face, means trusting that darkness is fertile. Light needs a source, but darkness holds it all. As a child who regularly spoke to dead people, I did not fear the dark until I was told that such conversations were "evil," until I had prayer cards filled out in my name at church and ceremonies performed to "cast out the evil spirits." Since then, I have fallen in love with the dark again, with the night, with the wild unseen. In *Where Science and Magic Meet*, Dr. Serena Roney-Dougal speaks about the prominent role of darkness, the literal absence of electric light, in psychic activity and magick making. Neglecting the beauty of the darkness has supported the social denigration of Witchcraft, of the hag, of the shadow — but darkness holds it all.

21. THERE IS MUCH MAGICK IN THE MUNDANE.

If there is a single truth that grounds my Witchcraft, it is this. We must see magick and mystery in everything. We need not attend grand rituals, purchase exorbitant materials for our spellwork, or decide how our Craft must be special, must be divorced from our everyday experience. I have been blessed to have many magickal moments in my life — that is, ones that made me sit up and pay attention, made me wonder if there was something to this Witchcraft of mine. None of them are climactic. All of them would sound quite ordinary if I were to describe them, small syn-chronicities, dreams, and nods from nature that showed me I was part of something greater than I could ever realize.

22. WINTER MAGICK WANTS DISCERNMENT.

Winter wants fire. Those long nights crave warmth, demand a glow of enduring hope. Our magick in winter asks that we not move too quickly. In *The Mist-Filled Path*, Frank MacEowen speaks of "setting the root," of simply deciding which direction to turn in, lest we lose our groundedness. Winter asks us to simply set the root; to discern just the very next step; to sense the quickening in our bellies, breathe, and trust.

23. BIRTH IS INEVITABLE.

If death is inevitable, so is birth. I remember the profound fear I faced when my belly was growing heavy with my first son. I wanted him to be born, of course, but I did not want to go through labor. I had read the books, taken the classes, booked the birth center, and done all the things I had decided were right. On the night when my contractions were intense, I remember visiting the midwife at her house and thinking that this was not the night, that I would go home and sleep, that this was yet another false alarm. She examined me, and she said, "You are having this baby tonight," and there was absolutely nothing I could do about it. There was no use wasting my energy on resistance. Birth was inevitable. At midwinter, we wonder if this will be the year that nothing happens, if this will be the most boring year yet, but it never is.

24. EVERY ENDING IS AN INITIATION.

If we look to those great endings in our lives, those moments when we could literally feel our old selves dying, we can see that these endings are initiations into a new way of partnering with the world, with our own souls. My Aquarian-ness always prompts me to ask whether a setback is an opportunity; sometimes it seems so, often not, but initiations are not the same as opportunities. They are invitations to belong, an acknowledgment not of achievement but of passage. When I watched my grandmother breathe slow and with much labor hours from her death, there was a profound sense of passage. I could feel the unseen others in the small room welcoming her to a new way of being in the world, and there was a primal rightness to it that I am blessed to have witnessed.

25. OUR BONES WANT BELONGING.

In the end, we all want to belong. We will go to all lengths to feel we belong to something, to some tradition or group. We will overidentify with flawed organizations, let ourselves be hazed, shun whole parts of ourselves, leaving them forgotten in shadow, while we put others in the spotlight in order to appear special or good. All the while, we do belong to great and immense collectives. We all have rich Earth-based ancestries if we go back far enough. We all have immense ancestral stores we can use to bolster our resilience and work for a broader, more just, more whole world. Our bones want belonging in a postcolonial world, and our grand story is not about questing and running, not about journeying so far from who we are or what we have become; it is a story of coming home to the house of the hag, returning to a place that part of us — the better part, maybe — never even left.

Acknowledgments

To my beloved babes, Bodhi and Sage, and my beautiful husband, Ryan, thank you for being in my world, for listening to nineties grunge albums start to finish on road trips, for making me laugh so hard it hurts, and for always coming back home with me to our haunted house. To those whom I have been blessed to call teacher this year — Bayo Akomolafe, Seán de Cantúail, and Dr. Clarissa Pinkola Estés — thank you for your immense wisdom and sacred work in the world. To the many councils of wild hearts I've been honored to know, to the fierce fireside circles at Wild Woman Fest, Ocean Earth Wind Fire, House of AUM, and my Moon House, *Yes, thank you — more, please.* To L. Rowan Crow, thank you for consulting on this book-baby of mine, for your friendship, and for all your invaluable work. To the team at New World Library, including my editor Georgia Hughes and publicist Tristy Taylor, and my agent, Sheree Bykofsky, the deepest bows and wildest howls to you for all you do. To my uncle Dwight, thank you for, literally and figuratively, keeping the fire burning at the mountain cabin. Lastly, to my beloved grandmother Grace, I miss you. Thank you for growing me up from my roots.

Notes

Introduction: Our Year of the Wild

p. 2   *"This breathing landscape..."*: David Abram, *The Spell of the Sensuous* (New York: Vintage Books, 2017), 260.

p. 3   *They feel into the* shaping: See Tom Cowan, *Yearning for the Wind* (Novato, CA: New World Library, 2003), 145, for the Celtic philosophy of the shape, shaper, and shaping.

p. 4   *"The times are urgent..."*: Bayo Akomolafe, "Making Sanctuary" (lecture, Jung Platform, starting March 7, 2019), https://www.jungplatform.com/2018/11/making-sanctuary-with-bayo-akomolafe.

p. 5   *racialized trauma and cultural context*: See Resmaa Menakem, *My Grandmother's Hands* (Las Vegas: Central Recovery Press, 2017), for in-depth understanding of racialized traumas.

p. 6   *"The Grandmothers teach us..."*: Carol Schaefer, *Grandmothers Counsel the World* (Boston: Trumpeter Books, 2006), 117.

p. 7   *"this old woman stands between..."*: Dr. Clarissa Pinkola Estés, *Women Who Run with the Wolves* (New York: Random House, 1992), 28.

p. 8   *she is the very shadow*: See Demetra George, *Mysteries of the Dark Moon* (San Francisco: HarperCollins, 1992), for information on the dark feminine shadow.

p. 8   *There are three lunar seasons*: See Bill Plotkin, *Soulcraft* (Novato, CA: New World Library, 2003), for an ecological psychology description of the shadow.

p. 9   *words that meant something very different*: For more information on intersectional feminism theory, see Dr. Maythee Rojas, *Women of Color and Feminism* (Berkeley, CA: Seal Press, 2009).

p. 10   *our language has not evolved*: See Abram, *Spell of the Sensuous*, for wisdom about language's shortcomings, evolution, and beauty.

p. 10   *on the land of the Lenni-Lenape*: See John Norwood, *We Are Still Here!* (Moorestown, NJ: Native New Jersey Publications, 2007), for the story of the Lenni-Lenape people.

p. 11   *housing long-standing traumas within our bodies*: For information on cultural somatics, see Tada Hazumi, SelfishActivist.com. In their article entitled "The Key to Healing Whiteness Is to Understand Cultural Somatic Context" (https://selfishactivist.com/the-key-to-healing-whiteness-is-understanding -cultural-somatic-context), they write, "Understanding cultural somatic context is important because it shows that practices cannot be separated from the bodies that practice them and the cultures these bodies are embedded in."

House of Initiation: The Beginning and the End

p. 17   *"God's transcendence..."*: Judith Plaskow and Carol Christ, eds., *Weaving the Visions* (San Francisco: HarperCollins, 1989), 95.

p. 21   *acknowledge the indigenous people*: When it is a group ritual, ceremony, or celebration, consider collecting monetary donations for the local tribal councils, and make regular donations to the indigenous people on whose land you live or to the Native American Rights Fund (NARF): narf.org.

Chapter 1. Season of Tender Roots

p. 31   *the scars we have inherited*: See Daniel Foor, PhD, *Ancestral Medicine* (Rochester, VT: Bear & Company, 2017), for more information on lineage repair.

p. 33   *where we meet the body electric*: See Walt Whitman, "I Sing the Body Electric," in *Walt Whitman: The Complete Poems* (London: Penguin Books, 1975), 127.

p. 44   *claim the choice as ours*: In Tantric philosophy, there exist the five actions of the gods, with these actions akin to the cycle of manifestation, concealment, fruition, dissolution, and grace. When we choose to manifest anything, we are concurrently choosing to conceal all other possibilities. For more on this topic and others within traditional Tantric philosophy, see Christopher Wall, *Tantra Illuminated* (Petaluma, CA: Mattamayūra Press, 2013).

p. 47   *eat when you're hungry*: See Adrienne Maree Brown, *Pleasure Activism* (Chico, CA: AK Press, 2019), for rich discussions of excess and sufficiency in a capitalist system.

Chapter 2. Season of the Elders' Altar

p. 51   *"The inside and the outside..."*: Bayo Akomolafe. *These Wilds Beyond Our Fences* (Berkeley, CA: North Atlantic Books, 2017), 6.

Chapter 3. Season of Mud-Caked Hands

p. 80   *"Regardless of religion or culture…"*: Danu Forest, *Celtic Tree Magic* (Woodbury, MN: Llewellyn Worldwide, 2018), 1.

p. 80   *better, ask the tree*: For more information on treespeak, see Peter Wohlleben, *The Hidden Language of Trees* (Vancouver: Greystone Books, 2015).

Chapter 4. Season of Wild Delights

p. 110   *"gratitude is the understanding…"*: David Whyte, *Consolations* (Langley, WA: Many Rivers Press, 2015), 89.

Chapter 5. Season of Holy Thunder

p. 123   *swallow all we can until we burst*: For more information on the myths of capitalism and scarcity, see Lynne Twist, *The Soul of Money* (New York: W. W. Norton & Company, 2003).

p. 136   *a holy trinity of artistry*: Tom Cowan, *Yearning for the Wind* (Novato, CA: New World Library, 2003), 145.

Chapter 6: Season of Midday Grace

p. 140   *"All action is communication…"*: Anodea Judith, *Eastern Body, Western Mind* (Berkeley, CA: Celestial Arts, 1996), 309.

p. 146   *"infinitely complex patterns…"*: Adrienne Maree Brown, *Emergent Strategy* (Chico, CA: AK Press, 2017), 51, 55.

Chapter 7. Season of Orphaned Dreams

p. 161   *one of the ghosts who stand*: See Daniel Foor, PhD, *Ancestral Medicine* (Rochester, VT: Bear & Company, 2017), for a succinct description of how the more primal ancestors, or beloved dead, are distinguishable from "ghosts."

p. 171   *"Transience is the force of time…"*: John O'Donohue, *Anam Čara* (New York: HarperCollins, 1997), 170.

p. 171   *We grieve not only for what we have lost*: See Frances Weller, *The Wild Edge of Sorrow* (Berkeley, CA: North Atlantic Books, 2015), for more information on the types of grief and the merit of grief ritual in our wounded world.

p. 172   *simply sit and gaze at these objects*: See Georg Feuerstein, *The Yoga Tradition* (Prescott, AZ: Hohm Press, 2001), for more information on the yogic practice of *samyama*, or the last four steps of the "eight-limbed path" from Patanjali's Yoga Sutras, written around 300 CE. The Western mind, in particular, is not accustomed to such focus, to directing one's attention fully to a single object for an extended period of time. Such practice facilitates a deeper connection with nature, with the material.

Chapter 8. Season of the Haunted Heart

p. 180   *Shadow work is an infinite task*: See Bill Plotkin, *Wild Mind* (Novato, CA: New World Library, 2013), for more information on shadow work from an ecological psychology perspective.

p. 189   *"Dolls are one of the symbolic..."*: Dr. Clarissa Pinkola Estés, *Women Who Run with the Wolves* (New York: Random House, 1992), 91.

Chapter 10. Season of the Thirteenth Moon

p. 217   *In the Celtic tradition*: For more information on the thirteenth moon cycle and the Celtic Wheel of the Year, see Liz and Colin Murray, *The Celtic Tree Oracle* (London: Connections Book Publishing, 1988), 52.

Chapter 11. Season of Salted Bones

p. 231   *"There is a moment of silence..."*: John Matthews, *The Winter Solstice* (Wheaton, IL: Quest Books, 2003), 6.

Chapter 12. Season of the Wild Wolf

p. 253   *As Imbolc approaches*: See Frank MacEowen, *The Mist-Filled Path* (Novato, CA: New World Library, 2002), xxii, for more information on Imbolc and the seed quickening.

Chapter 13. Season of the Cauldron Keeper

p. 271   *the main character, Athena*: Paulo Coelho, *The Witch of Portobello* (New York: HarperCollins, 2006), 83.

p. 287   *describes his experience watching a spider*: David Abram, *The Spell of the Sensuous* (New York: Vintage Books, 2017), 19.

Conclusion: Seasons of Moon and Flame

p. 301   *"There is an order and a structure..."*: Carol Schaefer, *Grandmothers Counsel the World* (Boston: Trumpeter Books, 2006), 146.

Epilogue

p. 305   *"Among the best teller-healers I know..."*: Clarissa Pinkola Estés, *Women Who Run with the Wolves* (New York: Random House, 1992), 509.

p. 308   *words stick to walls*: Dr. Maya Angelou, interview by Oprah Winfrey, "Dr. Maya Angelou," *Oprah's Masterclass*, OWN, season 1, episode 3, January 6, 2011.

Appendix 1. Hag Stories of Moon and Flame

p. 311   *The line is a fine one*: My dear friend wise woman Shine Blackhawk, daughter of a Choctaw mother and Nigerian father, said strongly to a group of white women in a lecture she was facilitating (Phoenixville, PA, March 22, 2019), that "[our white] ancestors are not here to pay, and [her black and indigenous ancestors] are not here to collect, so let's talk."

p. 316   *wise-woman*, bean feasa, *ways*: See Meda Ryan, *Biddy Early: The Wise Woman of Clare* (Blackrock, Ireland: Mercier Press, 1991).

p. 316   *The old myth of the selkie-woman*: One of my favorite retellings of the traditional selkie story is in Dr. Clarissa Pinkola Estés, *Women Who Run with the Wolves* (New York: Random House, 1992).

p. 318   *an old Irish folk tale*: See T. Crofton Croker, "The Soul Cages," in *Fairy and Folk Tales of Ireland*, ed. W. B. Yeats (London: Arcturus Publishing, 2018), 88–95.

p. 318   *Of old but unknown origin*: See "One Fine Day," in Iona and Peter Opie, *The Lore and Language of Schoolchildren* (New York: New York Review of Books, 2001), 24.

Appendix 3. Hag Lessons Unpacked

p. 327   *"My dream is a movement..."*: Adrienne Maree Brown, *Emergent Strategy* (Chico, CA: AK Press, 2017), 71.

p. 328   *equate distance with success*: Bayo Akomolafe, "Making Sanctuary" (lecture, Jung Platform, starting March 7, 2019), https://www.jungplatform.com/2018/11/making-sanctuary-with-bayo-akomolafe.

p. 331   *our anger is born of love*: David Whyte, *Consolations* (Langley, WA: Many Rivers Press, 2015), 13.

p. 332   *the prominent role of darkness*: Serena Roney-Dougal, PhD, *Where Science and Magic Meet* (Glastonbury, UK: Green Magic, 2010), 149–50.

p. 333   *"setting the root"*: Frank MacEowen, *The Mist-Filled Path* (Novato, CA: New World Library, 2002), xxiv.

Index

❧

for (waning moon practice), 213–14;
grieving (waning moon practice), 213,
324; human activities during, 8; initiation, 171–72, 324; journey overview,
155–56; magick of, 155, 160, 331;
moons of, 149, 179, 195; void following,
217; wild practices / sacred remem-
brances, 222–23; wild unseen and,
158–59; Witches and, 3. *See also* Sea
Hag; Season of Orphaned Dreams;
Season of Spice and Hearth; Season of
the Haunted Heart
autumnal equinox, 157, 160–61
Autumn's Eulogy, 214
awe, intentional, 295

Baba Yaga, 7
balance, 60, 121, 160, 295
balefires, 52
Bawdy Betty and the Lady in Beige (late
spring story), 28, 74–79, 313–14
becoming: author's experience, xvii;
collective story of, 6, 9, 12, 117, 219,
221–22, 301–2; continuance of, 309;
eternal, remembering as journey of,
2–3; lunar journey of, 7; midwifery to,
289; muse of, 221–22, 271; remembering and journey of, 2–3; Season of the
Thirteenth Moon and, 156, 217. *See
also* Season of the Thirteenth Moon
Becoming the Crone-Weaver (opening
practice), 287–88, 325
Beginning Again (waxing moon practice),
288–89, 325
beliefs, blocking, 212
belonging: ancestral, 311–12; desire for,
xvii, 68, 162, 170, 301, 302, 333; as hag
teaching, 1–2; in lived-out stories, 301;
loss of sense of, 6; magick efficacy and,
132; to nature, 80, 314; to a place, 192;
power in, 330; as Season of Tender
Roots nourishment, 27, 29; to stories,
117–18; trees and, 80. *See also* Season
of Tender Roots

"Beloved" (autumn central candle), 156
Beloved Dead, the (sunrise reflection),
31–32. *See also* dead, beloved
beloveds, living, 223
Beltane, 16, 52, 53–54, 93
Biddy's Retreat (late-summer love story),
90, 142–46, 315–16
birth: inevitability of, 269, 332; sea as
cauldron of, 173
birth-death-birth cycle, 156
Blessed by the Most Primal Rivers (Grandmother Speaks narrative), 65–66
Blessing Moon, 123, 131, 136
Blood Moon, 179, 191
body: caring for, 223; feeling (waning
moon practice), 68, 323; grounding in,
86; magick channeled through, 11–12;
presence in, 295; sanctity of, 17; wild,
68
Bone-Woman's Brew, The (midwinter
story), 227, 257–60, 320–21
book divination, 15
Book of Moon and Flame: blank book
set aside for, 22–23; reviewing writings
in, 250, 254; writing in, 32, 44, 52–53,
114–15, 122–23, 180–81, 192, 248,
253, 261–62
Bravest Gardener, The (full moon practice), 263, 325
Bread of Life and Death, The (Lughnasadh celebration), 123–24, 323
Bridal Bed and a Flame Alight, A (Imbolc
celebration), 253–56, 325
Bride's Brew, The (Imbolc salve), 252
Brighid (Celtic deity), 253
brokenness, 179
Brown, Adrienne Maree, 146, 326–27

Cailleach, 7, 271, 273
Calling in the Stubborn Dreamers (sunrise
reflection), 52–53
Calling on a Dream (dark moon practice),
137, 323

About the Author

Danielle Dulsky is a heathen visionary, Aquarian mischief maker, and word-witch. Author of *The Holy Wild: A Heathen Bible for the Untamed Woman* (New World Library, 2018) and *Woman Most Wild: Three Keys for Liberating the Witch Within* (New World Library, 2017), Danielle teaches internationally and has facilitated embodiment trainings, wild circles, communal spellwork, and seasonal rituals since 2007. She is the founder of the Hag School and the lead teacher for the Flame-Tender Facilitator Training, and she believes in the power of wild collectives and sudden circles of curious dreamers, cunning Witches, and rebellious artists as well as the importance of ancestral healing, embodiment, and animism in dismantling the long-standing systems supporting white supremacy and environmental unconsciousness. Parent to two beloved wildlings and partner to a potter, Danielle fills her world with nature, family, and intentional awe.

DanielleDulsky.com

TheHagSchool.com